EPHESIANS
Baptism and Pentecost

EPHESIANS
Baptism and Pentecost

AN INQUIRY
INTO THE STRUCTURE
AND PURPOSE OF
THE EPISTLE TO
THE EPHESIANS

J. C. KIRBY

Associate Professor of New Testament Studies
McGill University

LONDON

S · P · C · K

1968

First published in 1968
by S.P.C.K.
Holy Trinity Church
Marylebone Road
London N.W.1

Made and printed in Great Britain by
William Clowes and Sons, Limited
London and Beccles

SBN 281 02235 6

CONTENTS

ACKNOWLEDGEMENTS   vii

ABBREVIATIONS   ix

PREFACE   xi

PART ONE

General Survey of Recent Literature on Ephesians

A. BRIEF REVIEW OF MINOR WORKS ON EPHESIANS   3

B. CHARLES MASSON   9

C. ERNST PERCY   18

D. N. A. DAHL   40

E. E. J. GOODSPEED AND C. L. MITTON   44

F. G. JOHNSTON AND F. W. BEARE   49

PART TWO

The Jewish Liturgical Tradition and the New Testament

1. THE JEWISH LITURGICAL CALENDAR   59

A. THE CALENDAR IN THE OLD TESTAMENT CANON   61

B. THE CALENDAR IN THE INTERTESTAMENTAL LITERATURE, RABBINIC TRADITION, AND THE QUMRAN DOCUMENTS   64

C. THE ISRAELITE CONCEPT OF TIME AND ITS EXPRESSION IN THE LITURGY   69

D. THE CHRISTIAN CHURCH AND THE JEWISH CALENDAR   73

2. THE JEWISH LITURGY   83

A. THE FORM OF THE JEWISH BERAKOTH   84

B. THE READING OF SCRIPTURE AND SERMON   90

C. THE BETH MIDRASH PRAYERS AND THE QUMRAN HODAYOTH   94

D. PENTECOST IN WORSHIP AND TRADITION   97

3. THE JEWISH LITURGY AND THE NEW TESTAMENT   101

A. NEW TESTAMENT BERAKOTH   103

B. SCRIPTURE IN NEW TESTAMENT WORSHIP   110

CONTENTS

PART THREE
Ephesians
Baptism and Pentecost

1. EPHESIANS AND THE JEWISH TRADITIONS
   OF WORSHIP   125
   A. THE FORM AND LANGUAGE OF EPHESIANS   126
   B. THE EXALTATION AND SOVEREIGNTY OF CHRIST; THE SPIRIT 138
   C. THE CHURCH AND ITS UNITY   140
   D. EPHESIANS AND THE JEWISH PENTECOST   145
   E. PSALM 29   147
   F. EXODUS 19–20   147
   G. PENTECOST AND MARRIAGE   148

2. EPHESIANS AND BAPTISM   150
   A. DIRECT REFERENCES TO BAPTISM   150
   B. INDIRECT REFERENCES TO BAPTISM   154
   C. THE ESCHATOLOGY OF EPHESIANS   161

3. THE "LITURGY" BECOMES A LETTER   165

APPENDIX

NOTES   175
BIBLIOGRAPHY   191
INDEX OF NAMES   197
INDEX OF BIBLICAL REFERENCES   199

ACKNOWLEDGEMENTS

Biblical quotations from the Revised Standard Version of the Bible are copyrighted 1946, 1952, by the Division of Christian Education, National Council of Churches, and are used by permission.

Thanks are due to the following for permission to quote from copyright sources:

Henry J. Cadbury and the Editor of *New Testament Studies*: An extract from an article on Ephesians.

Martin Secker and Warburg Limited and Doubleday and Company: *The Dead Sea Scriptures*, by T. H. Gaster.

Singer's Prayer Book Publication Committee and Eyre and Spottiswoode Ltd: Extracts from Singer's *Translation of the Jewish Prayer Book*.

ABBREVIATIONS

BT	Babylonian Talmud (Eng. Trans., Soncino Press, 1935–1952)
CD	*Damascus Document*
CH	*Church History*
CJT	*Canadian Journal of Theology*
DBS.	*Dictionnaire de la Bible, Supplément*
Ep. aux Col.	*Epître aux Colossiens*
Ep. aux Eph.	*Epître aux Ephésiens*
Ev. Th.	*Evangelische Theologie*
ET	*Expository Times*
HDB	*Hastings Dictionary of the Bible*
HTR	*Harvard Theological Review*
HZNT	*Handbuch zum Neuen Testament*
ICC	International Critical Commentary
Int. Bib.	*Interpreter's Bible*
Int. Dict.	*Interpreter's Dictionary*
JBL	*Journal of Biblical Literature*
JBLH	*Jahrbuch für Liturgik und Hymnologie*
JQR	*Jewish Quarterly Review*
JSS	*Journal of Semitic Studies*
JTS	*Journal of Theological Studies*
Key	*Key to Ephesians*
Lit. Gut	*Liturgisches Gut im Epheserbrief* (microfilm)
Meaning	*The Meaning of Ephesians*
MNC	Moffatt New Testament Commentary
NTS	*New Testament Studies*
RGG	*Die Religion in Geschichte und Gegenwart* (3rd edition, 1957–)
SB	H. L. Strack and P. Billerbeck, *Kommentar zum Neuen Testament aus* Talmud *und* Midrasch
Stud. Theol.	*Studia Theologica*
ThB	*Theologische Blätter*
TLZ	*Theologische Literaturzeitung*
TWNT	*Theologisches Wörterbuch zum Neuen Testament* (ed. G. Kittel and G. Friedrich, 1933–)

ABBREVIATIONS

TZ	*Theologische Zeitschrift*
ZATW	*Zeitschrift für die Alttestamentliche Wissenschaft*
ZKG	*Zeitschrift für Kirchengeschichte*
ZNTW	*Zeitschrift für die Neutestamentliche Wissenschaft*

PREFACE

The discussion on the authorship of the Epistle to the Ephesians and the purpose for which it was written has been going on for over a century and a half without reaching satisfactory solutions to the major problems raised by the Epistle. I am not sanguine enough to think that any of these problems have at last been solved. What is offered here is hopefully a contribution to the discussion along a line that several scholars have mentioned, but none, as far as I know, has investigated.

The hypothesis here set out first took shape in my mind during a seminar on Ephesians conducted by Dr George Caird, now of Mansfield College, Oxford, but then Professor of New Testament Studies at McGill University, Montreal. Any person who has studied under him knows how stimulating an experience that can be. Since then I have received much constructive criticism from Dr Caird's successor, Dr George Johnston, with whom I now share the teaching of New Testament at McGill. I am deeply indebted to him not only for his help in the New Testament field but also for the contribution he has made to work that we have done together in the Faculty of Divinity and beyond it. I must also acknowledge gratefully the criticisms made by Professor C. F. D. Moule of Cambridge of an earlier draft of this material.

The material itself divides into three parts which are roughly equal in length. Part 1 is devoted to a survey of the critical work that has been done on the Epistle to the Ephesians, particularly during the last quarter of a century. It is hoped that this will serve a useful purpose, since the work of various scholars on this epistle has not been critically considered in any one article or book. If the lion's share of the space is given to Ernst Percy, it is because he has given us the most thorough investigation of the problem of Ephesians to date. Since many New Testament scholars are agreed that Ephesians is written in language and style that is most fittingly called liturgical, Part 2 discusses the form and content of Jewish liturgical worship with special reference to the Feast of Pentecost and also the possibility of liturgical influence in other parts of the New Testament. Part 3 applies these findings to Ephesians itself.

The final draft of this book was written in England while I was on leave, and I should like to express my thanks to the many people who showed more than a casual interest in the work that I was doing by making library facilities available and in helping me in any way that they could. Without being invidious, I would mention the staff and students of the College of the Ascension, Selly Oak, Birmingham, who, in their life and worship together, showed how Ephesians could still come to life.

J. C. KIRBY

PART ONE

General Survey
of Recent Literature
on Ephesians

A. *Brief review of minor Works on Ephesians*

Of all the letters in the New Testament which are attributed to Saint Paul, none produces such a sharp division of opinion as the letter to the Ephesians. There are few, if any, who would now say that Hebrews is the work of Paul, and while there are still some who claim that he wrote the Pastorals, they have not made a convincing case against the widely accepted opinion that these letters come from a time later than Paul.[1] With Ephesians, however, it is different. In his presidential address to the Studiorum Novi Testamenti Societas in 1958, H. J. Cadbury summed up what he called "The Dilemma of Ephesians" in this way:

> The persistently and widely shared doubt of Paul's authorship of Ephesians creates an embarrassment to our profession. Here is what the writer calls "a middle wall of partition" and it is not easily removed. Persons who otherwise agree on critical questions often differ sharply here. They may feel the strength of the arguments on each side, but are ashamed to make no choice. So they answer the question one way or the other, more because of their unwillingness to admit indecision than out of clear conviction. The same arguments are quite differently appraised by advocates of the same side. In the pressure to arrive at some decision, now one, now another, minor matter is given undeserved weight. Perhaps the individual scholar vacillates in his opinion, or over the years shifts from one side to the other. The book on the question he has read most recently may move him, but not always as the author intended.[2]

Even C. L. Mitton, who in 1951 wrote one of the major works on the side of non-Pauline authorship, felt compelled to admit five years later that while the problem of Ephesians may seem to some individuals to have been solved in one direction or another, it still remained open to discussion.[3]

It was not until the end of the eighteenth century that the authenticity of Ephesians was questioned, though it was known from very early times that ἐν Ἐφέσῳ (1.1) was not to be found in the best texts.[4] It was on the basis of this omission that Archbishop Ussher put forward the theory in 1654 that Ephesians was a circular letter. In 1792 E. Evanston expressed his doubts about the authenticity of this letter on the ground that Paul would not have written in such an impersonal way to a church where he must have known many of the members by name. But the first major work of criticism was that of De Wette who gave his fullest statement against the Pauline authorship of Ephesians in his *Exegetisches Handbuch z. N.T.*, published in 1843. His arguments have remained the basic ones down to our own time: (*a*) There is a close literary relationship between Ephesians and Colossians. (*b*) The style is verbose and dragging (*schleppende*), the sentences are unusually long and, for the most part, made up of clauses or phrases joined together by relative pronouns, participles, and prepositions. The only other place in the Pauline corpus where we find an approximation of this style is the first chapter of Colossians. (*c*) There are also many phrases which appear to belong to a time later than Paul, for example "the foundation of the apostles and prophets" (2.20), "his holy apostles and prophets" (3.5). The address of the letter shows that, even if it is genuine, it could not have been a letter to the church at Ephesus.[5]

It is not necessary for us to review the main works on either side of this argument at this point, for they are all summed up in the two works with which we shall deal in greater detail later on in this section. Only variations from the general consensus of opinion or additional arguments pro or con will be dealt with here.

One of the early variations from what may be called the critical norm is to be found in the work of H. J. Holtzmann. In his *Kritik der Epheser- und Kolosserbriefe* (1872), he put forward the theory that neither Colossians nor Ephesians as we now have them is prior to the other; there are parts of Colossians which appear to be prior to Ephesians and vice versa. This can be accounted for if we hold that the original Colossians was a much shorter letter written to combat the false theological beliefs and devotional practices of the church at Colossae. This "original" was written by Paul. On the basis of the "original" Colossians an unknown author wrote Ephesians; later still, either he or one of his readers expanded the "original" Colossians by borrowing extensively from Ephesians. We can therefore find primary and secondary material in both epistles.[6]

This theory did not gain a great deal of acceptance at the time or for many years afterwards but has found protagonists in more recent years. The main reason for rejecting it was that Holtzmann's judgement as to what was Pauline or non-Pauline could not be verified by objective tests. James Moffat's criticism is typical: "Such filagree-criticism has failed to win acceptance; the literary criteria are too subjective, and the evidence for bisecting the error attacked in Colossians is not convincing".[7] G. G. Findlay goes further and says that it is the most unconvincing book that he knows of, even though it is full of learning and subtly and scientifically written.[8]

More recent writers hesitate to be as sweeping as this. Writing in 1944, John Knox is "strongly inclined to believe" that though Paul wrote a letter to the Colossians, it later underwent considerable interpolation and that Holtzmann's work, particularly on the authenticity of Colossians, has been dismissed too quickly.[9] G. Schille[10] uses much stronger language.

> The modern attitude of passing over Holtzmann's observations in silence cannot be allowed. He has not only posed the question of the genuineness of Ephesians and Colossians; his observations have shown what the actual difficulties are. In the newer studies there is no serious discussion of the theses which he laid down.

It is too simple to say that Ephesians depends on Colossians. But though Schille agrees with Holtzmann that the relationship between the two letters is not a simple one, he thinks that there is a simpler explanation than the one which Holtzmann found.

According to Schille, the form-critical method can be of use to us here. We can now distinguish between the various types of material to be found in the Pauline letters, liturgical, parenetic, epistolary, and so on. Where a liturgical passage is found in one of the letters and the ideas contained in this passage are found in shortened form in the other, then the letter containing the liturgical passage is prior. As an example of this he gives Ephesians 2.4–10, which he calls a song of redemption (*Erlösunglied*), and compares it with Colossians 2.13–15, which says the same thing in a different way, but uses little direct language from Ephesians. The same is true in the parenesis. The admonitions in Colossians are much shorter than those in Ephesians. This would be natural if Ephesians, which may in fact be "the letter from Laodicea", was already written, and if Paul knew that the church at Colossae was

2—E.B.P.

going to read it. Again, if we turn to linguistic and grammatical considerations and compare Ephesians 4.16 with Colossians 2.19, for example, we find that Colossians has a masculine relative attached to a feminine noun. According to Schille, there is no difficulty over the text of Ephesians. The grammatical error in Colossians is due to the fact that its author shortened the text of Ephesians and left out "Christ". This is just as reasonable an explanation as to say that Ephesians improved the text of Colossians.

Schille thinks that the unique format of Ephesians—the first three chapters a thanksgiving, the last three an admonition—is accounted for by the fact that the letter is primarily catechetical in character.[11] He finds in chapters 1–3 at least four passages (1.3–12 and 20–3; 2.4–10 and 14–18) which he believes to be early Christian hymns; these have been incorporated into the letter by the author, because his readers are unknown to him (1.15), and he wishes to gain a hearing by appealing to a form of words which they already know.[12] Colossians follows the same general pattern as Ephesians except for the long polemic against the Colossian heresy (2.4—3.4); here matter dealing with a specific problem has been inserted into material which is quite general in tone.[13] Why does Colossians not follow the pattern of the other Pauline letters which deal with actual situations? Because, says Schille, the author of Colossians may have had Ephesians before him. If Colossians were prior, it is strange that it does not elaborate the doctrinal material as fully as Ephesians does. If Colossians is genuine, then Ephesians may also be genuine.

Nor will Schille allow such phrases as "the holy apostles" or "the very least of all the saints" to tell against Pauline authorship. Since Ephesians is written against a catechetical background, the epithet given to the apostles may be nothing more than a highly ceremonious phrase, one of the expressions used when the tradition is being handed over to new converts. In spite of Paul's critical attitude towards the leaders of the Church in Galatians 1 and 2, in 1 Corinthians 15.1–9 he includes them as those who can confirm his own teaching. If we see Ephesians as a letter in which tradition is being handed over, then the writer must speak not just on his own authority but on the authority of the whole Church; in that situation the apostles would be regarded as guarantors of the tradition and would not be spoken of in a critical manner. Again, Paul never denied the priority of Jerusalem and never broke with the Jerusalem church; in fact he gave himself a great deal of toil and trouble to bring an offering to it from the Gentiles. In the telling of the *Heilsgeschichte* and in giving its meaning to the Ephesians it would be perfectly natural to use "laudatory phrases".[14] The same is true for its opposite; the Apostle speaks of himself in a deprecating way in 1 Corinthians 15.9 and Ephesians 3.8, because he wishes to stress his subordination to the teaching upon which his own faith was based.

The long-drawn-out and unpauline style of Ephesians (and Colossians) is due to its quotation from hymns and from the parenetic tradition. The additions to, and the corrections of, the tradition, both in form and vocabulary, bear a genuine Pauline stamp. (Schille's dissertation is mainly concerned with differentiating between what he believes to be traditional material in Ephesians and the author's own comment on it.) He thinks that both of these letters are the work of one author, and if one is the genuine work of Paul, the other must be also. He ends his article by saying that the whole problem of Ephesians is now thrown into the open again; the statistical approach of Goodspeed and those who follow him has not solved it. The only thing it has shown is that the letters depend on each other. "In this doubtful case, I would hold that it is simpler to say that Ephesians is genuine than that it is spurious."

In a brief commentary of some seventy pages published in 1941, F. C. Synge arrives at the solution that Ephesians is a genuine letter of Paul and Colossians is an imitation. (Col. 4.10–18 is a genuine Pauline fragment which has been incorporated into a spurious letter, just as genuine fragments of Paul are embedded in the Pastorals.) The arguments he uses are those which are usually used to prove that Ephesians is not genuine. On grounds of style he says that Ephesians is superbly matched with the material: "The matter of the epistle is the building of many into One; the manner of the epistle is to build a unity out of variety."[15] In Colossians the sentences are much more complicated and the thought wanders more than in any genuine Pauline epistle; if Paul wrote Colossians he must have been "dejected and exhausted" when he wrote it. As for vocabulary, though both letters have a good many words in common, the way in which they are used shows that Ephesians is the work of a creative mind, while Colossians is not. As an example of this he compares Ephesians 2.12–14 and Colossians 1.21. The former makes apt use of such words as "aliens", "hostility", "peace", "reconcile", to describe the state of the Gentiles before and after God had reconciled them to himself and to the "commonwealth of Israel"; in the latter, words like "aliens" are not nearly so apt and the phrase, "having made peace", is redundant. The same is true if we compare Ephesians 1.12–13 with Colossians 1.5 or Colossians 3.25 with Ephesians 6.9. The only reason why certain words and phrases are found in both epistles is that the author of Colossians is so steeped in Ephesians that reminiscences of the latter are part of his own mind. In doctrine, too, Ephesians is more "primitive" and Pauline than Colossians: Ephesians 4.13 speaks of the concepts of corporate unity, "till we all come . . . to a perfect man", Colossians 1.28 only of mature individual orthodoxy. Indeed, Colossians as a whole is much more concerned with orthodoxy than Ephesians is; in this it strongly resembles the Pastorals. In opposition to a great many critics, Synge claims that μυστήριον in Ephesians has the same meaning as in the other Paulines, but in Colossians "it smacks of the mystery religions". He is also convinced that the author of Ephesians was a Jew, in fact, a Jew like Paul, who, though he accepted the great truth that Jews and Gentiles were equal in the Church, yet felt that there were some advantages in being a Jew; the same thoughts lie behind Romans 3.1–3 and Ephesians 3.4–6. He concludes by saying that Paul may well have written Ephesians and he is "the sort of person who must have written it".

This solution of the problem has received very little support from scholars, though a similar conclusion was reached by J. Coutts, purely on the basis of literary relationships (he does not discuss the question of authorship).[16] He takes certain passages from both epistles which appear to depend on each other, and argues that the simplest explanation is to say that Colossians depends on Ephesians. One example of his method may be given. If Ephesians depends on Colossians, then Ephesians 4.15b–16 is derived from Colossians 1.18, 2.19, and 2.2; if the reverse is true, then Colossians 2.19 is wholly derived from one passage in Ephesians. As a result of examining several passages like this, in which one passage in Ephesians is derived from two or more passages in Colossians, while passages in Colossians are derived from never more than two passages in Ephesians, generally in the same context, Coutts argues for the priority of Ephesians. At the same time, some of the doctrinal passages which seem to come in almost as asides in Colossians are worked out in Ephesians; the phrase "making peace through the blood of the cross" (Col. 1.20) is grammatically unconnected with what precedes and what follows it, for the author has to repeat δι' αὐτοῦ in order to show that the words which follow, "whether on earth or in heaven", go with "reconciliation" and not with "making peace". Coutts' explanation is that Colossians has conflated "in the blood of Christ" (Eph. 2.13), "making peace" (2.15), and "through the cross" (2.16). In Ephesians, too, the doctrinal argument is worked out thoroughly and the summary reference in Colossians would only be possible if "the process pre-supposed in Ephesians had already taken place in the author's mind".[17]

The difficulty about such theories is that they try to solve the problem mainly on linguistic grounds and either pass over, or find ingenious solutions to, questions which are raised by phrases or ideas which seem to indicate a later time than that of Paul. Synge says nothing whatever about the problem of the text in 1.1 or the "holy apostles and prophets" in 3.5, while he translates 2.20 as a subjective genitive, "being built upon the foundation laid by the apostles and prophets". While this interpretation has been given by others,[18] it does not agree with the context here, although it may be argued that it agrees with Paul's own teaching that Christ is the only foundation (1 Cor. 3.11). Schille finds that the material which is unlike Paul is taken from a baptismal liturgy, while the Pauline material is Paul's own correction of misunderstandings of the meaning of baptism which were held by those to whom he was writing.[19] The basis on which he recognizes liturgical or hymnodic material is open to question. W. Nauck,[20] for example, thinks that Ephesians 2.19–22 is a *tauflied*, a passage which Schille does not discuss at all.

B. *Charles Masson*

The most recent commentary which comes to approximately the same conclusion as Holtzmann is that of Charles Masson (1953). He rejects the theory of the circular letter because it presupposes a procedure which is otherwise unknown in the ancient world.[21] In writing to a group of churches, as he does in Galatians, Paul gives the name of the province; none of his extant letters is as impersonal as Ephesians. Even if the letter was not written by Paul, it is unlikely that it was originally addressed to Ephesus, for no disciple of the apostle would have been so maladroit as to write such an impersonal letter to a church which Paul knew so well.

Masson thinks that Marcion may well have had "To the Laodiceans" in one or more copies of his Ephesians, or that he knew of a tradition according to which it had been addressed to Laodicea. He had travelled through Asia Minor on his way to Rome in 140 and he would therefore know more on the subject of this epistle than the leaders of the Church at the end of the second century.[22] Masson quotes with approval the remark of J. Huby: "Il est difficile de croire que Marcion a imaginé de toutes pièces et qu'il n'avait aucun appui dans la tradition antérieure." If the objection is made that an impersonal letter would not have been written to Laodicea either, Masson's answer is that this objection does not hold good if this letter is not a genuine letter of Paul.

Masson's own theory is that the original letter of Paul to Colossae was not in the form that is now found in the New Testament. Paul had written a brief letter to Colossae dealing with the "deviationists" there. A disciple of Paul developed this letter into what is now our Ephesians, except that he addressed it to the church in Laodicea; he was inspired to do this by the reference to Laodicea in Colossians 4.15. He then interpolated some of the thought and language of his own letter into the original Colossians; one of these interpolations was Colossians 4.16 which recommends that Colossae and Laodicea exchange letters. The letters were so alike in outlook that they would naturally go together, and both of them, along with Philemon, were put into general circulation at the same time. How then did Laodiceans get changed into Ephesians? Masson thinks that the first step was taken at Ephesus where it was thought that this letter was not addressed to any particular church, and so "in Laodicea" was omitted. When it went out from the great metropolis of Asia Minor, it was regarded as having been addressed to that city, so it was given the title "To the Ephesians". This must have happened fairly early, since it appears always to have carried this title in the Pauline corpus.[23] From the title it passed into the text, for the text is incomprehensible without the name of a place. Marcion was the only known person who claimed that the original title was "To the Laodiceans", but, since he was a heretic, his witness was discounted by the orthodox.

It is highly doubtful whether Masson would have arrived at this ingenious theory if he had not been perplexed by difficulties which arose out of his comparison of Ephesians and Colossians. While it is generally agreed that the genuine letters of Paul underwent a certain amount of recension before they arrived at the form which they now possess, on the basis of this theory none of them has suffered such a radical change as Colossians. It is now widely held, for example, that the Corinthian correspondence is made up of parts of three, or more probably four, letters, but all the material, apart from some few phrases, is held to be genuinely Paul's. Romans 16 may not have been part of Romans; many scholars think that its original destination was Ephesus. Philippians too may be composed of parts of three letters sent at different times. If there were an original Colossians, would it have been "patched up" in the way that Masson suggests? This is not to deny that there is a problem here. If we look at one instance which Masson puts forward, we shall see how complicated the relationship between Ephesians and Colossians is. In the passage Colossians 1.3–7, verses 3 and 4 consist of introductory words of thanksgiving which are easily recognizable as Pauline. Verses 5 and 6 are complicated, and words are given a meaning which is unlike that found in the genuine letters. "Hope" appears to be brought in to complete the Pauline trilogy of "Faith, Hope, and Love", but it is not used in the ordinary Pauline sense of an eager looking forward to the final victory of God (Rom. 8.18–25); it is something already laid up in heaven. These two verses have parallels in Ephesians 1.13 and 18, and Masson thinks they are best understood in Colossians as borrowings from Ephesians which have been interpolated into the original Pauline letter.[24] This and similar instances require some explanation, but one wonders if Masson has hit upon the right one. The psychology of authorship is a notoriously difficult subject, but is it at all likely that the person who had such a grasp of his subject as the author of Ephesians would have done so pedestrian a job with Colossians?

But Ephesians is our main concern. As has been said above, Masson rejects the Pauline authorship. "Though the epistle is Pauline in language and thought, and this is not surprising, for the author wished the whole Church to hear the voice of the apostle of the Gentiles, it is not just Pauline."[25] The author is a child of his own time and it is not the time of the Apostle.

Language alone is not sufficient to prove that the letter is spurious, for in each of Paul's letters the vocabulary differs to suit the subject. Masson thinks, however, that the style of Ephesians decisively tells against Pauline authorship. We miss here the vigorous movement of the Pauline mind and the pungency of its thought; the author writes much more slowly and carefully, drawing out his ideas almost to the point of exhaustion. Again, while Paul has made use of liturgical language, he has not done so to the same extent as the author of Ephesians, who draws upon a longer liturgical tradition. (Masson thinks that 1.3–13 is a hymn which has been adapted as an introduction to the letter. We shall deal with this in a later section.)

In points of doctrine, too, Ephesians differs from Paul. For the latter, baptism is a dying with Christ, for the former, it is resurrection of those who were "dead through [their] trespasses and sins" (2.1; cf. 2.5 "dead through our trespasses"). Masson thinks that the authentic Pauline doctrine of baptism is found in Romans 6.3–5, which speaks only of being baptized into the death of Christ. When he goes on to speak of the resurrection, he uses the future tense: "If we have been united with him in a death like his, we shall certainly be united with him in a resurrection like his." He therefore regards as interpolations the passages in Colossians which speak of a dying and rising again with Christ (Col. 2.12b–13, and 3.1–2). The life of the believer is a manifestation of the power of the resurrection of Christ, but he must wait still for the resurrection of the dead.[26] "You were buried with him in baptism" (Col. 2.12); "With Christ you died to the elemental spirits of the universe" (2.20); "You died and your life is hid with Christ in God" (3.3—this is Paul). "You . . . God made alive together with him" (2.13). "If then you have been raised with Christ, seek the things that are above, where Christ is, seated at the right hand of God" (3.1—this is the Pauline interpolator). Ephesians appears to have forgotten, or not to have understood, that, for Paul, rising with Christ is impossible without first being buried with him; even where it proclaims the great doctrine of salvation by grace, it omits one of the principal affirmations of Pauline soteriology. This letter is so deeply coloured by Pauline thought that the omission can easily be overlooked, but it had disastrous consequences in later church history. "On verra . . . les impératifs de la vie chrétienne n'étant plus fondés sur l'acte rédempteur de

Dieu en la mort du Christ devenir les commandments d'une loi nouvelle." [27]

Masson may be right in saying that we miss in Ephesians the note of dying with Christ in baptism, but when he goes on to say that rising with Christ is not also part of baptism he appears to be speaking on dogmatic grounds rather than from the textual evidence. Can we so easily separate the first four verses of Colossians 3, where the resurrection of Christ, his ascension, his second coming, and Christian baptism are all mentioned together? Even in Romans 6, where Paul uses the future tense in verse 5, he uses the present in verse 11: "You are to consider yourselves as dead to sin and alive to God in Christ Jesus." The line of demarcation which Masson would draw between the present and the future cannot be as sharply drawn as he would have it, particularly in passages of an eschatological nature.

The doctrine of the "mystery" in Ephesians is non-Pauline, and for him the same is true in Colossians. In the letters generally regarded as authentic, the proclamation of the gospel to the Gentiles is not a mystery at all but "the truth of the Gospel" (Gal. 2.5, 14). The mystery which Paul imparts to the "mature" (1 Cor. 2.6) is an eschatological one; it is concerned with the participation of believers in the glory of the world to come (two examples of this use may be found in Romans 11.25 and 1 Corinthians 15.51). This idea, while not foreign to the gospel, does not belong to the core of it, nor did Paul ever consider it to be the main point of his preaching.[28] "I did not come proclaiming to you the testimony of God in lofty words or wisdom . . . and my speech and message were not in plausible words of wisdom" (1 Cor. 2.1, 4). What has happened in Ephesians (and Colossians) is that while "mystery" is used in the same sense as in Corinthians—a revealed secret—the content of the mystery is altogether different. The only difference between Colossians and Ephesians is that in the former we have only allusions to the mystery; in the latter these allusions are worked out in full. Further, only in Colossians and Ephesians do we find the phrases "the mystery of God" or "the mystery of Christ" (Col. 2.2; 4.3; Eph. 3.4). (The use of the plural in 1 Corinthians 4.1 —the mysteries of God—does not seem to have any bearing on the meaning of the words in Ephesians or Colossians.) In Colossians 1.26–7, the mystery is "Christ in you [the Gentiles], the hope of glory"; it is not a far step to "the Gentiles are fellow-heirs,

members of the same body, and partakers of the promise in Christ
Jesus through the Gospel" (3.6). Christ has accomplished this
in his death by abolishing the law which had caused the enmity
between Jew and Gentile (2.13–16). This springs from the mystery
of the will of God whose eternal purpose was to bring the whole
created universe under the lordship of Christ (1.9, 10). The mystery
was revealed after Pentecost to "the holy apostles and prophets"
and above all to Paul (3.3, 5, 8). Masson thinks that the language
of Ephesians may be drawn from 1 Corinthians 2.7–10: "We speak
the *wisdom of God* in a *mystery* which is *hidden* which God decreed
before the ages in order that we may be *glorified*, which none of the
rulers of this age understood, for if they had they would not have
crucified the Lord of glory. But, as it is written, 'What eye has not
seen nor ear heard. . . . God has *revealed to us through the Spirit*'."
While the language may be similar, the thought which it expresses
is very different.

Here is one place where there seems to be no possibility of agreement among scholars at the present time. Some say that there are
no differences in the meaning of the word "mystery" in the whole
Pauline corpus;[29] others, that Ephesians differs from all the rest
and especially from Colossians;[30] Masson, as we have seen, would
say that all the references to "mystery" in Ephesians and Colossians come from the hand of the same author. Under these circumstances, it cannot be used to prove either the Pauline or non-
Pauline authorship of Ephesians.

In Masson's view, the Ephesian doctrine of the Church is not
Pauline either. The local church is not present to the mind of the
author at all; he is thinking of the Church in its totality, which, like
Christ himself, is one (4.4). In the genuine Paulines, the Church is
the body of Christ and each Christian an organ of that body
(Rom. 12.4–6; 1 Cor. 12.4–6); in Ephesians, the Church is the
body of which Christ is the head (Eph. 1.22; 4.15). In Paul each
member of the body has his part to play, each his own ministry to
perform; in Ephesians the ministry has a more important role than
the ordinary members. In his exegesis of Ephesians 4.11–16, he
claims that in the working out of the metaphor of the body, the
ministers are the "joints", the means by which the body is kept
united, and by which, under Christ, its life is sustained. While the
ministers are subordinate to the head—like the other members
they belong to the body—they have a more important position than

the rest of the Christian community. The apostles and prophets are the foundation on which the Church is built (2.20), and evangelists, pastors, and teachers are those through whom it is built up (4.11–12). It is through them that grace is given to every believer; it is through them that believers are shaped in the Christian life, nourished by the Word and Sacrament until they come to spiritual maturity. The believers benefit from the work of the ministry, but they do not take part in it at all. They live by the grace received from Christ through (*par le moyen*) the ministers. Ephesians draws a sharp line between ministry and laity (*le peuple*). The charismatic ministry had disappeared by the time Ephesians was written.[31]

The eschatological aspect of the Church's life is also missing. The body grows by the life which it receives from Christ by the channel of the ministry until all believers attain their perfection; there is nothing to indicate that the present relationship of the head in heaven and the body on earth is temporary, and that the Church will be reunited with its Lord. For our author the eschatological event is the creation and growth of the body of Christ in which mankind will find its unity; already united to Christ, it is growing towards him. There is nothing here of the Lord returning to his Church.

There are few exegetes who would agree that this doctrine of the Church and, particularly, of the ministry, is to be found in Ephesians. Masson can do this only by saying that $\chi\acute{\alpha}\rho\iota\varsigma$ in 4.7 has nothing to do with $\chi\acute{\alpha}\rho\iota\sigma\mu\alpha$, and that if the author were thinking of the latter he would not have used the aorist of $\delta\acute{\iota}\delta\omega\mu\iota$ but the present, in conformity with 1 Corinthians 12.7–9. For Masson this verse is a reference to baptism which is performed by the ministry. "The aorist looks back to baptism, the purpose of which is to communicate personally to each believer the grace of the redemptive act."[32] In disagreement with this, all the other current commentaries say that, having dealt with the unity of all believers in 4.1–6, the author now turns to the place of the individual in his relationship to the body, and that verse 7 refers to the particular endowment given to each individual (cf. Rom. 12.3, "I say through the grace which was given to me"). Once more, in order to prove that in the Ephesian doctrine of the Church it is the ministry which is all-important, he punctuates 4.11 and 12 in this way: "His gifts were that some should be apostles, some prophets, some evangelists, some pastors and teachers for the perfecting of the saints, for the work of ministry in building up the body of Christ." He claims that since various orders of ministers are mentioned here, the phrase "for the work of ministry" cannot refer to all believers, for the community benefits from the ministry but does not exercise it. The task of pastors and teachers is to perfect the saints, just as the task of apostles, prophets, and evangelists is to found the Church and to spread the gospel. When converts have been made, they are to be trained by pastors and teachers. Since the work of apostles and prophets has been mentioned previously (2.20; 3.5), their work did not need to be mentioned here. The last two phrases, "for the work of ministry in building up the body of Christ", are meant to refer to the work of all five ministries. Since the Church in Ephesians is the universal Church, the author can speak at the same time of the two orders of ministers who are the founders, and of the three who are continuing the work.[33]

Surely this is a very forced piece of exegesis; in one minor detail at least, it is contradictory. Masson includes the evangelists with apostles and prophets in the earlier part of the section, and with the pastors and teachers in the later. True, as he himself says, "cette péricope est probablement la plus difficile à expliquer dans une épître qui ne manque pas de péricopes difficiles". Nevertheless, does this marked distinction between the *kleros* and the *laos* go back as far as the end of the first century, the date which Masson gives to the epistle?[34] It is much more probable that *diakonia* in 4.12 does not refer to any specific function within the Church but rather to the service that is given to the Christian community by its individual members. The ministry is given to the Church in order to equip the saints for the work of service so that the body of Christ may be built up.[35] The institutional aspect of the ministry may be slightly more stressed here than it is in 1 Corinthians or Romans, but certainly not to the extent that Masson says.

Here we find ourselves involved in a circular argument. For, since Masson insists that the references to the Church in Colossians were interpolated by the author of Ephesians,[36] it follows that the doctrine of the Church as the body of which Christ is the head, a doctrine found in Colossians and in a much more developed form in Ephesians, is not a doctrine which we owe to Paul. "It is a singularly bold elaboration of the simile of the body and its members which Paul made use of in his ethical teaching."[37] Consequently, if Colossians is accepted as genuine, this doctrine cannot be accepted as an argument against Pauline authorship, for it is on this that Masson mainly rests his case. The same may be said of the idea that in the genuine Paulines it is the local church that the Apostle is thinking of, whereas in Colossians (that is, in the non-Pauline parts) and in Ephesians it is the universal Church. For in no fewer than three places in 1 Corinthians (10.32; 12.28; 15.9) the word "Church" has universal overtones (cf. Gal. 1.13 and Phil. 3.6). The other metaphors—symbol is perhaps the better word in the ancient sense in which there was a definite relationship between the two objects compared—of the temple and the bride are not foreign to Paul's thinking (2 Cor. 6.16 and 11.2). This is not to say that there is no development in the doctrine of the Church in Ephesians; it is to say that the ideas that are found are genuine growths from seed-thoughts in the other letters, including Colossians. As K. L. Schmidt puts it: "Der Eph. ist in der Sache durchaus paulinisch." [38]

Masson's final argument is that demonology has an importance in Ephesians which is not found in the authentic letters of Paul. While Paul occasionally speaks of Satan, the tempter and the accuser, as the adversary of the believer and the Church (2 Cor. 12.7; 1 Thess. 3.5; 1 Cor. 5.5), he never uses διάβολος, nor do we find in his writings such phrases as "the prince of the power of the air" (2.2). Here is indeed one difficulty which those who accept Pauline authorship find hard to explain, for in the rest of the New Testament the word is found only in books which are generally held to be later than Paul.

Two other points are mentioned by Masson without a great deal of elaboration: the eschatological outlook which is found so frequently in Paul's letters has almost disappeared, and the ethical imperatives are here not so closely tied with the indicatives of the gospel. While he is right in saying that we do not find the same kind of eschatological language in Ephesians that we find in some of the earlier epistles (1 Thess. or 1 Cor.) it may seriously be questioned if he is altogether right in his other assertion (see 4.25, 30, 31).

It is not always easy to follow the trend of Masson's argument, for he has not stated his case at any great length in his two short commentaries on Colossians and Ephesians. It is discussed only in brief excursuses scattered here and there, and also in occasional foot-notes. Apparently he is unacquainted with the works of Goodspeed and Mitton, and has given very little attention to the linguistic relationship between the accepted epistles and Ephesians. While there are many illuminating comments on certain passages, his case would have to be presented much more thoroughly to convince anyone who thoughtfully holds the traditional view of both epistles.

C. *Ernst Percy*

If Masson gives his position in rather sketchy fashion, the same cannot be said of Ernst Percy, who has given us the most thorough defence yet of the Pauline authorship of Ephesians.[39] With painstaking care he deals with all the arguments that have been brought against the genuineness of the epistles and tries to prove that they can be overcome.

As the title of his book indicates, Percy investigates the authorship of both Colossians and Ephesians. "In any case one thing is certain: The question of the authenticity of Ephesians cannot be considered apart from the question of the authenticity of Colossians."[40]

Starting with Colossians, he acknowledges that there are very striking differences between it and the other Paulines; the style with its lengthy and verbose sentences, its piling up of relative clauses and participial phrases, is markedly different from the vigorous and vivid style which is characteristic of the genuine writings of Paul.[41] Though there are a good many *hapax legomena*, the proportion is very little higher than in Philippians and some of them are accounted for by the attack on the Colossian heresy in the second chapter. It is no argument that some of the favourite words of Paul are missing in Colossians (e.g. δικαιόω), for they are not found in every genuine epistle. Vocabulary cannot be used as argument against authenticity.[42]

The real problem is the style. In order to prove that Colossians is genuine, Percy takes the peculiarities in the style of Colossians—the heaping up of synonyms, fondness for repeating the same idea in another form, series of two or three genitives depending on each other, nouns with ἐν at the ends of sentences, prepositions followed by anarthrous nouns, final infinitives—and shows that parallels to all of these can be found in the genuine Paulines. The main difference is in the frequency of their occurrence; in the commonly accepted letters they are met with only occasionally, while in

Colossians they are much more frequent (the one peculiarity of Colossians so far as style is concerned is the use of ὅ ἐστιν to make the meaning of a word more explicit, e.g., 3.14). From the stylistic point of view, Colossians can be explained as a gradual development of traits which are already present in Paul's writing rather than as the work of another author. There is the further explanation that the theme of Colossians, which is so very different from those of the other epistles, may account for some of the peculiarities. When we have taken into consideration also that words and phrases are found in Colossians which are found in Paul, but not in any other early Christian writing, we may safely say that the style and vocabulary of this epistle tell for, rather than against, Pauline authorship.[43]

The same is true of its thought, for it agrees on all points with that of the authentic epistles, even in minor details. This is partiticularly true in its view of reconciliation and of the contrast between "this age" with its offer of salvation through the Law, behind which stand the *Geistermächte*, and the "new age" which is shared with Christ by those who have died to the old. Out of this springs the tension in the life of the believer between "being" and "becoming", a concept that is Paul's own. While there is a greater emphasis on "knowledge" (*gnōsis*) in Colossians, this is only a continuation of thoughts expressed in other epistles, for example, I Corinthians 2.6–8; 4.9. These agreements are all the more striking because they have no actual parallel in early Christian literature after Paul. True, there are developments in Colossians, in the sense that ideas which are touched on only briefly by Paul in earlier letters are here made more explicit, for example, the relationship of the "heavenly powers" to the salvation wrought by Christ or the idea of Christ as the goal of creation. Even the strange expression in 1.24, "In my flesh I complete what is lacking in Christ's afflictions for the sake of his body", could not have been written by anybody else, for it can be understood only as an expression of the consciousness of his vocation which is one of the hall-marks of the genuine Pauline writings. "The thought world of Colossians is Pauline to such a high degree that the hypothesis of another author is highly unlikely, and in the light of such a passage as 1.24 it is quite impossible."[44] This may be said in spite of the fact that the ethical admonitions in 3.18—4.11 have no parallel in the other letters.

We need make no comment on Percy's defence of the genuineness

of Colossians, for this question is not part of our main theme.
It has been given briefly here because Percy's treatment of Ephesians proceeds along similar lines, though he appears to be less
confident of Pauline authorship. He admits at the outset that,
though Ephesians and Colossians have much in common from the
point of view of style, yet Ephesians differs from Colossians in that
the stylistic peculiarities are more emphasized and there are also
some places where Ephesians has a style all its own. "Man konnte
beinahe sagen, dass der Epheserbrief in stilisticher Hinsicht sich
zum Kolosserbrief verhält, wie der Kolosserbrief zu den aner-
kannten Paulusbriefen."[45]

We shall first of all state Percy's case and then give our criticism
of it, rather than deal with each point as it arises. His method is
to take all the peculiarities of Ephesians and deal with them one
by one, in order to show that they are not incompatible with the
genuine letters. He first of all dismisses the high number of rare
words in Ephesians—40 not found elsewhere in the New Testament, 51 not found in Paul, and 25 found only in Colossians—by
saying that the percentage in Philippians is almost as high. The expression ἐν τοῖς ἐπουρανίοις—6 times in Ephesians and nowhere else
in the New Testament—is used because of its solemn tone and because the author wishes to denote heaven as a sphere of life rather
than as a place; διάβολος—not in the other letters—because this is
the only place where individuals are warned against his attacks,
and this name would indicate his *function* to Greek-speaking
readers; αἷμα καὶ σάρξ—a *hapax legomenon*—in order to avoid mis-
understanding in the light of the usual Pauline meaning of σάρξ,
and also to avoid two sigmas coming together.[46] The use of διὸ
λέγει to introduce a quotation is not found in Paul; his usual expression is καθὼς λέγει. But since he uses λέγει by itself, we cannot
say that διὸ λέγει is unpauline. None of these words or phrases can
be used, then, as an argument against genuineness.[47]

As in Colossians, the great difficulty is the style. Indeed the
problem here is accentuated, for the sentences are longer; consequently relative clauses and participial constructions are more
frequent. There are also more ἵνα clauses, infinitive constructions,
and phrases beginning with a preposition; the heaping up of ad-
verbial, wordy statements makes the style more drawn out than in
Colossians. The fondness for synonyms is more marked and this
expresses itself in joining together words of the same or similar

meaning by the use of the genitive case, for example, τὴν εὐδοκίαν τοῦ θελήματος αὐτοῦ (1.5), ἐν τῷ κράτει τῆς ἰσχύος αὐτοῦ (6.10). Not only are single words used in this way, but also whole phrases: ὁ δὲ Θεὸς πλούσιος ὢν ἐν ἐλέει, διὰ τὴν πολλὴν ἀγάπην αὐτοῦ, ἥν ἠγάπησεν (2.4). The wealth of attributive adjectives is meant to give the letter a more solemn tone, the article with Χριστός is used more frequently, particularly in cases other than the genitive, and the whole epistle is replete with genitives. This case is used in the expression of abstract ideas, e.g., τὸν λόγον τῆς ἀληθείας and τὸ εὐαγγέλιον τῆς σωτηρίας (1.13), and in metaphors, ἐν τῷ συνδέσμῳ τῆς εἰρήνης (4.3) and τὴν μάχαιραν τοῦ Πνεύματος (6.17); sometimes we find three genitives following each other, μέτρον ἡλικίας τοῦ πληρώματος τοῦ Χριστοῦ (4.13). In common with Colossians, though again used more frequently, are nouns with ἐν at the ends of sentences, parallel clauses, for example, ἀπηλλοτριωμένοι τῆς πολιτείας τοῦ Ἰσραηλ, καὶ ξένοι τῶν διαθηκῶν τῆς ἐπαγγελίας (2.12), and the combination of two words from the same stem, παντὸς ὀνόματος ὀνομαζομένου (1.21). Quite without parallel in Colossians is the use of indirect questions.

Percy now goes on to show that examples of all these different forms of expression may be found in the authentic letters. Clauses linked by prepositions can be found in 2 Corinthians, several times in Philippians, and in 2 Thessalonians; the tendency to tautology, in both Corinthian letters and Philippians; and the use of abstract nouns, in all the epistles except 2 Thessalonians and Philemon. Abstract nouns with the genitive are found in all the letters—no fewer than twenty-six in Romans—but indirect questions and attributive adjectives are rare.[48] If we add to this the fact that the vocabulary is predominantly Pauline in the sense that words are used in Ephesians which are rare outside the Pauline corpus, then on grounds of style alone we cannot deny Pauline authorship. The more frequent use of all these forms of expression is due to the form and content of Ephesians which have no exact counterpart in the other letters. The thanksgiving and prayer in the other epistles are much shorter—only five verses in 1 Corinthians and Philippians —than the doxology which takes up almost one half of Ephesians. The tone of rapture which runs all through Ephesians apart from the straightforward admonitions (5.21–5a; 6.1–9) is found only here and there in the other letters, but that is because nowhere else does Paul speak so much about the greatness of the divine plan of salvation and of the power of God.[49] Indeed, according to Percy, the way in which the mind of the author appears to jump back and forth in the first three chapters may be considered a good indication that they were written by one who cared little about style—a person like Paul.

Nor can we argue that Ephesians is non-Pauline because its thought is different from Paul's. As there are developments in the style of Ephesians when compared with Colossians, so here there are contacts with Colossians, but the thought is more fully developed. There are also striking resemblances to the other epistles which are either not found in Colossians or are mentioned only in passing. The two features which distinguish Ephesians are the place given to demonology and the great emphasis on the reconciliation of Jew and Gentile which was accomplished by the cross. Neither of these is new; the novelty lies in new thoughts on old themes.

The peculiarities of the demonology are as follows:

1. The Church is the instrument by which the gospel will be preached to the heavenly powers.
2. The evil spirits live in "the heavenly places".
3. Christians must be equipped to fight a vast army of them.
4. The moral, or rather the immoral, life of unbelievers is attributed to the influence of "the prince of the power of the air".

None of these can be regarded as arguments against Pauline authorship. The first is the development of ideas found in 1 Corinthians (2.6–8; 4.9) that the angelic powers are concerned with human affairs and that God's plan of salvation was unknown to them, and in Colossians (1.20, 26) where the reconciliation of all creation is the theme. In 1 Peter the angelic powers are well disposed towards man (1.12); thus Ephesians is like the Pauline writings, not the post-Pauline. While the second is not found in any of the other letters, it was an idea widely held in Judaism (Job 1.6; Zech. 3.1). As for the third, while Paul normally mentions Satan only as the enemy of man, he does speak of an "angel of Satan" (2 Cor. 12.7) or of "demons" (1 Cor. 10.20–1). The enumeration of the demonic powers is meant to show the greatness of the enemy with which the Church has to fight, and that all her strength must therefore be mobilized against him. The fourth peculiarity has affinities with 2 Corinthians 4.4, where it is said that the "god of this Age" has blinded those who do not believe; with 1 Corinthians 12.2, where Paul tells the Corinthians that in their pre-Christian days they were led astray to "dumb idols"; and with 2 Thessalonians 2.7 which speaks of "the mystery of iniquity" being already at work (cf. 1 Thess. 2.18 and 2 Cor. 12.7).[50]

The Ephesian doctrine of salvation is equally Pauline. $\Sigma \acute{\alpha} \rho \xi$ in Ephesians has the usual Pauline meaning of man living in a state of opposition to God, his unregenerate human nature. The phrase, "doing the desires of the flesh and of the mind" (2.3), does not intend to draw a distinction between the sensual and the intellectual, for it is in exact parallel with the preceding phrase, "the desires of the flesh". $\Delta \iota \acute{\alpha} \nu o \iota \alpha$ is added for the sake of variety and explanation. It defines how the impulses of the "flesh" express themselves in the total life of the non-Christian. "Gentiles in the flesh" (2.11) does not mean physically Gentiles, but those who live in an area of existence where the law of circumcision is still valid, in the "old age". If we examine the usage of $\sigma \acute{\alpha} \rho \xi$ in other early Christian writings, we find that it never means the "old age" where Sin, Death, and the Law still reign.[51]

The emphasis which Ephesians places on the love of God as the motive for our salvation is not found in the other Paulines, but the idea is there in Romans (5.5, 8; 8.38–9; 15.9) and in 2 Corinthians (5.18–21). The other motive which Ephesians gives—the honour of God—can be found in Romans (9.23; 15.7,9), in 2 Corinthians (1.11; 4.15), and in Philippians (2.11). The love of God as the basis of man's redemption is the theme of the Johannine writings, and can be found in other early Christian literature, but the thought of the honour of God is not found outside Paul. The doctrine of election is spoken of by many early Christian writers and is not just a Pauline idea (John 15.16; Jas. 2.5; 1 Pet. 1.2; Rom. 8.28; 1 Cor. 1.27). What is unique in Ephesians is the concept that believers have been chosen in Christ before creation (1.4). This is a genuine development in the doctrine; if Ephesians is not Pauline, then it was written by a disciple of Paul who heard this doctrine from his master. At any rate, it is not something with which Paul would have disagreed.[52] Behind this doctrine lies the idea of a pre-ordained plan of salvation which is called in Ephesians the $o \grave{\iota} \kappa o \nu o \mu \acute{\iota} \alpha$ of God; while the word is not used in this sense in the other Paulines, the thought is there (1 Cor. 2.7; Gal. 3.22; Rom. 5.20). The means by which the plan is realized on earth is the blood of Christ; this is not a particularly Pauline idea, but the word καταλλάσσω is (Eph. 2.16, ἀποκαταλλάσσω). While Ephesians does not speak directly of "peace with God" as the result of the death of Christ, this result is implied in the passage which speaks of Jews and Gentiles being reconciled (2.14–18) and this is in line with Romans 5.1, 10. It may also be said that the purpose of the sacrifice of Christ is the consecration of the Church (5.2, 26); this thought is implied in 1 Corinthians 6.11, "You were washed, you were sanctified, you were justified"; the words used in 5.2 are found in Philippians 4.18 and an idea similar to 5.26 is found in 2 Corinthians 11.2 (Percy is constrained to admit that these may be questionable parallels).[53] On the other hand, the thought that the resurrection is the manifestation of the power of God is not found outside Paul (Eph. 1.19; 1 Cor. 6.14; 2 Cor. 4.10–12; Phil. 3.10).

Ephesians does not use "justification" to describe the result of Christ's work. But it does speak of the forgiveness of sins (1.7) which is not earned by man, but is wholly due to the gift of divine grace. The good works which are done in the new age are not of man's own doing, for God has prepared them beforehand (2.10). Though Paul never used the phrase "good works", there is nothing in this passage which contradicts him. In fact it is Pauline throughout with its emphasis on faith as the only stipulation for receiving salvation. Again, Paul never speaks directly of the Christian's access (προσαγωγή) to God (Eph. 2.18; 3.12), but he does speak of our access to grace (Rom. 5.2) and he alone used the word adoption (υἱοθεσία) to describe our new relationship to God as that of children to their father (Rom. 8.15; Gal. 4.6; Eph. 1.5).

As was said above, one of the ideas peculiar to Ephesians is the reconciliation that Christ made between Jew and Gentile by his death on the cross (2.11–21). Many have said that the great interest of the author is in this fact. According to Percy this is not so; the main point of this passage is that the Gentiles now have a share in the divine grace from which they were formerly estranged (verses 11–12 describe the former condition of the Gentiles, 14–18 the act of Christ, 19–21 the result). The key to the meaning of the passage is therefore to be found in 14b and 15a: "He has broken down the dividing wall of partition, the enmity, for he has destroyed in his flesh the law of commandments consisting of ordinances." The Law was the cause of the enmity, seeing that it separated the Jew from the Gentile, and it cut off the Gentile from salvation, attainment of which was possible only when he submitted to circumcision as the Law demanded. The same Law had validity even for Christ so long as he belonged to the sphere of σάρξ, but when he died he was free from its demands. Since he died as the representative of mankind, all men died in his death. In his body on the cross all men were reconciled, for all became free from the claims of the Law, and the way of salvation was therefore open to all. They died as two groups divided on the basis of nationality, and rose again with him to a new life; they became one new man. The whole process is called "making peace" because the whole section is a Christian interpretation of Isaiah 57.19 (LXX): "I gave to him true consolation, peace upon peace, to those far off and to those near." Originally the passage referred to the Jews in Palestine and to those of the Dispersion, but the rabbis had interpreted the "far off" as proselytes.[54] Ephesians has gone a step further, the "far off" are now the Gentiles. The basis of this section of Ephesians is found in the letters of Paul, especially Romans and Galatians (Rom. 3.30; 11.17; Gal. 3.14, 26-8). The great stress which is placed on the equality of Jews and Gentiles before God indicates that the letter must belong to a very early time in Christianity, for Christians after Paul's time would have taken it for granted. The idea that the Law was abolished in the death of Christ is also Pauline; later Christianity either distinguished between the moral law and the ceremonial law, or it allegorized the Pentateuch. Paul occasionally does the latter (Gal. 4.21-3), but never the former.

Paul's favourite expression for the result of Christ's redeeming work is ἐν Χριστῷ [55] which occurs some thirty-six times in Ephesians. Not all the various Pauline uses of it are found in our epistle, the most striking omission being the death of the believer with Christ (Rom. 6.3-5; Col. 2.12), but according to Percy it lies behind 2.14-16, as we have seen. It is not directly mentioned here because the question of the relation of the believer to sin and the law is not the main thought in the author's mind. But it is expressly said that the believer has been raised with Christ (2.6; cf. Col. 3.1), and, further, that he is already sitting with Christ in the heavenly places (2.6). This is but another way of saying that already with Christ he is living in the "new age". This finds only indirect expression here and there in the other letters (2 Cor. 5.17; Gal. 6.15); what is implicit in these passages is explicitly stated here. We must therefore say that if Paul did not write Ephesians, it was written by one who understood the heart of the Pauline doctrine of salvation better than the Apostle himself. Since nobody before Irenaeus understood it, and he did not understand it clearly—the Fourth Gospel and the Johannine Epistles may be an exception to this—is it likely that anyone other than Paul had grasped its full meaning? [56]

Ephesians also goes beyond normal Pauline usage when it uses σώζω in the perfect tense (2.5). In the other letters it is found in the present (1 Cor. 1.18; 2 Cor. 2.15), but much more frequently in the future (Rom. 5.19–20; 1 Cor. 3.15; Phil. 1.19; 1 Thess. 2.16, etc.). The aorist is found only in Romans 8.24 where it is said that "we were saved through hope"; but since Christians possess this hope only as members of the body of Christ (1 Cor. 15.19), and those outside of Christ are without hope (Eph. 2.12), it cannot be said that the use of the perfect tense is a contradiction of Paul. For Paul speaks of justification as past (Rom. 5.9; 1 Cor. 6.11) and as future (Gal. 5.5), and of "adoption" as something we have (Rom. 8.15) but still wait for (Rom. 8.23). The same tension between salvation as present possession and future hope is seen in 1.22 where it is said that all things have been subjected to Christ, and in 6.10–12, where the Christian still has to struggle against the powers of evil. This is also true of the Pauline antinomy between "being" and "becoming", for Ephesians has it no less than the genuine epistles: "You have been saved" (2.8), yet "the old man" must be put off and the "new man" put on (4.22, 24). It is even carried over into what may be called the ontological, as distinct from the moral, life of believers. In 1.23 the Church is the fullness (πλήρωμα) of Christ, which must mean that it includes within itself the whole fullness of the being of Christ, but in 3.19 the apostle prays that his readers "may be filled with all the fullness of God". The tension here is between faith and experience, between what the believers are as a result of their incorporation into Christ, and their earthly existence; what they already possess they must make their own more and more. In the prayer (3.14–19) the intention is that all which is said to have happened in 1.3—2.22 will happen. This is the same pattern that we find in the thanksgiving and prayer in Colossians 1.4–14.[57] The "inner man" (3.16) is not simply the part (*Punkt*) of man on which the Spirit can work and to which it can join itself. Behind this phrase lie the ideas expressed in Romans 7.13–25. There Paul is describing the tension which continually exists in the Christian life—the believer knows that he belongs to Christ though he still lives in the "old age"; if he is to "actualize" within himself what he knows himself to be, then his faith must continually be renewed. The "inner man" is not a part of the "natural" man, but the spiritual side of the believer in so far as it belongs to the "new man", that is, to Christ, though it cannot be completely identified with him. On the other hand, the believer already has the "new man" because of his membership in the body of Christ. So when the Apostle prays that the recipients of his letter may be "strengthened with might through his Spirit in the inner man", he is asking that they may have the power to realize within themselves what they already are, and the Spirit is the agent through whom this will come about. No idea could be more Pauline than this (Rom. 8; Gal. 5.16–18; 2 Cor. 3.18).

The Ephesian teaching about the Spirit is also similar to the other Paulines. The Spirit is the "seal" (1.13; 4.30; cf. 2 Cor. 1.22), the "guarantee" (1.14; cf. 2 Cor. 1.22; 5.5), the source of knowledge (1.17–18; 3.5; cf. 1 Cor. 2.10–12), the sphere of prayer (6.18; cf. Rom. 8.15; Gal. 4.6), the bond of unity (4.3; cf. 1 Cor. 12.13). The only place where Ephesians differs from the remaining Paulines in its teaching on the Spirit is in 5.18 where his readers are exhorted to be filled with the Spirit; Paul's usual prayer is that they may show in their lives the fruit of the Spirit which they already possess.[58]

Nor is the Ephesian emphasis on knowledge proof that it is non-Pauline. When Paul appears to minimize the value of knowledge in 1 Corinthians 8 and 13, it is only because the church in Corinth was strongly inclined to overrate knowledge at the expense of love. Paul places a high value on Christian knowledge (Rom. 15.14; 2 Cor. 8.7; 11.6; Phil. 1.9). The reason for this is seen in Ephesians 4.14—it is a shield against error—but especially in 3.14–19. The deeper the knowledge the believer has, the more he makes the knowledge his own, the more he understands the divine revelation, the nearer he comes to fulfilling the purpose of his creation, which is to be filled with all the fullness of God. To grasp the divine plan of salvation in all its "breadth and length and depth and height" means to come to an understanding of the love of God which is manifested in that plan. It is to make his own what he already possesses as a member of Christ. This is beyond the capacity of the human mind to grasp completely. Knowledge therefore reaches its fulfilment when it becomes aware of its own insufficiency (cf. Phil. 4.7).

Where Ephesians differs from the other epistles in this respect is that it regards the revelation of the divine plan as the highest proof of the riches of God's grace. Nothing like this appears in early Christian literature; the exuberant language used can only mean that the idea was quite new; this would not be so in the generation after Paul.[59]

The Christology of Ephesians is not essentially different from that of Colossians. The difference lies in using language about Christ which in the Old Testament is used of God. "The fullness of him who fills all in all" (1.23) and "in order that he might fill all things" (4.10) are borrowed from Jeremiah 23.24, "Do I not fill heaven and earth?" But this is only a development of the idea in Colossians that all things were created in, through, and for Christ (1.16–20). The only parallel to this in the other letters is found in 1 Corinthians 8.6, where it is said that all creation exists through Christ; a similar thought is found in 1 Corinthians 15.27 and Philippians 2.10 which speak of all things being subjected to Christ. If this idea does not occur elsewhere, it may be only because there was no need to bring together the doctrines of Christ and creation.

Nor does the phrase "the kingdom of Christ and of God" (5.5) mark an advance in Christology, for Colossians 1.13 has "the kingdom of the Son of his love", and 1 Corinthians 15.25 says that Christ is now reigning and will reign until the parousia, when he will hand over the kingdom to the Father. Paul is not consistent on this point. In Romans 14.17 and 1 Corinthians 4.20 the kingdom of God is at present in existence. Equally, Christ or God can be the source of redemption (2.5–7; Rom. 15.7; Gal. 2.20).[60]

The doctrine of the Church as the Body of Christ in this epistle is the key to the teaching on this subject found in the other epistles. It is in the death of Christ, where all men die to the "old age", that all men—Jews and Gentiles—are incorporated into his body, and become one organism, the members of which are endowed with many different gifts. Ephesians 5.29–30 and 1 Corinthians 12.12–14 express the same idea, for in both passages Christ himself is the body and believers are members of that body; the thought here is the relationship between Christ and the individual Christian. Only where the relationship between Christ and the Church is discussed is the head–body image used (Col. 2.19; Eph. 1.22; 4.15).

The spiritual gifts that are given to the Church in Ephesians 4.7–9 resemble the lists that we find in Romans 12.3–5 and 1 Corinthians 12.28, particularly the latter. Corinthians and Ephesians have apostles, prophets, and teachers; Corinthians alone has workers of miracles, healers, helpers, administrators, those who speak with tongues. This appears to be a fluid list, and it does not mean to suggest that one person has only one gift. Ephesians alone has evangelists and pastors. Percy thinks that Ephesians is different from 1 Corinthians because the Apostle is concerned here only with the gifts which make for unity and the growth of the Church.[61] The role played by these men is to equip the saints, that is, the members of the body, for "the performance of service that the body of Christ may be built up". Every member has his special gift (4.7; cf. 1 Cor. 12.7), and his own special task (4.16), but since some gifts are more important than others, inasmuch as they contribute more to the up-building of the Church, those who have received them play a more important part than others. The final goal is that all the members, through gradual growth in knowledge and through co-operation, will arrive at a complete possession of the contents of the Christian faith, and so be unified in Christ. The stress in this letter is not therefore on the external growth of the Church but on the spiritual maturity of those who already belong to it. The officers mentioned in 4.11 have a greater measure of faith and knowledge for the sole purpose that they may help the average member to come to full maturity. The difference between Ephesians and 1 Corinthians is that the latter speaks of the necessity of all the gifts of the Spirit for the life of the Church, while the former stresses the necessity for the greater gifts of the leaders. The group is to comply with the instruction and direction of these leaders whom Christ has placed in the Church in order that it may be saved from error and come to fullness of faith (4.14–16). This protection from error is similar to the teaching in Colossians 2.

Nowhere except in Colossians and Ephesians do we find the idea of the Church as an organism healthy in its growth (Eph. 4.16; Col. 2.19). For the author of Ephesians, the individual finds his life only as a member of the body. But the idea of mutual caring for one another and the desire that all should use their gifts for the common profit are frequently expressed in Paul (Rom. 14.19;

1 Cor. 8.11; 1 Thess. 5.11, etc.). The great stress on unity (4.13–14) would seem to suggest that the letter was written at a time when false teaching was spreading; we do not know if this was the case in the time of Paul, though Colossians offers an example of it. In some parts of his letter, the author of Ephesians seems to have in mind the Church as a whole; therefore it may be that, when writing to Ephesus, he realizes that his readers have not yet reached maturity of faith, and he is warning them against the influence of false teaching which may spread to them from another part of the Church. He is also exhorting them to show forth in this age the unity which they already possess as members of Christ. The Church must become what it is.

The concept of the Church as the bride of Christ is a peculiarity of Ephesians (5.22–4), and therefore some would say that it is the importation of a Gnostic idea. Percy will have none of this; the idea of a pre-existent Church is not found in Ephesians, for the Church is born when Christ dies on the cross (2.15). The same thought is found in this passage: "Christ loved the Church and gave himself up for her". There is no need to look beyond the early Christian community for the source of this idea. Paul must have had it in mind when he said: "I betrothed you to Christ to present you as a pure bride to one husband" (2. Cor. 11.2).

The third picture of the Church given in Ephesians is that of a building with the apostles and prophets as its foundation and Christ as the corner-stone (ἀκρογωνιαῖος). Percy will not admit that this word may be translated "keystone", on the ground that this passage (2.20–2) is based on Isaiah 28.16, the only place where the word occurs in the Septuagint, and also that it destroys the whole picture of a building not yet finished. Christ cannot be the stone put in last. This is not a parallel to the head–body analogy, for it is quite differently oriented. In the picture of the Church as a body with Christ as its head, the dominant thought is the unity of the Church; in the picture of the building, it is growth that is in the foreground of the writer's mind.

Percy admits that this passage is one of those most frequently used to deny the Pauline authorship, because Paul had said in 1 Corinthians 3.10–11 that Christ alone is the foundation of the Church, but he does not think there is any contradiction here. In the Corinthian letter it is a question of the relationship of the Apostle and his work to those who succeeded him in Corinth; in Ephesians it is a matter of the relationship of the believers to apostles and prophets. This is expressed in the picture of a building in which all are stones. In the one case the Apostle laid the foundation, in the other he himself is part of the building in which Christ has the most important place—the corner-stone. It is strange that Paul—if it is he—should mention the apostles as a group without saying anything about his own relationship to them, but this has also happened in Romans 16.7 and 1 Corinthians 12.28. The stress in this section of Ephesians may be on the necessity of the faithful to maintain a continued relationship with those from whom they originally received the faith. Paul had a high consciousness of vocation and more than once asserted his authority when his enemies tried to deny it (Gal. 1.1; 1 Cor. 9); this was especially true about his authority in the Gentile churches. Even though it may be said that the linking of apostles and prophets points to a time before the apostles were given a unique position (as in Ignatius), it cannot be denied that there are two strange things here: the apostles are the bearers of the Christian revelation and the prophets are part of the foundation of the Church. In 1 Corinthians 14 and 1 Thessalonians 5.20 they are ordinary members of the local church. It is with some hesitation, then, that Percy accepts this passage as Pauline.[62]

The phrase "his holy apostles and prophets" (3.5) creates no difficulty. Where all the believers are holy (1.1; 3.18; 6.18), it would be natural to apply the same adjective to their leaders. In Colossians 1.26 it is said that "the mystery hidden for ages and generations is now made manifest to his saints". In Ephesians 3.1–13 the author is dealing with the call of Paul to be the apostle of the Gentiles and therefore does not think of the whole Church as the bearer of the revelation. He has here taken the thought in Colossians and combined it with the "apostles and prophets" of Ephesians 2.20.

A greater difficulty arises over the titles "apostles" and "evangelists" (4.11). It has been thought that all who preached the gospel were called apostles at the beginning (Rom. 16.7), and that the word was later limited to Paul and the Twelve. Attempts have also been made to trace the idea of apostleship to the Jewish *shaliach*—a man sent out to perform a service for a community and given authority to act on behalf of the community. But two facts militate against this: the *shaliach* was given this authority only for the duration of his mission, while the apostle had a permanent standing; the *shaliach* was appointed by the community, but the apostle was called by the Lord himself. We cannot distinguish between apostles in the local church, who have received a special gift of the Spirit, and apostles over the whole Church, who were commissioned by the Lord; at any rate Paul makes no such distinction (1 Cor. 12.28). (The only "apostles" appointed for a special task are those made responsible for the gift to the Jerusalem church, and they do not appear to have a special *charisma* for this purpose.)

But there are others who preach the gospel who are not called apostles—Priscilla and Aquila, Timothy, Epaphras, to name only a few; Paul makes it clear in Colossians (1.25) that he is their apostle, though he has never seen them. It would therefore appear that evangelists are mentioned in Ephesians because the letter was written to churches which had been founded by those who did not bear the title of apostle. So we cannot say that it belongs to a later time than Paul.

Percy admits that the section 3.1–13 contains apparent contradictions. In 2–3 and 8–9 it appears as if Paul alone had received by revelation the message that the Gentiles had an equal share in salvation with the Jews, while in 5–6 the same message is revealed to the "holy apostles and prophets". But he claims it is easier to understand the difficulty if we think of Paul as the author of the letter. When Paul is thinking of his relationship to the recipients of the letter, of his commission to preach the gospel to them, then he speaks of himself alone as the one who received the revelation; but when he speaks of the epoch-making revelation itself, then he associates with himself those who have had the same experience or received the same commission. If Ephesians was written by a later author to magnify the name of Paul in the Christian tradition, would he have said that others had shared the same experience? If by "apostles" is meant the Twelve, then we have not overcome the difficulty; but if it includes all those who were commissioned by the Lord, which is Paul's usual meaning, then he simply means all who received the special duty of preaching to the Gentiles. It should also be noted that in Acts, prophets had sent Paul and Barnabas on their first missionary journey (Acts 13.1–3), and that prophets from Jerusalem had worked in the Gentile mission in Antioch (Acts 11.27; 15.32). In these significant events Paul may

well have seen the working of the Spirit, and he has here gener-
alized out of his own experience with those who worked in the
Gentile mission or were benevolently disposed toward it.[63]

The καθὼς προέγραψα ἐν ὀλίγῳ (3.3) does not refer to a collection
of the Pauline letters as Goodspeed claims, but to the two fore-
going chapters and especially to the mystery (1.9; 2.11–22) of the
share of the Gentiles in salvation. It is on the basis of the knowlege
of the mystery which he has received by the grace of God that he
has the right to preach the gospel; the same point of view is expressed in Romans, though the same language is not used. Nor is
"less than the very least of all the saints" necessarily unpauline,
for he uses the expression "the least of the apostles" in 1 Corinthians 15.9. In Percy's view, nobody else would have thought of
putting such a strong expression of humility in the mouth of Paul.
And when the Apostle tells his readers that his sufferings are their
glory, he is only saying again what he has said in 2 Corinthians 1.14
and Colossians 1.24.

So this passage cannot be used as an argument against authenticity; it cannot be explained as an attempt by a later author to re-
habilitate Paul's position at a time when it was in eclipse in Asia
Minor. Nobody in the time after Paul would have made so much of
the Gentiles' privileges in the Church, for by that time they would
have been taken for granted. To say that an author other than Paul
would insert in his letter a plea for his readers not to lose heart over
the Apostle's sufferings (3.13) is to credit him with far too much
subtlety of mind. Nor is it likely that anyone other than Paul could
have written about Paul's understanding of the mystery of salvation as it is expressed in 3.1–13.

The ethical instruction in Ephesians differs in many ways from
that of the other Pauline epistles, though there are resemblances.
The most striking difference is the great emphasis on unity; both
the gifts of the Spirit and moral conduct are directed to that end
(4.7–16, 25–9). The lack of detail on the relationships within the
congregation may be due to the fact of Paul's imprisonment
(Colossians and Philippians are like Ephesians in this respect); lack
of knowledge leads him to generalize. There is also a marked difference between the teaching on marriage in Ephesians and that
found in 1 Corinthians 7, while the exhortation to be joyful and
patient in suffering which is found in almost all the other letters is
missing here.[64]

As a result of this investigation, Percy holds that the thought of Ephesians is not essentially different from that of the other Paulines, while it differs markedly from the post-Pauline literature. The greatest stumbling-blocks to the acceptance of its authenticity are the role of the apostles and prophets (2.20; 3.5) and the section on marriage (5.25–33), but these cannot be allowed to outweigh the rest of the evidence. If anyone other than Paul wrote it, then he had a greater insight into the mind of the Apostle than any other Christian before Luther.[65]

Percy now turns to the literary relationship between Ephesians and Colossians, which has been one of the main sources of argument against Pauline authorship. While he agrees that there is a direct literary connection between the two letters, the most important part of his book is this section which attempts to refute the arguments of those who hold that Ephesians can be shown on a literary grounds to be post-Pauline.

He first of all claims that the literary relationship between the two letters is not as great as some scholars suppose. While there are definite connections between Ephesians 3.1–6 and Colossians 1.23–27, Ephesians 4.2–6 and Colossians 3.12–15, and Ephesians 6.21–2 and Colossians 4.7–8 (these last two passages agree almost word for word), the other contacts between the two epistles are limited to passages which are quite different in order and which are seldom in complete textual agreement—for example, the parenetic section of Colossians begins with a warning against sexual sins and then continues with warnings against anger and sins of speech (3.5–8), while the corresponding section in Ephesians begins with a warning against the sins mentioned at the end of the list in Colossians, and inserts a warning against stealing which is not found in Colossians at all (Eph. 4.25–8). While the *Haustafel* follows the same order in both letters, the two verses of Colossians on husbands and wives are expanded to eleven in Ephesians, and the phrase about partiality which is addressed to slaves in Colossians is transferred to masters in Ephesians. Phrases which occur in the "prayer" in Ephesians (1.3—2.22) are found in the admonition in Colossians (Eph. 2.1–2 is paralleled by Col. 2.13 and 3.7); Ephesians 1.15–16 follows Colossians 1.4, 9, but the content of the sections which are respectively introduced by these verses is different. Ephesians 5.15, 19 is closely related to Colossians 4.5 and 3.16–17, but these latter passages precede and follow the *Haustafel* in

Colossians; in Ephesians they precede it and are linked together by two verses which have no parallel in Colossians. These and other examples, according to Percy, show that Ephesians does not borrow from Colossians; it merely makes use of thoughts and expressions which, apart from the three sections noted at the beginning of this paragraph, may be nothing more than reminiscences of Colossians.[66]

There are a few phrases in Ephesians which appear to have been borrowed from Colossians, but these, says Percy, may be no more than habitual phrases which come naturally to the author's mind, since in nearly every case they are used in different contexts. In Percy's opinion, if they were deliberate borrowings, the borrower would have been careful to give the total idea rather than just a few of the words. Two examples of the ten that Percy gives are here briefly discussed.

1. Ephesians 3.16; Colossians 1.11. In the former the author prays that his readers may be given strength in the inner man through the power of the Spirit, in the latter that they may be given the power of God to endure patiently. Though some of the words are the same, both context and meaning are different.
2. Ephesians 2.12 and 4.18; Colossians 1.21. These are the only places in early Christian literature where the participle ἀπηλλοτ- ριωμένος is found. Here again the contexts are quite different. In Colossians it is "estranged and hostile in mind" while in Ephesians 2.12 it is "alienated from the commonwealth of Israel" and in Ephesians 4.18 it is "alienated from the life of God".

These and the other examples, according to Percy, are more easily explained as one author's use of the same words and phrases than as borrowings by one author from another.[67]

At this point Percy admits that there are several contacts between Ephesians and Colossians which make it appear as if they were written by different authors. He notes no fewer than twenty-five places where the author of Ephesians appears to have taken a word or phrase from Colossians and either misunderstood it, or changed its meaning, or given it a different application. Of these twenty-five, six are especially difficult. The six are:

1. Ephesians 4.3, "The bond of peace"; Colossians 3.14, "The bond of perfection".

2. Ephesians 5.20, "Giving thanks in the name of our Lord Jesus Christ to God the Father"; Colossians 3.17, "Do everything in the name of the Lord Jesus, giving thanks to God the Father through him".

3. The phrase "submitting yourselves to each other" which acts as the bridge between the admonitions and the *Haustafel*, Ephesians 5.21; it is repeated in the following verse, which is almost the same as Colossians 3.18.

4. Ephesians 5.22–33; Colossians 3.18–19. The duties of husbands and wives.

5. Ephesians 6.8; Colossians 3.24–5. The duties of slaves to their masters.

6. Ephesians 6.19; Colossians 4.3. The important phrase in Colossians is "a door for the word".

Since Percy's method is the same in dealing with all these passages, it is not necessary to consider them all. Three of them may be used as examples.

1. Ephesians 5.20. This is the only place in early Christian literature where "in the name of our Lord Jesus Christ" is used with giving thanks; the normal preposition is "through". According to Percy, "in the name" and "through the name" have different meanings in the Pauline corpus. His only explanation of this unique phrase in Ephesians is that the author wished to end the phrase with a dative, "to God the Father", as the previous phrase had also ended with a dative.[68]

2. Ephesians 6.19. In this passage Ephesians is dependent upon Colossians for its language, but the meaning is different. In Ephesians the writer asks his readers to pray that he may be given the right word to say; in Colossians, either that men may be receptive to the gospel, or that external hindrances to preaching it may be removed. The two epistles are not saying the same thing here, as some have thought, for in Colossians 1.29 Paul says that the energy he possesses is inspired by God; it is not the Apostle who speaks, but God who speaks through him. Percy's conclusion is that no disciple of Paul, with Colossians before him, would have given the same phrase two different meanings. But it would be quite possible for Paul to use the same metaphor in two different ways in two different letters, since it is not likely that he had copies of his own correspondence.[69]

3. Ephesians 5.22–3. Here the greatly developed comparison of marriage with the relationship of Christ and the Church has no parallel in Colossians. Since, says Percy, there is nothing specifically Christian in the admonition on husband-wife relationships in Colossians, it may be that the non-Christian ethical material of Colossians has been combined with Christian material in Ephesians. Indeed, the main point of interest in the Ephesian section is Christ and the Church, not husband and wife. While he admits that it is strange that Paul should give instruction on this point in only one of two letters which he wrote at the same time, this cannot be maintained as an argument against Pauline authorship. Ephesians may have been written to a new church which needed more instruction on this point.[70]

Dr Percy's conclusion after dealing with all these passages is that while they do present some obstacles to the acceptance of Pauline authorship, these obstacles are not as insurmountable as those which are raised on the assumption of non-Pauline authorship.

There are also clear indications of literary relationship between Ephesians and the letters which are generally accepted as Pauline. Phrases similar to those in Ephesians may be found in Romans, 1 and 2 Corinthians, and Galatians; this must mean that the author, if not Paul, knew and used these letters. But why then is Colossians used much more than the others? Because, says Percy, Colossians is the only Pauline letter which, apart from the sections dealing with the Colossian heresy, is general in tone. Apart from this, it describes the greatness of salvation in liturgical language, which is what Ephesians does also. Yet this does not explain the literary relationship. The question then arises why Ephesians has relationships with Colossians both in form and content. It is absurd to think that it was composed by someone on the basis of the mention of a letter to Laodicea in Colossians 4.18, for this is too transparent a fiction. Nor could a secretary have written it at Paul's order, for this does not explain the contacts with the other Paulines. The most likely hypothesis is that Paul wrote Ephesians shortly after he had written Colossians (Goodspeed is dismissed as being "allzu naiv").[71]

But even apart from these literary relationships which lead

4—E.B.P.

Percy to think that the weight of evidence falls on the side of
Pauline authorship, there is the further fact that there is no trace in
the letter of any set of circumstances which would make post-
Pauline authorship acceptable to him. The various theories that
have been put forward—that Ephesians was written as an introduction to the Pauline corpus, that it was written to promote
the unity of the Church when Jewish and Gentile Christians were
beginning to drift apart or to warn against the disruptive influence
of incipient heresies, that its purpose was to revive the influence of
Paul at a time when that influence was dying in the church in Asia
Minor—all these are dismissed with a few brief comments, on the
ground that while they may explain certain aspects of the letter,
they do not explain the letter as a whole. The most tenable explanation for Percy is that Ephesians was written to deepen the faith of
believers—probably recent believers—and to encourage them to
live lives worthy of their faith. This, together with the precise
claim that Paul is the author (3.1), leads him to think that the
genuineness of the epistle has more to be said for it than the
opposite view.[72]

It has been thought necessary to give so much attention to
Percy's book because it is the most detailed defence of Pauline
authorship that has yet appeared. The general impression that the
book as a whole gives is that it "protests too much". All scholars
admit that the language of Ephesians is Pauline, though it is remarkable that certain of Paul's key words, such as "justification",
are omitted. Parallels to its style also can be found in the rest of the
Pauline corpus. But the really difficult question, that raised by both
vocabulary and style, Percy does not answer at all. Where else in a
single letter of Paul do we find such sustained, sonorous sentences
and such a large number of tautological phrases?[73] It is not the type
of phrase but the frequency of its occurrence that raises doubts in
our minds, and it is no argument to say that it is the content of the
letter which controls the style, for, on Percy's own admission, the
content is not different from that of the other Paulines. He has not
answered those who, like Moffat, have rejected Pauline authorship
on grounds of style alone; he has simply taken the varied forms of
expression one by one and does not deal with the problem which is
raised by their frequency.

He has no difficulty in showing that the thought of Ephesians
can be found in Paul, and that its main themes are Pauline. But

when he goes on to say that the only difference is a development in the thought, he does not allow any time for that development in the Apostle's mind. To say that Ephesians marks the same sort of advance on Colossians that Colossians does on the other letters implies that some time must have elapsed between the writing of the two letters. Yet at several places in his book Percy says that the similarity of language between Ephesians and Colossians can be accounted for by the hypothesis that both letters were written at about the same time. A great deal of his argument is thereby vitiated. Here too Percy uses the same method as he used in the argument on style. Each individual passage which has caused others to think that the letter as a whole is unpauline is taken by itself and shown to be either a legitimate development of Pauline thought, or else a variation on a theme from one of the other epistles; again the question is not faced as to why there are so many of these passages in one letter. It may be possible to explain the appearance of an occasional phrase which arouses our suspicions, but when these phrases occur in every section of the Epistle, then no amount of explanation devoted to each one separately is going to give a satisfactory answer to the problem.

In the comparison of parallel passages in Ephesians and Colossians this method is carried to extremes. Here Percy takes the twenty-five passages which appear to point to two different authors, examines each of them, and, confidently in some cases, with hesitation in others, proves to his own satisfaction that there is no strong reason why any one of them could not have been written by Paul. But some of his reasons are dubious, to say the least. He has no real answer to the problem raised by the admonition on marriage (5.22–32), nor why the section on slaves and masters should be so radically changed from Colossians (Eph. 6.5–9; Col. 3.22—4.1). The same may be said of Ephesians 5.20 and Colossians 3.17, or of Ephesians 6.4 and Colossians 3.21. Again, the real stumbling-block to the acceptance of Percy's thesis is that he never attempts to deal with the problem which is raised by all of these passages together; he deals with each one by itself, as if unaware that there were twenty-four others which needed to be explained—six of them, on his own admission, extremely difficult. Unless the solution offered covers a fairly high percentage of the twenty-five, we are justified in looking askance at it, especially when we are told of some of the passages that an imitator could not have written them because he would have been more careful (5.20 is cited as an example), or that he would not have used rare words (as in 2.12).

Neither has Percy answered the problem of the impersonal nature of the letter. All other letters ascribed to Paul, even those addressed to people whom he does not know personally, have warm personal greetings (Rom. 1.8–15; Col. 4.7–14) and references to real problems (Rom. 14, 15; Col. 2.8–16). Indeed, the *Sitz im Leben* of this epistle is one of the main reasons why there has been so much difference of opinion about it. Is it at all likely that in only one of his extant letters Paul would have become as impersonal as he does in Ephesians?

Finally, Percy uses far too strong language when he says that it is "scarcely possible to understand Ephesians as a whole as a post-Pauline fiction",[74] for he is applying modern moral and literary standards to a time which had a different set of standards. It was considered highly laudatory in the ancient world for a disciple to publish his own work under his teacher's name, as Tertullian tells us.[75] Further, to say that the main difficulty in rejecting Pauline authorship is that we cannot reconstruct a set of circumstances in the first century which would cause a close follower of Paul to publish a letter in the Apostle's name is to place more weight on this difficulty than it can possibly bear. While it is true that no hypothesis put forward by modern scholars to account for the writing of Ephesians has won general acceptance, the failure to find a universally acceptable solution cannot be used as a weapon to destroy the formidable case which has been built up by those who reject Pauline authorship.

Though this book displays a wealth of learning, though it is written with painstaking care, and every problem discussed, sometimes in the most minute detail, the verdict on it must be "not proven".

D. *N. A. Dahl*

The one other person on the side of Pauline authorship whose work must come under review is N. A. Dahl. His contribution to the debate is that Ephesians was written by Paul to newly founded churches in order to instruct their members more fully in the meaning of their baptism. The passages on which this thesis especially depends are 1.14; 4.5, 30; 5.8, 26.[76] It was written not as a general letter to all churches, but specifically to those in Asia Minor which Paul had not founded; in this respect it is similar to Colossians except that no specific problems had arisen like those which made Colossians necessary. Its main purpose is to remind these Asian Christians of the great blessings which they had received and of the responsibilities which are entailed in becoming believers.

In Dahl's opinion Ephesians opens with a benediction which is modelled on a liturgical form, not with a hymn placed at the beginning of a letter.[77] Primitive Christian blessings are bound up with certain acts, as in Judaism, but a variety of forms of blessing developed out of one main form. Just as the eucharistic prayer originated in the Jewish blessings at meals, so blessings at baptism may well have developed out of blessings which were always said before a Jewish ritual bath; the introductory section of Ephesians, which contains within itself the main ideas of the letter, may look back to a benediction said before a baptism. It opens with a traditional form, "Blessed be the God and Father of our Lord Jesus Christ" and continues with a traditional adjectival clause. Verses 4-6a speak of salvation from the point of view of the gracious will of God, verses 6b-12 speak of the gracious acts of God by which his will is made known, while the last two verses apply what has been said to those who heard, believed, and were baptized. The style of introduction—a prepositional phrase followed by an adjectival clause—helps to tie all these thoughts together and enables the author to apply what he says of all Christians to the specific group who are going to receive the letter. The contents may be set out in summary form as follows:

3   The praise of God
4-6a   His eternal gracious purpose
6b-7   Grace as forgiveness
8-9a   Grace as revelation
9b-10 Universality of salvation
11-12 Share of Christians in this salvation
13-14 The application to those who will receive the letter

The remainder of the letter develops out of this section. The readers are reminded of what has happened to them through the act of God in Christ, through their own baptism and through the calling of Paul to be the apostle to the Gentiles. In his admonition he refers not only to the beginning of their call—one Lord, one faith, one baptism—but several times points to the contrast between what they were earlier as heathen and what they are now to do as Christians. The admonition, in fact, is the type of teaching that would be given to new converts. The letter is therefore a logical whole, with the main idea stated in the benediction and then expounded in the rest of the letter.

On the question of authorship, Dahl does not think a decision is possible either on theological or stylistic grounds alone, or on the relationship between Ephesians and Colossians. The peculiarities of Ephesians are no greater than in any letter of Paul's which is regarded as authentic. If Colossians is accepted, then it is no greater step to accept Ephesians than to accept 2 Thessalonians. He thinks that the most important question is the situation in which the letter originates, and that if we can find a satisfactory answer to it, we can make the peculiarities of the letter, both singly and together, intelligible; he believes that the situation outlined above does provide this answer.

On the vexed question of the salutation, he does not think that the solution is to be found in attempts to emend the text. The text as in B, S, and P46 must be considered as the original text in the Pauline corpus, but cannot be the text in the original letter which must have had a place name or names, and must have been sent to a definite circle of readers (1.13; 2.21-2; 6.21)—he dismisses the hypothesis of a blank space into which the place name could be inserted either orally or in writing, as having no parallel in the ancient world. If Ephesians is not genuine, he thinks that the best hypothesis that has been put forward is that it is a "catholicized version" of Colossians which had "in Colossae" in the text. This was struck out when it was discovered that there was a genuine Colossians.[78] But for Dahl this presents difficulties; the figure of a reviser only complicates the history of the letter before it was accepted into the Pauline corpus, for it must have been read in Ephesus without the place-name before the letters of Paul were collected. This alone would account for the superscription "To the Ephesians"; a letter sent from Ephesus without a place-name was thought to be a letter to Ephesus when it was added to the collection. It is not likely that it was a pseudonymous letter to Laodicea, for there is no reason why the place-name would have been omitted from it; besides, this is not the kind of letter that would be written to a single community even by an imitator. It must be an encyclical.

How then does Dahl account for the omission of the place-name or names, if Galatians is any criterion of the way in which Paul began an encyclical letter? His theory is that Paul, after writing Colossians, wrote a letter to the other churches of Asia Minor that were personally not known to him. Copies of this letter, with individual place-names, or the letter itself with all the place-names for which it was intended, were brought to Ephesus by Tychicus on his way to the other cities. There it was read to the church by Tychicus, or some of the members read it for themselves, and thought that it would be good to have a copy of it for their own community. Since it was not addressed to them and they did not wish the encyclical nature of the letter to be overlooked, they could not retain one place-name nor could they insert the name of their own church. But they could make a copy and use it; since the Apostle had ordered the churches in Laodicea and Colossae to exchange letters, they felt that he would not object to Ephesus having a copy of his general letter. Hence arose the difficult text that has come down to us. This hypothesis can also account for Marcion's ascribing "Ephesians" to Laodicea. The copy he possessed still retained the name of one of the churches for which the letter was originally intended. This, like the letters sent to Hierapolis and possibly to other churches, has now been lost.

If Ephesians is accepted as genuine, this seems to be the best hypothesis yet put forward to account for the present text of 1.1, but it is not without its difficulties. It is not easy to see why, if there were several place-names in the original, they were not retained; or if there were only one place-name in several copies, they were not all combined, after the manner of Galatians or 1 Peter, in the copy which was made at Ephesus. If the place-name or names were taken out, why was not τοῖς οὖσιν omitted as well, for the text as it stands does not make good sense without "in" followed by a place-name? Nor does Dahl give any reason why a letter written by Paul contains only one personal reference (6.21), when Colossians, written also to a church not founded by Paul himself, devotes almost all of the last chapter to personal greetings and news. It is highly unlikely that Paul, after writing such a letter to Colossae, could write such an impersonal one to other churches in the same area, particularly when he has mentioned some of the members of the Laodicean church in Colossians.

With regard to the purpose of the letter as expounded by Dahl, there can be no doubt that membership in the Church is one of the main themes of the letter; consequently baptism is bound to be one of the subsidiary themes. But if the letter is written to remind new converts of their privileges and responsibilities, it is strange that nothing is said about the Eucharist, particularly when the readers are exhorted to unity (4.3) and Paul held the Eucharist to be the means of unity (1 Cor. 10.17). Why is there so much stress on the reconciliation of Jew and Gentile and nothing whatever in the admonition about the way in which Jews and Gentiles ought to behave to one another? Is it at all likely that the churches which were so close to Colossae had no difficulties similar to the Colossian heresy? (Epaphras is well known to them all—Col. 4.13.) Further, to pass over the problems which are raised by style, language, and thought is a counsel of despair. Attractive as Dahl's thesis is, it must be rejected, for while it looks at Ephesians from a fresh point of view, it does so at the cost of overlooking the difficulties which some have found to be the greatest obstacles in accepting the epistle as genuine.

E. *E. J. Goodspeed and C. L. Mitton*

We now turn to the work of two scholars who have put forward the best case, at least in the English-speaking world, for non-Pauline authorship, E. J. Goodspeed and C. L. Mitton. Mitton's work is an expansion and development of Goodspeed's, though he does not accept many of the details of the latter's work nor all of his conclusions.[79]

Briefly stated, Goodspeed's theory is as follows: Paul's letters to individual churches, written as they were for a specific purpose, were forgotten even by the churches to whom they were written. Towards the end of the first century a Christian at Colossae who knew both Colossians and Philemon received a copy of Luke–Acts. This aroused in him a desire to search for other letters of Paul in the Christian churches mentioned in Acts; as a result he received letters from seven of the churches. He studied this collection until he knew the theology and ethics of Paul almost by heart and then decided to give to the whole Church the letters he had found. He realized that a great many parts of them were no longer relevant, since some of the problems which confronted the churches almost half a century before had either been solved or by-passed, but that there was still much that was as valid as when it was written. In order to underline the great values that remained and to arouse the Church to listen again to the great Apostle, he wrote an introductory letter to the collection in which he set out, in Pauline language, Paul's own presentation of the Christian faith. In this letter Colossians—with which he was most familiar—was the basic document, but almost all the other letters were drawn upon and also a few passages from Luke–Acts. The result was our "Ephesians".[80]

Goodspeed goes further, and conjectures that the person who did this was none other than Onesimus, on whose behalf Paul had written to Philemon. He identifies him with the Onesimus who was bishop of Ephesus in the early part of the second century. This bishop, together with Polycarp of Smyrna, was responsible for the collecting of the letters which Ignatius of Antioch wrote on his way to Rome and martyrdom. He bases this conjecture on two grounds:

1. He thinks it is historically more probable that the Onesimus of Philemon later became bishop of Ephesus rather than another person by the same name; Paul saw great possibilities in Onesimus, who could well have become a bishop.
2. Since he was interested in collecting the letters of Ignatius, he could equally have been interested in collecting the letters of Paul. He would have revered the man who had done so much for him and would have cherished copies of the letters that Paul had written about himself and to his home church at Colossae.[81]

To identify the author in this way is indeed a conjecture. Onesimus had spent some time in Rome with Paul. Would he not have known that Paul had written a letter to the church at Rome, to say nothing of the fact that he must have known of Paul's journeyings?[82] It is highly unlikely that Paul would never have mentioned anything of his past life and his "children" in his conversations with Onesimus, and it would be completely natural for other correspondence to be mentioned when the letters were being written for Colossae and Philemon. This identification of the author must be dismissed as pure speculation.

For purposes of discussion, Goodspeed's reasons for rejecting

Pauline authorship may be divided into two parts: doctrinal–
ethical and literary.

On the doctrinal–ethical side, he thinks that the whole letter
bears the marks of a time later than Paul. The controversy between
Jew and Gentile has come to an end and the Gentiles are now
thinking of themselves merely as Christians (2.2, 11). The ministry
is assuming a definite form which means that the Church is becoming "institutionalized". The hope for an early return of the Lord
is waning, for fathers are admonished to train their children in the
Christian faith (6.4). The Church is being threatened by sectarian
heresies and needs to be warned against them (4.14); hence the
great stress that is laid on unity (4.3–6). Tradition is beginning to
play a role in maintaining the true faith; the apostles and prophets
are now the foundation of the Church (2.20), as they were the
means through which God has revealed his eternal purpose (3.5).
The stress in the letter is on the Church Universal, not on the local
church, as it is with few exceptions in Paul. The descent into Hades
(4.9, 10) has no place in the thought of Paul and in all likelihood
belongs to a later time (cf. 1 Peter 3.19).[83]

But it is in his literary analysis of Ephesians that Goodspeed has
found his strongest support, though that support is seldom un-
qualified. He claims that out of 618 phrases into which the letter
may be divided, 550 have unmistakable parallels in the other
letters "either in word or substance".[84] This for him proves that
the author must have been acquainted with the Pauline collection.
The only other books drawn on are Luke and Acts and some
Septuagintal texts. The *hapax legomena* are more closely related to
late first century Christian writings than to earlier. The style is
sonorous and liturgical and not at all like the direct and rapid style
of Paul. The interest in hymnology (5.14, 19) also shows a developing interest in purely Christian forms of liturgical worship, which
up to this time had been dominated by Jewish forms.[85] Many of
the words, though used by Paul, are used in Ephesians with a meaning different from his. The phrase "as I have written briefly" (3.3)
must refer not to Ephesians itself, but to the other letters of Paul,
for it would be meaningless if it referred only to the preceding
section of Ephesians. It is the liturgical style of Ephesians, however, that Goodspeed continually stresses. This letter is the
Pauline gospel in the form of a liturgical meditation; it is a "magnificent liturgy" and the fullness of expression shows its liturgical

character. It is this "combination of deep religious insight with lofty liturgical expression that constitutes the distinctive genius of Ephesians".[86] Such passages as 4.30 and 5.14 in the ethical section are examples of a developing genius for liturgy.

Mitton's work is, as G. Johnston says, a refinement and improvement of Goodspeed's theory.[87] Where Goodspeed had expounded his ideas in two short monographs of some seventy-five pages each (*The Key to Ephesians* is little more than a minor revision of *The Meaning of Ephesians* with the parallels in English instead of Greek), Mitton has given us a thorough exposition, with six appendixes showing all the relationships possible between Ephesians and the material in the New Testament that is relevant to his hypothesis.

In his doctrinal section Mitton sets out the usual arguments against Pauline authorship; the doctrine of the Church, the place of the apostles and prophets within it, the omission of the hope of an early parousia, the teaching on marriage, the change of meaning of such words as οἰκονομία and μυστήριον. To these he adds the arguments adduced by Goodspeed, though he does not appear to be as confident of the validity of all of them as Goodspeed is. He hesitates to accept the latter's exegesis of "as I have written briefly" (3.3), though he thinks that it is the best one that has yet been put forward; the same is true of the explanation of πατριά as individual churches within the one ἐκκλησία, which, he says, "may well prove the least unsatisfactory of the suggested interpretations".[88] He admits that we cannot be certain that Ephesians 4.8–10 refers to the descent into Hades, though he infers that the passage probably would mean this if we could show on other grounds that Ephesians is late first century. He accepts wholeheartedly the suggestion that the general tenor of the Epistle, with its emphasis on the supreme worth of the Christian faith and its earnest exhortation to live lives worthy of it, shows that it must have been written to those who were in danger of taking the Gospel for granted because they had known it all their lives.

But it is the literary difficulties that Ephesians raises which cause Mitton to come down decisively on the side of Goodspeed. While he finds that Goodspeed has overstated his case in saying that almost three-fifths of Colossians can be found in Ephesians, and that more than 400 phrases from the other Paulines are reflected there, and would reduce the figures to slightly more than one-third and slightly less than 250 respectively—the latter including

passages which are found both in Colossians and one or other of
the remaining Paulines—he still thinks that even with these reduced figures the Goodspeed theory can be proven.[89]

He does this first of all by making a comparison of Philippians
with the other letters and showing that there are twice as many
parallels in Ephesians as there are in Philippians. What is more remarkable is that the phrases which are found in Philippians are,
with four or five exceptions, commonplace phrases such as might
be found in any Pauline letter. In Ephesians, on the other hand,
there are some twenty phrases which are borrowed from the other
letters; these are the significant phrases which would be retained in
the memory and would be bound to be reproduced if an author
wished to convey to others the main points of what he had read. It
is not a matter here of looking through the Pauline letters to find
the striking phrases, for there is no mechanical copying. Rather the
ideas have passed through the crucible of the author's own mind
and have been reproduced in his own way, with words drawn from
the passage as a whole.[90]

What is true of the other epistles is even more true of Colossians. Though the extent of dependence is higher than that of all
the other letters combined, we have only one instance where more
than seven words are borrowed consecutively (Eph. 6.21-2;
Col. 4.7-8). For the most part, the borrowing seems to be from
memory, and a phrase from one part of Colossians may be linked
with a phrase from another part by association of words or ideas.
"Therefore, having heard of your faith in the Lord Jesus and
(your love) toward all the saints, I do not cease to give thanks for
you, remembering you in my prayers" (Eph. 1.15-16) is a combination of two different passages in Colossians: "Therefore, from
the day we heard it, we do not cease to pray for you" (1.9) and
"Having heard of your faith in Christ Jesus and your love toward
all the saints" (1.4). Mitton lists seven places in Ephesians where
this phenomenon occurs,[91] the best example being Ephesians 5.19-
20, where the readers are urged to give thanks "in the name of our
Lord Jesus Christ"; this is a non-Pauline idiom, for Paul always
gives thanks through Christ (Rom. 1.8; 7.25). In Colossians 3.16-
17, the Colossians are told that all their actions should reflect the
Lord whose name they bear, and that their thanks should be
offered to God through him. The phrase which refers to action in
Colossians is placed in the context of thanksgiving in Ephesians.

Although Mitton does not say this, it was "through Christ" that the early Christian prayers were normally addressed to God. The author of Ephesians in quoting from memory appears to have slipped from the norm.

For these reasons Mitton believes that a post-Pauline authorship of Ephesians answers more of the difficulties that this letter raises than Pauline authorship does. It gives a more intelligible account of its likenesses to the other letters of Paul and at the same time its dissimilarities from them.

Though Mitton holds to Goodspeed's theory that the author of Ephesians knew Acts, he does not think that it was the publication of Acts which led him to search for the letters of Paul. He believes that they came gradually into his hands, that he read them and pondered over them, and that after Acts was published, he decided to draw up a summary of Paul's message. He confided his idea to Tychicus, now an old man, who gave it his blessing. This would account for Tychicus being mentioned in the final verse. The author must have held an important position in the Church or his writing would not have been accepted into the collected letters of Paul as readily as it was. Mitton puts this theory forward with some hesitancy, but thinks that it, or something like it, gives us a possible theory of origins. The author may also have had worshipping communities in mind when he wrote the letter; this would account for its "somewhat rhetorical style".[92]

F. G. Johnston and F. W. Beare

Before commenting on the Mitton–Goodspeed hypothesis, mention must be made of the work of two scholars who have dealt with it, G. Johnston and F. W. Beare.[93] The former accepts the basic thesis and says that "the case for the dependence of Ephesians on an existing Pauline collection is unanswerable". But he believes that the Pauline corpus had probably been in existence for some time before Ephesians was written and that Luke–Acts has had no influence on the text of our letter; he therefore dismisses the publication of Acts as the immediate cause of writing. He thinks that the liturgical material in Ephesians should be treated cautiously since the Epistle itself may have influenced the early liturgies. He dismisses Mitton's theory about the author as pure fancy.

Beare is much more reserved in his acceptance. While he agrees that the purpose of Ephesians is to commend Paul's teaching to the Church of a later time, there is nothing in the letter which would lead us to conclude that Paul's correspondence had been neglected until the publication of Acts sent a devout reader of Colossians and Philemon in search of other letters. Indeed, 3.2 implies that the readers of Ephesians already knew something of Paul's teaching. Nor is there very much indication that the Christians of the author's time had lost their enthusiasm and were beginning to break up into sects. The admonitions are directed against walking "as the Gentiles do" (4.17). The more positive aspect of the whole letter is to deepen the Christians' understanding of their faith in order that they may see the place which the Church has in the design of God and so be drawn more closely together. This unity must express itself in the actions of the individual Christians towards each other.

Nor does Beare think that Colossians is used more than the other epistles because the author of Ephesians was more familiar with it, but because the language and thought of Colossians are more closely allied to the theme which he wishes to discuss. The Colossian doctrine of the cosmic Christ, taken out of the context which called it forth, becomes the thread on which Ephesians is strung. By means of it Paulinism is reduced to a more systematic form than is found in any of the Pauline letters. The other letters are brought in only in so far as they serve this main purpose, for "many, if not most of [Goodspeed's] alleged correspondences do not indicate literary dependence in the slightest degree".[94] While it is true that many of the expressions in Ephesians cannot be properly understood except by reference to the other epistles, this does not necessarily mean that it was written as an introduction to them all; if it were, Colossians, which is so different from the others that its authenticity is doubted by many, would not have been drawn upon to the extent that it is, and the theological content of the others would have been put to greater use. There is also some textual evidence that all the letters which now form the Pauline corpus circulated separately before they were issued as a collection.

Beare is also highly sceptical of attempts to reconstruct the occasion on which Ephesians was written. All that may have happened is that a close personal disciple of Paul—the mastery of technical Paulinism that is found in Ephesians cannot be explained on the grounds of literary influence alone—felt that he should commit to writing the result of his own ponderings on his beloved master's teaching. But he is not slavishly tied to Paul, though he uses Pauline materials; out of them he has developed thoughts of his own. The finished work may have been sponsored by one of the leading churches, but where it was written or how it circulated among the churches we cannot say. It received its title in the second century when a scribe made a connection between Ephesians 6.21 and 2 Timothy 4.12: "Tychicus have I sent to Ephesus."

It is clear that Beare's agreement with Goodspeed lies in areas of purpose, doctrine, and the use of Colossians, with much less use of the other epistles than Goodspeed finds.

Not all the arguments which have been put forward by this group of writers can be unhesitatingly accepted, though their cumulative force is strong. Nor is there agreement among themselves as to the value of each argument. Whereas Goodspeed places equal value on doctrinal and literary arguments, Mitton and Johnston stress the literary argument—Mitton is extremely cautious about some of Goodspeed's doctrinal arguments, and Johnston thinks that "the crux of the matter is the relationship between Ephesians and Colossians".[95] For Beare it is doctrine and the use of Colossians. Neither Beare nor Johnston thinks that the liturgical language of Ephesians should be stressed.

The main difficulty here lies in the apparent contradiction of some of the arguments. If Goodspeed is right in saying that the influence of Paul on Ephesians is literary, how can its author have grasped so clearly the essentials of Paul's teaching? No other person in the early Church appears to have done it. The Pastoral Epistles written also in the name of Paul are far from understanding Paulinism, and the same is true of the Apostolic Fathers. Is it possible for one man to enter so completely into the mind of another without the give and take of deeply personal conversation? (Here Beare is surely right.) If Ephesians 6.21 is copied almost verbatim from Colossians 4.7, as it appears to be, this means that the author had a copy of Colossians before him. Why did he not use it more often instead of jumping back and forth from one passage to another? (This is not to say that there are not passages from Colossians reflected in Ephesians.) If Ephesians was written in deliberate imitation of a Pauline letter, why is it so unlike any other letter of Paul's?

Goodspeed appears to think that Christians broke away from Jewish forms of worship towards the end of the first century and created forms of their own. But such is not the case. The continuity between Jewish and Christian worship in the early Church is just as marked as is its refusal to give up the Old Testament. Without doubt it was enriched and deepened by the new experience and understanding of God in Christ, but it was still full of the devotional language of scripture and synagogue, and even the pattern was retained.[96] A good many of the phrases which Goodspeed would say are drawn from other letters may well have come from this source. "Holy and without blemish", "an offering and a sacrifice to God for a sweet-smelling savour", "to the praise of his glory", "things in heaven and things on earth", "to all generations for ever and ever"—these are the very stuff of liturgy. The prayer for wisdom and knowledge is one of the oldest prayers in the worship of the synagogue. And how could a Christian writer avoid using such phrases as "raised from the dead"? Mitton's argument against liturgical sources for some of the phraseology of Ephesians, which he considers to be "conflations" of passages in Colossians, is that "liturgies teach people fixed forms of words rather than ideas of such flexibility that they can be variously expressed in different words".[97] But this is the very opposite of what liturgies actually do. Rigid liturgical uniformity is unknown even in Western Europe until the sixteenth century, and the early history of the liturgy shows a great deal of variation on a pattern that was more or less fixed.[98] On the other hand, to say that Ephesians was written for worshipping congregations rather than for private readers, and that this is the best explanation for its style,[99] appears to infer that the rest of Paul's letters were not read in public. None of the New Testament documents is a private document, yet none of them is "stylized" in the manner of Ephesians. We may not therefore say that Ephesians as it stands could have been written with this purpose in mind. In reply to Johnston that Ephesians may have been a source for later liturgies and that we should be cautious about a "liturgical" approach to Ephesians, it may be said that the earliest extant liturgical text which shows the influence of Ephesians is *The Prosphora* of Sarapion of Thmuis in the middle of the fourth century. Reflections of biblical texts appear with increasing frequency from this point onwards and they can easily be distinguished from their contexts. It is true that we may easily get involved in a circular argument here, arguing back from later liturgies to the New Testament text and then saying that the text itself is liturgical in origin, but it is possible to break out of this circle if it can be shown that the passages with which we are concerned have a relationship with forms of prayer which can be traced back to pre-Christian Judaism.

Again, many of the phrases in the ethical section of the Epistle which Mitton, Goodspeed, and Johnston regard as marks of dependence on the other letters, may be drawn from a common stock of teaching material which could be used in a more or less free fashion by any Christian teacher and adapted by him to suit his particular circumstances.[100] Mitton does not do justice to this hypothesis in his chapter on the relationship between Ephesians and 1 Peter, for he does not consider all the New Testament material; he does not take sufficiently into account the amount of variety to be found amid the many similarities and he reads modern ideas of catechetical material back into the first centuries. While we now have abundant evidence from Qumran that the use of written material as a means of handing on the tradition goes back far earlier than has sometimes been supposed, it is doubtful if this can be used as the basis of an argument for literary dependence in the case of the New Testament epistles. To give only one example from the Ephesians–Colossians material: while there is ample evidence that the ethical teaching of Ephesians has many affinities with that to be found in Colossians—Mitton finds some thirty verses reflected in eighty, but some of these are not certain—there are also variations from it, particularly in the passage dealing with the relationship between husbands and wives. Nor would it appear likely that as capable a person as the author of Ephesians would borrow phrases from the other epistles and extract them completely out of their context (he never appears to do this in the case of Colossians, and there is widespread disagreement as to whether he changes the meaning of words or phrases). In 1 Corinthians 4.12, Paul uses the phrase "we labour, working with our own hands" in a deprecating way, and the purpose of his labour is to support himself. In Ephesians 4.28, labour is regarded as honourable and its purpose is to help the poorer members of the Christian community. Other samples of this type of "dependence" are to be found in Galatians 4.4 and Ephesians 1.10, and Philippians 4.18 and Ephesians 5.2.

If Beare is right in his assertion that the author of Ephesians knew Paul personally, then the question of literary dependence—apart from Colossians—cannot be answered, for there is no way of distinguishing between what the author of Ephesians heard from Paul himself and what he might have read in a letter. The opening "Blessing" which Beare says is taken from 2 Corinthians 1.3 is hardly likely to be a phrase which Paul used only once (cf. 2 Cor. 11.31). Would Paul have used the metaphor of "sealing" or the word ἀρραβών only on the occasion of writing 2 Corinthians (1.21–2)? The repetition of a telling metaphor is hardly a sign that a person is not "a strong original genius".[101] The fact that the "seal" became part of the traditional language of baptism may be due as much to Jewish influence as to Paul's use of it, although ἀρραβών appears to be his own coinage.

It may therefore be said that these scholars have given us a strong case against the Pauline authorship of Ephesians but that it has not been strong enough to convince many of their confrères who still hold the traditional position.

H. Chadwick[102] has recently suggested that, since the question of the authorship of this epistle appears to be an insoluble one, some progress may be made in our understanding of "one of the most difficult of the New Testament documents" by a more careful consideration of the purpose for which it was written. His own view is that this profoundly theological document was written for a pastoral purpose, in response to a spiritual crisis in Gentile Christianity. It was addressed to "everybody in general and nobody in particular", because the crisis itself was widespread. Since the Christian Church had appeared so "late in time", there were some who thought that its message could not be true. "In the ancient world it is a generally accepted truth that nothing new can be true." The answer of Ephesians is that Christianity is an old faith. It springs out of Judaism and is, in fact, Judaism which has broken out of the narrow nationalism of the past and is now ready to accept all men into its membership. Yet the old Judaism has not been destroyed; a Jew who accepts Jesus as Messiah does not have to abandon the past history of his own people. Nor does a Gentile have to become a Jew; the old Judaism has been transformed in such a way that the Gentile is now offered an approach to God which formerly was denied him. Through the death of Christ both Jew and Gentile are reconciled to God and to each other. This reconciliation is proof that God's ultimate purpose, to unite all things in Christ, will be accomplished.

The unity of mankind and the Church as the instrument of that unity had always been part of God's eternal plan. The Church had appeared in the world, not as the result of a series of accidents, but at the time predetermined by God.

By expounding the doctrine of the Church in this way, the author of Ephesians answered certain objections "which arose out of the uniqueness of the Incarnation and the obvious limits of the empirical Church".

A no less important motive, according to Chadwick, is the assertion of Paul's authority over all Gentile churches, including those not founded by him. Since Paul had been appointed the apostle of the Gentiles by a special revelation (Eph. 3.7 ff), all Gentile churches should submit to this authority.

A position diametrically opposed to this is taken by Stig Hanson.[103] He thinks that the problem of the *Sitz im Leben* is quite insoluble. While it may be possible to see both Ephesians and Colossians as Paul's own reactions to the religious syncretism of Asia Minor, it is "more plausible to think that the particular character of Ephesians is connected with the theological speculation of the Pauline circle",[104] and it is not necessary to postulate a crisis of any kind. This theological speculation may have been going on before Colossians was written and its language used to refute the Colossian heresy, though this, of course, cannot be proved. Nor can we find in Ephesians itself the reason why the theme of unity is the dominant theme. It may be due to the influence of the Johannine circle. The practical exhortation to unity in the second half of the epistle is a natural result of the theological speculation of the first half. More than that cannot be said.

In all this welter of argument and counter-argument, there is at least one area of agreement which has not been given serious consideration, so far as I know. Percy, Goodspeed, and Chadwick, to mention only three representatives of the three possible positions on the question of authorship, all detect the influence of worship on the language of Ephesians. The remainder of this book will be devoted to an investigation of this area of agreement in the hope that a little more light will be thrown on both the form and content of this enigmatic document. But before we begin, mention must be made of a short article in *Die Religion in Geschichte und Gegenwart*

(3rd edn) by Ernst Käsemann. He rejects the Pauline authorship of Ephesians and thinks that, though the letter stands in the Pauline tradition, it is not the result of the literary influence of Paul. Its main components are liturgical and hortatory material drawn from traditional sources. This hypothesis will be considered as our argument proceeds.

PART TWO

The Jewish Liturgical Tradition
and the New Testament

1

THE
JEWISH LITURGICAL
CALENDAR

Three active movements within the Church of our time, which at first glance appear to be entirely unrelated to each other, are in point of fact having a great deal of influence on each other. These are the Ecumenical Movement, the Liturgical Movement, and the revival of Biblical Theology with its increasing awareness of the essential unity of the Old and New Testaments. The second of these has no organization outside the Roman Catholic Church, while the third has no organization at all. It is only from occasional meetings, or books and articles emanating from the studies of many scholars in different parts of the Church, that we are being made aware of what is going on in both these fields. The Ecumenical Movement is in the process of making Ecclesiology as important for us in the twentieth century as Christology was for the Church of the fourth century. The Liturgical Movement has for its main aim the bringing to life of the doctrine of the Church in the place where doctrine should fully come to life—in worship. Its chief proponents are now saying that true progress in worship is possible only when the worshippers are at the same time being trained in the proper understanding and use of the Bible.[1] One of the interesting trends in recent New Testament research is the rediscovery of the Bible as the book of the worshipping community. Investigation into the liturgical forms that may lie behind the books of the New Testament has given us an increasing flow of writing on this subject. Few of the writers are obscurantists; they accept wholeheartedly the critical method and the general findings of critical research, while they act also as a corrective to those critics who at times give the impression that they regard primitive Christianity as primarily a literary movement.[2] Faith and order, worship, and the study of the raw materials out of which both grow, are therefore complementary, each to the other; and insights into one ought ideally to influence the others. This is happening, but not in open and direct ways.

Our concern is with the third of these movements. The hypotheses that have been published to date have not been widely accepted, although there appears to be a growing body of opinion that further investigation of them may throw more light upon the New Testament documents and also upon the stages by which Christianity transformed its inheritance from Judaism. In a field where a great deal is still unknown, the predilections of the individual scholar may lead him to stress the continuing Jewish or the peculiarly Christian aspects of this period of the Church's life, and it is only by critical consideration of all hypotheses that truth will be separated from fanciful exegesis.

A few examples of what may be called the liturgical approach to the New Testament are given here, in order to show how much has been written on this subject and how many of the New Testament documents have been treated in this way. G. D. Kilpatrick has put forward the suggestion that the Gospel of Matthew was composed for reading at worship, but he does not make any attempt to divide it into a detailed lectionary.[3] Philip Carrington has gone much further than this with the Gospel of Mark and claimed that it is made up of a number of pericopes which fit into an annual cycle of Sabbaths and feasts.[4] Over thirty years ago, B. W. Bacon thought that Roman liturgical usage lay behind the Gospel of Mark and particularly the Passion narrative.[5] David Daube is strongly inclined to think that Mark 12.13–37—the three questions asked of Jesus and one which he himself asks—reflects the structure of the Passover Haggadah where questions of a similar type are asked, *in that order*.[6] While nobody has dealt with Luke from this point of view, C. F. Evans believes that the central section (9.51—18.14) is deliberately patterned on the Book of Deuteronomy.[7] Oscar Cullmann contends that one of the chief purposes of the Gospel of John is "to set forth the connexion between the contemporary Christian worship and the historical life of Jesus",[8] and Miss Aileen Guilding has tried to show that the discourses in the first twelve chapters of this Gospel are based on the lections and psalms used at the Jewish feasts, while chapters 14–17 are comments on all the lections used in the first twelve chapters.[9] Less sweeping

statements are to be found in B. W. Bacon and F. C. Grant.[10]
T. W. Manson has suggested that the early part of Romans takes its
form—confession of sin and expiation—from the liturgy of the Day
of Atonement, and that 1 and 2 Corinthians contain reminiscences
of Passover, New Year, and Tabernacles.[11] Carrington, in the work
referred to above, says that some of the themes of Paul's Corinthian
correspondence are derived from a synagogue lectionary used during the fifty days from Passover to Pentecost.[12] He also thinks that
Hebrews may be a Megillah for the Day of Atonement;[13] W.
Manson expresses a similar thought in his Baird Lecture. It is now
widely held that the main part of 1 Peter (1.3—4.11) is a baptismal
homily; F. L. Cross goes well beyond this with his thesis that this
material is liturgical rather than homiletical and was used at the
initiation of converts at the Christian Pascha.[14] M. H. Shepherd
holds that the structure of the Apocalypse is based on the order of
the paschal liturgy as it is found in the *Apostolic Tradition of
Hippolytus*, on the ground that Hippolytus is following a tradition
which does go back to apostolic times.[15]

This is an imposing list of witnesses for this point of view; most
of them put it forward with a great deal of diffidence and are more
or less prepared to admit, as T. W. Manson says, that their conclusions may be "too far fetched".[16] Nevertheless, they do give us
good grounds for examining Ephesians along this line of inquiry;
we do not expect to prove a case beyond all doubt, but simply to
put forward an hypothesis which gives a reasonable explanation of
some aspects of this document. "C'est en multipliant les tentatives
de ce genre qu'on peut espérer parvenir un jour au but."[17] We
shall begin with a brief discussion of the place of the calendar in
the worship of Israel and then proceed to look at the more important calendar references in the New Testament.

A. *The Calendar in the Old Testament Canon*

Three annual festivals form the basic structure of the Jewish
liturgical year: the Feast of Unleavened Bread, the Feast of
Harvest or Weeks (Pentecost), and the Feast of Ingathering,
Booths, or Tabernacles.[18] These are clearly agricultural festivals,
marking the beginning and the end of the grain harvest and the
gathering of "the wine and oil" respectively. The Feast of Passover, which probably goes back to Israel's nomadic period and

which centred in the sacrifice of a young sheep or goat, merged with the Feast of Unleavened Bread at some point in pre-exilic times, and by the time of the Synoptic Gospels had become identified with it;[19] one of the ceremonies connected with this double feast was the waving before the altar of the first sheaf of the newly ripened grain. It has been strongly argued by the "Myth and Ritual" school that the Feast of Booths was also a New Year festival, a feast of the Kingship of Yahweh; but this theory is still regarded as doubtful by some scholars.[20] The Feast of Purim is generally regarded as the "Judaizing" of a Babylonian New Year festival;[21] Hannukah, or Dedication, marks the annual commemoration of the cleansing of the Temple by the Maccabees (164 B.C.). The Day of Atonement—a fast, not a feast—comes from post-exilic times. There are no direct references to either Atonement or Purim in the New Testament and only one to the Feast of Dedication (John 10.22); our main concern will therefore be with Passover, Pentecost, and Tabernacles.

In the Books of Chronicles these feasts are described as having been kept by Solomon, but they are no longer "nature festivals"; they appear to be nothing more than days on which the Law requires that sacrifices be offered. "Then Solomon offered up burnt offerings . . . as the duty of each day required, offering according to the commandment of Moses for the sabbaths, the new moons and the three annual feasts—the feast of unleavened bread, the feast of weeks, and the feast of tabernacles" (2 Chron. 8.12 f). The same books also describe the keeping of the Passover by Hezekiah and Josiah (2 Chron. 30 and 35). In neither of these accounts is any connection made with Exodus. Hezekiah's invitation to all Israel to keep the feast contains the words: "Yield yourselves to the Lord, and come to his sanctuary which he has sanctified for ever, and serve the Lord your God, that his fierce anger may turn away from you" (2 Chron. 30.8). It is to be noted that the feast must be kept in Jerusalem and not elsewhere (verse 13). The same is true of the Passover kept by Josiah. In Ezra the Passover is kept in Jerusalem as an act of thanksgiving, "for the Lord had made them joyful and had turned the heart of the King of Assyria to them, so that he aided them in the work of the house of God" (Ezra 6.22). The Feast of Tabernacles was the day on which Solomon dedicated the temple (2 Chron. 5.3) and it was observed by the exiles shortly after their return to Jerusalem (Ezra 3.4). In the former case it is given as a date, and in the latter the text simply says that "they kept the feast of booths, as it is written". There may be a reference to the Feast of Weeks in 2 Chronicles 15.8–11, where there may be a play on the words *shabuoth* and *shebuoth*.[22] But it is indeed curious that the Books of Chronicles contain no reference to Israel in Egypt or to the giving of the Law; only in one passage connected with the ark is it said that "the Lord made a covenant with the people of Israel when they came out of Egypt" (2 Chron. 5.10). It is also strange that in the list of feasts given in the Book of Ezekiel (Ezek. 45.21–5) there is no mention of the Feast of Weeks. Thackeray thinks that this may be due to some older connection of this feast with Tammuz and sun-worship.[23]

The beginning of the "historicizing" of the festivals appears to be given us in Nehemiah, where we are told that after hearing and studying part of the Law, "the people made booths for themselves . . . and all the assembly of those who had returned from the captivity made booths and dwelt in the booths; for from the days of Jeshua the son of Nun to that day the people had not done so" (Neh. 8.16–17).

By the time that the Torah had assumed its final form, these originally nomadic and agricultural feasts had been incorporated into the history of Israel and historical explanations had been provided for them, or at least for two of them, and the explanations draw our attention to an all-important aspect of Israel's faith. The eating of unleavened bread, which is a normal part of an agricultural festival, is now ordered because it commemorates the time when the nation came out of Egypt (Exod. 13.3); the ceremony of sprinkling the door-posts with the blood of the paschal lamb, which probably in origin was a prophylactic against demonic powers, now takes place because the Lord "passed over the houses of the people of Israel in Egypt, when he slew the Egyptians but spared our houses" (Exod. 12.27). The way in which the lamb is to be eaten—in haste, with loins girded and with staff in hand—is to be a vivid recollection of the night of deliverance before the departure from Egypt. The booths at tabernacles, the origins of which are lost in antiquity, but which certainly were not replicas of the tents of nomads—according to Nehemiah, the booths were made of the leafy branches of olive, myrtle, and palm—came to represent the wanderings in the wilderness. "You shall dwell in booths for seven days . . . that your generations may know that I made the people of Israel dwell in booths when I brought them out of the land of Egypt" (Lev. 23.42–3). These feasts are no longer bound up with the cycle of nature alone, but serve as a means by which the redemptive acts of God are recalled. The sacrificial offering of all male firstlings of cattle and the "redemption" of the first-born son are both ordered for the same reason: "By strength of hand the Lord brought us out of Egypt" (Exod. 13.14). Yahweh is the Lord of nature (Hos. 2.8) but he is also the Lord of history and Israel's faith is in a Saviour God who has acted in history; the manifold material which has been gathered together in the Pentateuch—myth, cult, legend, law, custom—is all adapted to show forth this primary aspect of her faith; her theology is found in her calendar. "Denkgesetz alttestamentlichen ist . . . das die Mannigfaltigkeit der Erscheinungen zu einer ideologischen Einheit zusammenbindet durch das Band der Geschichte." [24]

Though the Law later became the centre of Israel's life, there is no explicit reference in the Pentateuch itself to a commemoration of the day when it was given at Sinai. The Feast of Weeks alone of the three feasts is not historicized in the Pentateuch, though there may be an indirect reference to it in Exodus 19.1: "On the third new moon after the people of Israel had gone forth out of the land of Egypt, on that day they came to the wilderness of Sinai . . . and encamped before the mountain". This calendar reference can hardly be an historical reminiscence, and since the Feast of Weeks always takes place in the "third month", the writer may have wished to indicate it in this way. Later tradition says that "that day" was the first day of the month and that the Law was given on the following sabbath; Exodus also implies that the pattern of the tabernacle was given to Moses at the same time. [25]

B. *The Calendar in the Intertestamental Literature, Rabbinic Tradition, and the Qumran Documents*

If the Feast of Weeks does not appear to be as important as the other feasts in the Old Testament canon, the same cannot be said of it in the Book of Jubilees. In this document it is the most important of all the festivals; though it still retains its original significance as a harvest festival (Jub. 6.21), it has now become the day on which many of the great events of the past took place. The author places great stress upon the fact that it is to be celebrated for one day, which would seem to imply that some groups were celebrating it for more than one day (Jub. 6.17–22)—this custom probably arose in the Diaspora because of the difficulties involved in making exact calendar calculations, and was then copied by Palestinian Judaism.[26] Tradition held that this feast had been celebrated in heaven from the days of creation till the time of Noah. "And Noah and his sons swore that they would not eat any blood that was in any flesh, and he made a covenant before the Lord God for ever throughout all the generations of the earth in this month" (Jub. 6.10, Charles' translation). Noah's children did away with it, but it was renewed at the time of Abraham, in the middle of the third month. "On that day we made a covenant with Abram, according as we had covenanted with Noah in this month; and Abram renewed the festival and ordinance for himself for ever" (Jub. 14.20). The reference here is to the covenant mentioned in Genesis 15; the covenant described in Genesis 17 is also made "in the third month, in the middle of the month" (Jub. 15.1). Other important events which took place on the same day of the year were the birth of Isaac (Jub. 16.13), the meeting of Abraham, Isaac, and Ishmael at "the Well of the Oath" to celebrate the Feast of Weeks (Jub. 22.1–24), the making of the covenant between Jacob and Laban (Jub. 29.1–8), the appearance of Yahweh to Jacob before he went down to Egypt (Jub. 44.4–8), again at the Well of the Oath, and also, very significantly, the covenant of Sinai. According to Jubilees, the feast had been forgotten until "the children of Israel celebrated it anew upon this mountain" (6.19). "On this account [because of the covenant with Noah], God spake to thee that thou shouldst make a covenant with the children of Israel upon the mountain with an oath, and that thou shouldst sprinkle blood upon them because of all the words of the covenant, which the Lord made with them for ever" (Jub. 6.11—this is clearly a reference to the covenant described in Exod. 24). This covenant is to be renewed annually. "For this reason it is ordained and written on the heavenly tables, that they should celebrate the feast of weeks in this month once a year, to renew the covenant every year" (Jub. 6.17). On the day after the feast, Moses was called up to the mountain and for forty days was instructed by God in order that "the generations may see how I have not forsaken them for all the evil which they have wrought in transgressing the covenant which I establish on this day on Mount Sinai" (Jub. 1.5). Pentecost is therefore a feast of revelation.

Passover and Tabernacles do not appear to be as important as this for the author of Jubilees, although both feasts are instituted by Abraham. It is at Passover that Abraham is tested by being asked to offer his son (Jub. 18.1–19); the reason given here for the seven-day festival in the first month is that Abraham went and returned in peace from his journey to the mountain of sacrifice. In Jubilees 49, however, the reason given is because of the deliverance from Egypt. No specific reason is given for Abraham's celebration of Tabernacles. We are simply told that "Abraham built booths for himself and his servants on this festival, and he was the first to celebrate the Feast of Tabernacles on earth" (Jub. 16.21). One of the ceremonies he performed was to go around the altar seven times on every day of the feast with palm branches in his hand (Jub. 16.31).

We may say then that Jubilees, which is dated between 135 and 105 B.C. by R. H. Charles and well before 100 B.C. by J. T. Milik,[27] has gone further than the Pentateuch in linking the history of Israel with its cult festivals. The other books of the Apocrypha and Pseudepigrapha need not detain us; where they show any calendar influence, it is the same calendar as Jubilees, and very much the same connections are made.[28]

One minor point may be made here. The calendar of Jubilees is a solar calendar, divided into four quarters of ninety-one days each. The other calendar in use was a lunar calendar; since this calendar would be eleven and a half days wrong at the end of every twelve-month period, an additional month was intercalated at the end of every three years. The day on which Pentecost fell, according to the calculation of the Pharisees, would be 5, 6, or 7 Siwan depending on whether the months between Nisan 15 and Pentecost had twenty-five or thirty days; this would not happen in the case of the solar calendar. To confuse matters even more, a difference arose between the Pharisees and the Sadducees about the meaning of the phrase in Leviticus 23.15 which states that Pentecost is to be observed fifty days after "the morrow after the sabbath"; the Sadducees took this to mean that the counting of the days began at sunset on the sabbath in Passover week, while the Pharisees said

that it meant Passover day itself, which was a day of rest and therefore a sabbath. By Sadducean reckoning, Pentecost would always
be on the first day of the week, but for the Pharisees it would depend on the day of the week when Passover fell. The Pharisees
finally won the battle. In the Book of Jubilees the counting of the
omer begins at sunset of the first sabbath which occurs after the
seven days of unleavened bread. Since the year always begins on
the same day of the week and the number of days in the months
does not vary—each quarter is divided into months of 30, 30, and
31 days respectively—Pentecost for Jubilees will always fall on
Siwan 15, exactly a week after the Sadducean reckoning, which
appears to be the most ancient of them all.[29]

In the rabbinic tradition the first definite connection that we
have between Pentecost and the Law-giving is in Seder Olam
Rabba which is dated around A.D. 150. There it is said that "The
Israelites killed the Passover lamb in Egypt on the fourteenth of
Nisan which was a Thursday. . . . In the third month on the sixth
day of the month the Ten Commandments were given to them and
it was a sabbath day."[30] Rabbi Eleazer (c. A.D. 270) said that Pentecost was the day on which the Law was given.[31] Another reference
is found in the Mishna,[32] where we are told that Tammuz 17 is a
fast day because it was the day on which Moses broke the two
tables of the Law. Since Moses broke the tables forty days after he
had received them, he must have been given them on Siwan 6,
though this is not stated explicitly. Since most of the material in
the Mishna and in Seder Olam is traditional material, we may say
that Pentecost became the feast of the commemoration of the Law-
giving for rabbinic Judaism early in the second century or late in
the first. Neither Philo nor Josephus makes the connection; for the
former, the Law was given on the Feast of Trumpets in the
autumn.[33] It may be that a new meaning was given to the feast of
Pentecost when the destruction of the Temple made it impossible
to fulfil the pentecostal ceremonies, the most important of which
was the offering before the altar of two loaves made from the new
grain (Lev. 23.15–17). The material for this new meaning lay
ready to hand, as we shall see.[34]

It is in the Qumran community that we find a close connection
made between the Feast of Weeks and the Sinai covenant.[35] In the
last two pages of the Damascus Document the writer speaks of the
way in which a postulant enters the community, or, rather, takes

his final vows after one year of postulancy and a novitiate of two years.

> On the day that he speaks to the superintendent of the many, they shall enroll him with the oath of the covenant which Moses made with Israel, the covenant to return to the law of Moses with the whole heart and the whole soul. . . . And on the day that the man obligates himself to return to the law of Moses the angel of enmity (Mastema) will depart from behind him if he makes good his words. Therefore Abraham was circumcised on the day that he received knowledge.[36]

As we have seen, the Book of Jubilees states that Abraham made two covenants, both on the Feast of Weeks; the second of these covenants was the covenant of circumcision. This implies that new members are admitted into the community on this feast. There was also an annual renewal of vows. "So shall they do year by year all the days of the dominion of Belial."[37] J. T. Milik thinks that all the members of the Essene sect gathered at the mother-house at Qumran for this Feast of the Renewal of the Covenant.[38] Since it took place in the third month of the year,[39] and the Book of Jubilees, the guide book of the community in all matters pertaining to the calendar, expressly orders an annual renewal of the covenant (Jub. 6.17), we should appear to be on safe ground in saying that, for the covenanters of Qumran, Pentecost was the day when they made the annual renewal of the oath which they took when they entered the community.

The liturgy for this annual event is given us in the Manual of Discipline (1QS). It begins with a berakah—a telling forth of the mighty works of God and of his "steadfast love and mercy upon Israel". This is said by the priests; it is immediately followed by a confession said by the Levites, confessing the sins of the nation, and all those who are entering the covenant identify themselves with sinful Israel according to a prescribed form. The priests then bless all those who are members of the community: "May he bless you with all good and keep you from all evil; may he enlighten your heart with life-giving prudence and be gracious to you with eternal knowledge; may he lift up his loving countenance to you for eternal peace." The curse on "all the men of Belial's lot" is given in a twofold form, the first by the Levites and the second by the priests and Levites together (1QS1.7—2.19). This ceremony is reminiscent of the one which is ordered to take place on Mount Gerizim and Mount Ebal in Deuteronomy 27.11–26.

Summing up, we may say that, while there is little direct evidence in rabbinic Judaism in the first century to connect Pentecost with the giving of the Law, the evidence is clear in the "apocryphal" tradition and in the Qumran literature.

C. The Israelite Concept of Time and its Expression in the Liturgy

One of the great differences between Greek and Hebrew modes of thought lies in the concept of time. For the Greek, eternity is a timeless state; for the Hebrew, eternity is a kind of synthesis, a gathering up of the past, the present, and the future. When man comes face to face with God who maintains within his grasp the whole course of history from beginning to end, then for man the past and the future have been gathered up into the present; ephemeral man is caught up into God's "eternity" and God and man share common ground. An old Midrash on the divine name says that when God spoke to Moses he told him to tell the Israelites that his name was "I am he who will be". When Moses inquired why God placed himself in the future, the reply was given that the Israelites would have need of him to help them out of their troubles. To this Moses objected that to speak about trouble to come would only discourage a people who had had enough troubles already. "God, recognising that this was a pertinent remark, changed the definition to 'I am he who has been and I am he who is'".[40] The implication here is that past, present, and future are all one. While the Israelite liturgy is tied to the past by "remembrance", it is also bound up with a "waiting" for the future. We can tell only from their context whether the words *Malakh Yahweh* mean "God has reigned", "God reigns", or "God will reign"; they may mean all three together.[41] In Hebrew syntax the addition of a "waw consecutive" to the verb can change it from a past into a present.

Illustrations of this may be seen in the cult forms which have been embedded in the Old Testament and also in the traditional rites of Judaism. In Deuteronomy 26.1–11 we are given an old cultic form to be said at the offering of first-fruits,[42] in which the

worshipper is told to say that his father had gone down to Egypt
and there had become a great nation; but then the liturgy suddenly
changes into the first person:

> The Egyptians treated us harshly, and afflicted us, and laid upon us
> hard bondage. Then we cried to the Lord the God of our Fathers, and
> the Lord heard our voice, and saw our affliction, our toil, and our
> oppression; and the Lord brought us out of Egypt . . . and he brought
> us into this place and gave us this land. . . . And behold, now I bring
> the first of the fruit of the ground, which thou, O Lord, hast given me.

Here the worshipper not only thanks God for the food that he has
received; by the use of the first person plural he identifies himself
with those who had come from bondage into freedom. The divine
act of redemption in the past has become the present possession of
the one who has appropriated it to himself by means of the prescribed cultic act. In Joshua 24.1–28 all the tribes of Israel "present
themselves before the Lord" and a covenant is made. Joshua,
speaking on behalf of Yahweh, tells the assembly:

> I brought your fathers out of Egypt, and you came to the sea; and the
> Egyptians pursued your fathers with chariots and horsemen to the
> Red Sea. And when they cried to the Lord, he put darkness between
> you and the Egyptians, and made the sea come upon them and cover
> them; and your eyes saw what I did to Egypt; and you lived in the
> wilderness a long time (Joshua 24.6–7).

The movement in this liturgy from the past to the present and
back again shows how impossible it was for the Hebrew mind to
make a line of demarcation between what God had done for his an-
cestors and what God had done for succeeding generations; all
shared in the "mighty acts of God". Similarly, in the Passover
liturgy the head of the household is ordered to say to the "simple"
son who asks the meaning of the rite, "It is because of what the
Lord did for me when I came out of Egypt" (Exod. 13.8).[43] The
same idea is given expression in a more admonitory form in another section of the Passover Haggadah:

> Every man in every generation is bound to look upon himself as if he
> personally had gone forth from Egypt. . . . It is not only our fathers
> that the Holy One redeemed, but ourselves also did he redeem with
> them. For does not the Scripture say: And he brought us out thence
> that he might bring us in, to give us the land which he swore unto our
> fathers (Deut. 6.23).[44]

In the study of the Law, which the rabbis also called "the service of the altar", the same experience occurs.

> The Law is not to be regarded as an antiquated edict to which nobody pays any attention, but as a new one which everyone runs to read. Every day when a man busies himself with the study of the Law, he should say to himself, it is as if this day I received it from Sinai. . . . In what seems to us fanciful forms, the rabbis sought to impress on themselves and others that the student is receiving the Law from the lawgiver as really as if he stood at the foot of Sinai amid the awe-inspiring scenery depicted in Exodus 19 and Deuteronomy 4.10ff.[45]

S. B. Frost has expressed this idea succinctly when speaking of the Coronation Psalms: "The famous tag *Urzeit wird Endzeit* can be paralleled by another equally true: *Urzeit wird Nunzeit*, the beginning has become now".[46]

It is (equally) true that *Endzeit wird Nunzeit*, the end has become now. To share by "remembrance" in the past is also to share by "anticipation" in the future. The rule or reign of God which he has established by his power in the present means that his ultimate victory is also here.

> O sing to the Lord a new song,
>   for he has done marvellous things!
> His right hand and his holy arm
>   have gotten him victory.
> The Lord has made known his victory,
>   he has revealed his vindication in the sight of the nations.
>
> Let the sea roar, and all that fills it;
>   the world and those who dwell in it!
> Let the floods clap their hands;
>   let the hills sing for joy together
> before the Lord, for he comes to rule the earth.
>
> (Ps. 98. 1–2, 7–9a)

In the prophetic literature it is not always easy to distinguish between the present judgement of God on the wickedness of his people and his final judgement, for the one shades off into the other. Amos can speak of the punishment that is coming upon Israel as the result of social and economic injustice, and in the same breath speak about the "Day of the Lord" (Amos 5). The temporal judgement, because it is the foreshadowing of the final judgement, becomes the final judgement; all events that are significant are, from one point of view, final events. Because Yahweh is the God of past, present, and future, wherever he is present the future is present, either for condemnation or for salvation.

> The Lord of hosts has sworn:
> "As I have planned,
>   so shall it be
> and as I have purposed
>   so shall it stand . . .
> This is the purpose that is purposed
>   concerning the whole earth;
> and this is the hand that is stretched out
>   over all the nations.
> For the Lord of hosts has purposed,
>   and who will annul it?
> His hand is stretched out,
>   and who will turn it back?"   (Isa. 14.24–7)

> Arise, shine; for your light has come,
>   and the glory of the Lord has risen upon you . . .
> And nations shall come to your light,
>   and kings to the brightness of your rising.
> Lift up your eyes round about, and see;
>   they all gather together, they come to you.   (Isa. 60.1–4)

There is salvation, so close that it can be seen.

Yet from another point of view, the ultimate salvation must wait until "the latter days". After the judgement and the purification a new Israel will arise, with whom Yahweh will make a new covenant (Jer. 31.31–4). The Law which had been promulgated from Sinai for the benefit of Israel will then be promulgated from Mount Zion for the benefit of all mankind (Isa. 2.3). The presence of Yahweh which had manifested itself at Sinai in "thunders and lightnings and a thick cloud . . . and a very loud trumpet blast" (Exod. 19.16) will then be seen on Mount Zion as it was seen in the halcyon days in the wilderness, in the form of "a cloud by day and smoke and the shining of a flaming fire by night" (Isa. 4.5). As Israel now confessed her faith in the one Lord, so on that day "the Lord will become King over all the earth; on that day the Lord will be one and his name one" (Zech. 14.9). Because Yahweh had promised to David that the throne of Israel would forever belong to him and to his descendants (Ps. 89.27 ff), a descendant of David will be the Anointed on *that* day. While Ezekiel would confine the future gift of the Spirit to those who physically belong to Israel (Ezek. 37.1–14), the promise of God through Joel is that it will be poured out on all flesh (Joel 2.28). The Reign of God which is here and is acclaimed in worship is still "to come". Nowhere is this tension more clearly expressed than in the passover Haggadah: "Though this year we are here, next year may we be in the land of Israel; though this year we are slaves, next year may we be free men." [47] The implication of this passage is that Passover, which commemorates the Exodus and blesses God for having redeemed his people from bondage, is in one sense commemorating an event which has not yet taken place!

D. *The Christian Church and the Jewish Calendar*

The relationship of the early Church to the Jewish calendar is an extremely difficult subject, mainly because our evidence is extremely scanty; scholars are therefore driven to conjecture, and often a person's conjectures are the result of his own presuppositions. We can only set forth and discuss the evidence here as we see it, knowing that indisputable proofs cannot be provided. The best method appears to be to begin with the direct evidence of the second century and work backward to the New Testament period. This method saves us from starting with conjecture.

Since we are not greatly concerned with the place of Sunday in the Christian calendar, it may be briefly said that its centrality in Christian worship does go back to the New Testament, though here again we are not told when the change was made from the Sabbath to Sunday. The reason for the change is obvious and it may be that it was made by the Jerusalem church itself, or at least by certain members of it. Though Stephen's polemic against Jewish institutions does not include an attack on the Sabbath, the accusation against him that "Jesus of Nazareth will destroy this place, and will change the customs which Moses delivered to us" (Acts 6.14) would seem to imply that he had condemned Judaism root and branch. At any rate, while Paul went to the synagogue for worship, specifically Christian worship seems to have been on Sunday (Acts 20.7–11; 1 Cor. 16.2). Neither Paul nor the author of Acts calls it "the Lord's Day"; they use the Jewish terminology, "the first day of the week". By the last decade of the first century "the Lord's Day" (Rev. 1.10) was coming into use and by the middle of the second century the pagan name—the day of the sun —was used by Justin Martyr (*Apol.* I. 67). Justin gives the reason for its observance: "It is the first day on which God, having wrought a change in darkness and matter, made the world; and Jesus Christ our Saviour on the same day rose from the dead" (ibid.). The author of the Epistle of Barnabas adds that the ascension took place on Sunday (Bar. 15.9); he also calls Sunday "the eighth day, because it is the beginning of another world". This appears to be his way of saying that on Sunday the Church steps across the border of time into eternity, or better, perhaps, that on Sunday the Christian enters upon the experience of the age to come. Attempts were made at various times from the first century on to make the Sabbath a day of worship also; these were resisted for a time, but appear to have won out in the fourth century.[48] In consequence of adopting the Ten Commandments as a basis for moral teaching in the Middle Ages, the rules of the Jewish Sabbath were adopted by some as the rules for the Christian Sunday, and by some groups during and after the Reformation, Sunday was practically identified with the Sabbath.

Of the festivals of the Jewish calendar, Passover and Pentecost were the only ones retained by the Church. The elimination of the others, Tabernacles, Day of Atonement, Dedication, and Purim, seems to have occurred at the very beginning. Purim as a nationalistic feast would naturally have gone; the Dedication of the Temple was dropped for the same reason, and also because the Church had now taken the place of the Temple (John 2.21; Eph. 2.21; 1 Pet. 2.5). Atonement was connected with the death of the Lord, not with the fast in the autumn, and Tabernacles had found its fulfilment. The Christian was no longer on his way to the Promised Land; he had already "tasted . . . the powers of the age to come" (Heb. 6.5). Tabernacles therefore had no significance in the new chapter of the *Heilsgeschichte*. (Perhaps an exception to this may be made in the case of the Fourth Gospel. It is not easy to say whether Tabernacles and Dedication were still observed by the Church in the milieu where John was written. The teaching which he connects with them may be anti-Jewish polemic—the feasts are fulfilled in Christ and no longer have any validity—or it may be a Christian explanation of ceremonies connected with the feast. When John's whole bias against Judaism is taken into account, it is probably the former.)

Our first definite evidence of a Christian Passover is to be found
in the second century, when a controversy arose over the date on
which it should be kept. (Justin Martyr in his *Dialogue with
Trypho* refers several times to Christ as the paschal lamb, but this
may be because he is arguing with a Jew; it does not prove that he
observed the Passover.) The churches of Asia Minor observed it on
the same day as the Jews, Nisan 14; hence they were called
"quartodecimans". All other churches observed it on the Sunday
following. Our evidence, though definite, is scanty, and many interpretations of it have been given.[49] A. A. McArthur thinks that
quartodecimanism began when the Fourth Gospel was published.
John had altered the date of the crucifixion for theological reasons,
and the churches in Asia Minor, wishing to keep the paschal feast
at the same time that the Lord had held the Last Supper, changed
from Sunday to whatever day of the week Nisan 14 fell.[50] (If
McArthur is right in thinking that the quartodecimans kept the
night of 13–14 and not 14–15, this would not be a paschal meal; but
I have been unable to discover anyone else who holds this.) But
other evidence would lead us to believe that the ancient traditions
were held more tenaciously in Asia Minor than in any other part of
the Church. It was the home of Papias, the lover of oral tradition,
of Polycarp who had received the tradition of "John" through
Ignatius, and of "John" himself. Furthermore, Polycarp claimed
that he had kept the *pascha* from his childhood and this would
mean that there was a Christian *pascha* in the seventies of the first
century.[51] The Jewish traditions were most influential in this area,
as Colossians, the Apocalypse, and Ignatius' letters tell us. But the
strongest argument against McArthur's position is that, while the
influence of Sunday as the weekly recalling of the resurrection
might well lead to the change from Nisan 14 to the following
Sunday, the reverse is extremely unlikely. Moreover, there is a
large number of scholars who think that John gives us the original
Palestinian chronology of the passion, and that the synoptic tradition is erroneous. It is not likely that John replaced an earlier tradition in Asia Minor, when we also take into consideration the
present trend on the dating of John—the last twenty years of the
first century. It would appear then, that the change in the date of
the *pascha* took place outside Asia Minor, which held fast to the
traditional date. If this is so, Passover may have been celebrated as
a Christian festival from the very beginning.[52] The adoption of a

Jewish custom in such an area as Asia Minor, where the Christian leaders were so strongly conscious of the difference between Christianity and Judaism, is highly improbable.

M. Goguel says that Christianity, because of its Jewish origins, was ultimately bound to have some kind of liturgical calendar. The fact that the Jerusalem disciples continued to frequent the Temple would lead us to conclude that they also celebrated the traditional feasts of Judaism, even though their outlook on them would be changed because of their faith in Christ. The Jewish–Christians had, "at least, a seed out of which an annual liturgical calendar could grow. But this is not valid for Hellenistic Christianity." [53] He goes on to argue that for Gentile Christians the paschal feast had its origin in Asia Minor after the destruction of Jerusalem. Large numbers of Jewish–Christians had come from Palestine where they had continued their old customs. The separation between Church and Synagogue was taking place at the same time—the gulf between them had been gradually widening and it now had become impassable—and it was natural that over a period of time the Eucharist would have been substituted for the Passover meal. This festival was then adopted by all Christians in the area. "The Paschal feast and the Paschal Eucharist could have been born out of Christian meditation on the typological meaning of the Jewish Passover." [54] J. Boeckh agrees that the Palestinian church had the fixed custom of an annual *pascha*, but he thinks that the custom was first adopted by Rome from Palestine or from the Jewish–Christian community in Rome. [55]

But the typological interpretation of the Passover is much older than this; it goes back to Paul (1 Cor. 5.6–8). The Corinthian church had a case of incest in its midst and had done nothing about it. In the course of warning its members that they must not make compromise with sinners, he tells them:

> Do you not know that a little leaven ferments the whole lump of dough? Cleanse out the old leaven that you may be fresh dough, as you really are unleavened. For Christ, our paschal lamb, has been sacrificed. Let us, therefore, celebrate the festival, not with the old leaven, the leaven of malice and evil, but with the unleavened bread of sincerity and truth.

Here Paul takes it for granted that his readers know the story of the Passover and will identify the paschal lamb with Christ; indeed the knowledge of the Old Testament which Paul presupposes in the case of this church and the connection which he had made between the old and the new covenants (see 1 Cor. 10), lead us to think that Jeremias is right when he says that the comparison between Jesus and the paschal lamb was "probably an established part not only of the Pauline but also of the early Christian *Passa-Haggadha* in general".[56] Would this have happened if the Jewish Passover had not been transformed in the earliest days by Christian preachers and teachers? Further, would the transformation have happened if the Christians were not observing their own Christian *pascha*? The whole point of the comparison would be lost on those who knew about the Passover only by word and had not experienced its Christianized version themselves. The fact that Paul wrote 1 Corinthians shortly after Passover (1 Cor. 16.8) may have suggested the illustration to him, but to say, as Goguel does, that "we can be assured that Paul would not have expressed himself as he has done, if a Christian Paschal feast existed in Corinth at that time" appears to be an unreasonable assumption.[57] The passing reference to the first-fruits in 1 Cor. 15.20 is inexplicable without the meaning of the custom being known.

As has been mentioned above, B. W. Bacon has suggested that the form of the passion narrative in Mark is influenced by the Roman liturgical celebration of the *pascha*. The precise time indications in 13.35 and the three-hour periods of the crucifixion in 15.25, 33, and 34, which are so uncharacteristic of the rest of the Gospel, led Bacon to think that by the time Mark was written, the *pascha* in Rome had already set the pattern which was followed in the Paschal celebration of the later Church, the all-night vigil preceded by the all-day fast. Some commentators have suggested that a further reference to the fast of one day preceding the *pascha* is to be found in Mark 2.20: "The days will come when the bridegroom is taken away from them, and then they will fast *in that day*."[58] Certainly, Tertullian appealed to it as the source of the custom of the Church (*de Ieiunio*, 2.13). If this interpretation is right, it means that the *pascha* was of long enough standing (perhaps in Rome) for the saying to have developed, for it could not be an authentic word of the Lord. We cannot deduce from Mark whether the *pascha* at Rome in his time was held—if it was held—on Nisan 14 or on Sunday. Both sides in the quartodeciman controversy appealed to "apostolic tradition" which means that the tradition they held went back beyond living memory. M. H. Shepherd thinks that the change was made from Nisan 14 to Sunday when Matthew's became the favoured Gospel, probably by the end of the first century or early in the second.[59]

The great objection to any festivals in the first-century Gentile Christian churches—other than Sunday, which all agree was a day of worship—is that Paul is apparently adamant in insisting that the Gentile converts were to be free from any observance of festivals. "Let no one pass judgment on you in questions of food and drink or with regard to a festival or a new moon or a sabbath. These are only a shadow of what is to come; but the substance belongs to Christ" (Col. 2.16–17; cf. Gal. 4.10). Though he himself still continued to observe the Law in certain instances, and does not appear to have insisted that Jewish Christians give up their old customs, the above quotation from Colossians would seem to say that festivals are unnecessary in the new dispensation. Paul is not always consistent, but he would never have countenanced a division of the Christian community on the basis of race and racial or religious custom. His angry outburst in Galatians was occasioned by the desire on the part of some to adopt the whole Jewish Law; his angry outburst in Antioch when he argued with Peter about the Jewish and Gentile Christians participating in different Eucharists (as G. Johnston says, "Gal. 2.12 has little point if it has no bearing on the sacrament"),[60] shows that two worshipping communities in the same city, divided on a basis of religious custom, would have been anathema to him. (The tolerance which he advocated in Romans 14 has to do with fast days; this is probably the earliest record we have of what were later called "stations", voluntary days of fasting undertaken by individuals and not compulsory for anybody.) Would he have advocated a community life where certain members kept Sunday only as their "holy day" while others met for the Eucharist on certain special days? The outcome of this over a short period of time would have been a divided congregation, each part going its own separate way. The attack in Colossians and Galatians is more probably directed against those who think that the fulfilling of legal requirements can assist in the winning of salvation; in Colossae they had also taken up certain ascetic practices which were Gnostic, not Jewish, but in both cases they were bringing themselves into subjection to the "elemental spirits of the universe" (Col. 2.20; Gal. 4.3). If Paul is to be taken literally in the passages under consideration, it means that any special day of any kind would have to be given up and this would include the first day of the week, which must have derived its custom of weekly worship from the Sabbath worship of the Synagogue. It was therefore not festivals *per se*, but the keeping of festivals for the wrong reason, or the keeping of festivals which no longer had any significance since they were "only a shadow of what is to come", against which Paul is declaiming. It is to be noted that he mentions in his letters only the feasts of Passover and Pentecost. To say that Jewish and Gentile Christians in the same city or town went their separate ways of worship, at least on certain occasions, is to bring the ghost of Tübingen into the field of liturgy after it has been exorcized in the field of doctrine.

It may be concluded, then, that Paul in these passages is not forbidding Christians to have any festivals whatever, but forbidding only those which have lost their meaning. It is much more reasonable to suppose that the "meaningful" feasts were continued from the beginning, rather than brought in at a later date from some obscure Jewish–Christian source. By the time this could have happened, probably in the last quarter of the first century, the membership of the Church was so predominantly Gentile that such an innovation would have been impossible, and we may add that the name the Passover bore—*pascha*—has no meaning in Greek, but is simply the attempt of the Septuagint translators to transliterate the Hebrew. "The whole system [of the paschal cycle] arose in a Jewish milieu and not a Hellenistic one; but the Jewish meaning of the whole has been transformed by a Christian eschatological interpretation."[61]

Our earliest references to Pentecost outside the New Testament are found in Hippolytus and Tertullian. One passage in Tertullian refers not to one day but to the whole period of fifty days between the *pascha* and its conclusion at Pentecost;[62] another refers to the day itself: "We count fasting or kneeling in worship on the Lord's day to be unlawful. We rejoice in the same privilege also from Pascha to Pentecost."[63] In his *de Baptismo* he says that, while the most fitting day for baptism is the *pascha*, the Day of Pentecost may also be regarded as a proper time, since it was the day on which the resurrection was made widely known among the disciples, the gift of the Spirit was begun, and the hope of the Lord's return suggested.[64] References in the later Fathers make it clear that Pentecost was for them the festival of the ascension and of the giving of the Spirit.[65] This is what it must have meant for Tertullian also. Hippolytus does not describe the festival but merely says that if anyone is not at home at the time of the paschal fast—the Saturday before Easter—and therefore misses it because he does not know the proper date, he "may keep the likeness of it after it has passed by", by fasting for one day after he arrives home, but that this ought not to be done till after Pentecost.[66] Pentecost is therefore a recognized Christian festival by the end of the second century.

The fact that Pentecost is not a source of disagreement at the time of the quartodeciman controversy does not mean that it did not exist then, as Jurgen Boeckh argues.[67] This quarrel was not about the meaning of a feast or whether a feast should be kept, but about its dating, and there was no difficulty over the dating of Pentecost. If the Johannine dating of the crucifixion is right, as we believe, then on the Pharisaic counting of the days after Passover, Pentecost in that year would have fallen on a Sunday. If we accept the synoptic chronology, there still need be no difficulty, as the most ancient method of counting the omer was to begin on "the morrow of the Sabbath in Passover week", that is, on Saturday after sunset; by this counting, Pentecost always fell on a Sunday (in the Jubilees calendar, Pentecost always fell on Sunday, but a week later than the ancient reckoning). The argument from silence in this case is not an argument at all.

We turn now to the New Testament, where Pentecost is mentioned three times: Acts 2.1 and 20.16, and 1 Corinthians 16.8. In the last of these Paul speaks of remaining in Ephesus "until Pentecost". Is this merely a time reference? Many scholars think that it is and there is certainly no suggestion in the text that it is a Christian feast. Perhaps we can say only that it does not tell us whether there was a feast or not, but merely that the church in Corinth was familiar with the Jewish calendar. Yet we have to remember that when 1 Corinthians was written the church in Corinth was four or five years old at the most, and that the majority of its members had come out of paganism and would have known nothing of the Jewish calendar before their conversion. Would the date have meant anything to them unless it had some association with their Christian life? Goguel forgets this when he says that people can use a calendar which is religious in origin and not think about its religious character. He cites as an example the fact that we think of Saturday without ever thinking of Saturn.[68] Would any of us not think of Saturn if we had been told four years ago that the faith which we had newly embraced had sprung from another faith which honoured Saturday as a festival, and that our faith gives the true meaning of its ancestor? Would Paul have said that he would remain in Ephesus until Pentecost unless he wished to keep the festival with the church there, a church which was in all probability predominantly Gentile?[69]

Paul's desire to keep Pentecost at Jerusalem (Acts 20.16) may be only the desire of a Jew to keep one of the pilgrimage feasts at the place where the Law orders it to be kept, but there may also be a deeper reason. Pentecost was the least "popular" of the three great feasts, lagging far behind Tabernacles, which was known as "The Feast", and Passover; this is shown also by the fact that it was the last of three to be connected with the great events of Israel's past. If Paul was anxious to keep at least one of the feasts at Jerusalem, would he not have chosen one of the others? Kretschmar thinks that the Book of Jubilees was known in Galilean circles and that, like the Qumran community, the Jerusalem church held an annual feast of covenant-renewal which had been inaugurated after the resurrection; the disciples had been scattered after the crucifixion, but after the appearance of Jesus in Galilee they went back to Jerusalem to renew the covenant and to receive the promise of the new one.[70] If this is so, then there would have been a Christian Pentecost as well as a Christian Passover; but in the light of our present knowledge this hypothesis is still a conjectural one. Paul was anxious to present "the offering of the Gentiles" to the Jerusalem church at the Feast of Pentecost and there must have been some reason for this. If he wished to demonstrate the unity of the Church, and this must have been part of his reason, there would have been no more fitting time than when the Jewish–Christians were gathered together, and he must have known that they would be assembled at Pentecost. The reason for the gathering we do not know.

We shall be concerned with the meaning of Acts 2.1–11 at a later stage in this book. Here we shall deal only with the date mentioned in Acts 2.1. As we have said, the Feast of Pentecost at the end of the second century was a recalling of the ascension and the gift of the Spirit. This must mean that the feast had been established before Acts was well known in the Church, for Luke has separated these two "events" by a period of ten days. By the time that Acts had become well known, the liturgical tradition was too strong to be overcome, and it did not break down till the last quarter of the fourth century when the eschatological celebrations were being replaced by historical commemorations.[71] Whatever tradition lies behind Acts 1 and 2, it is not the tradition which the first centuries accepted as liturgically correct. W. Knox thinks that there is an Aramaic original behind the Pentecost story,[72] which would mean that it goes back to a very early period.

Some corroboration of this is found in the history of the text itself. Henry J. Cadbury and Kirsopp Lake point out that the text of Acts 2.1 is extremely difficult to translate.[73] Literally, it reads "in the completion of the day of Pentecost", whereas the event described took place in the morning (v. 15). They therefore translate it "At the completion of the 'Weeks'", namely, the weeks which ended with Pentecost. *Codex Bezae* has, "And it came to pass in those days of the completion of the day of Pentecost", while the Latin, Syrian, and Armenian have "the days of Pentecost". The last mentioned clearly reflect the liturgical Pentecost of the fifty days and this is probably true also of Bezae. J. H. Ropes believes that the "western" reading of Bezae "was made before, and perhaps long before, the year 150, by a Greek-speaking Christian who knew something of Hebrew, in the East, perhaps in Syria or Palestine".[74] This means that a pentecostal feast was known in the Christian tradition before the time of the "Western" text, and it is not likely that its author would have changed the text if the feast had been new in his own time.

The results of our investigation lead us to assert that there is a high probability that Easter and Pentecost were feasts of the Christian Church almost from the beginning.

2

THE JEWISH LITURGY

At the beginning of the Christian era two institutions dominated the worshipping life of Judaism—the Temple and the Synagogue. The Temple with its minutely regulated sacrificial system was a priestly preserve, but a link between it and the Synagogue was formed by the Ma'amadot (the standing men). These representatives of Israel were drawn from all parts of the country and were divided into twenty-four groups to correspond with the twenty-four courses of priests and some of each group took their turn in "standing by" while the sacrifices were being offered. Before the sacrifice they met the officiating priest in the "hall of stones" (in Acts this is called Solomon's portico), where he blessed them in the presence of the congregation. After the sacrifice was completed, they returned to the hall where they held a service of their own consisting of Scripture reading and prayer. That this was primarily a lay institution is shown by the fact that the High Priest was granted the privilege of reading the proper lesson on the Day of Atonement.[75] At the same time at which the sacrifices were offered, the representatives who had remained at home met in the synagogue for worship.

The Mishnah gives us the order of service at the daily offering of sacrifice.[76] It begins with a call to worship; then follow the recital of the Decalogue, the Shema with its three benedictions—two before and one after—a petition for the acceptance of the sacrifice, and a prayer for peace. After the priestly benediction (Num. 6.24–26), the service ends with the proper psalm for each day of the week sung by the Levitical choir.

The synagogue morning service followed a similar pattern. While a certain amount of freedom was given to the leader, certain fixed forms had already come into use by the time of Christ,[77] and the substance of these was expected to be said. Since they were handed down by oral tradition—written prayers were frowned on by the rabbis—they would probably vary slightly from day to day. The service began with the Shema and its benedictions, and it was continued by a set of eighteen prayers which had become canonical in the first century. They were known as the *Amidah*, because they were said standing, or the *Tephillah*, because they were regarded as the prayer *par excellence*, or the *Shemoneh 'Esreh* (the Eighteen). On certain occasions one of the penitential psalms was said at this point and the service concluded with a kaddish, or doxology. On the Sabbath the *Amidah* was followed by the reading of Scripture, which was then explained to the congregation. One lesson was always read from the Law; it is a matter of debate among scholars of the Jewish liturgy whether there was also in the first century a reading from the prophets as a regular part of synagogue worship, that is, readings from a set lectionary system. The reading from the prophets was known as the *Haftorah*, or Dismissal, because it took place at the close of the service. The afternoon and evening services followed this order with variations—there was no set pattern of Scripture reading, for example, with the possible exception of the Psalter—but these variations need not concern us here.

The liturgical pattern set by public worship was reflected in the Jewish home. Meals were preceded and ended by blessings which were similar in style to the synagogue and Temple prayers. On ordinary days they were very simple in form, but the great days of the year were marked by elaborate variations on the central themes of Israel's faith.

A. *The Form of the Jewish Berakoth*

The characteristic notes of Jewish prayer are praise and thanksgiving to God for his mercies vouchsafed to Israel, primarily for creation and for his choice of her as his own people; actual intercessions and petitions are placed in a very subordinate position. The root from which *berakah* comes means "to bend the knee"; in prayer it sometimes implies both a physical act and in a wider sense an act of adoring wonder at the graciousness of God. "Thanksgiving" in the modern sense of the word may be involved in this, but this is not its primary note. It is noteworthy that the Greek verb εὐχαριστέω is not found in the Septuagint in any of the books which form the Hebrew canon;[78] the translators use either εὐλογέω or ἐξομολογέομαι. There are only three instances in the rest of the Septuagint where εὐχαριστέω is addressed to God. In the

New Testament these three verbs are practically synonymous when explicitly addressed to God, and in the light of the Old Testament it is doubtful if the primary meaning of all three is other than the usual meaning of *barûk*.[79]

There are two types of this prayer to be found in the Old Testament. The first arises out of a situation where some amazing thing has happened and one of the persons involved expresses his amazement at the goodness of God. When Abraham's servant is sent to seek a wife for Isaac (Gen. 24), and finds immediate success, he exclaims: "Blessed be the Lord, the God of my master Abraham, who has not forsaken his steadfast love and his faithfulness toward my master" (v. 27). When Jethro is told of all that God has done for Israel and of the marvellous escape from Egypt, he utters his berakah with which he couples his confession of faith: "Blessed be the Lord, who has delivered you out of the hand of the Egyptians and out of the hand of Pharaoh. Now I know that the Lord is greater than all gods, because he delivered the people from under the hand of the Egyptians" (Exod. 18.10). A similar sentiment is placed in the mouth of Hiram, king of Tyre, when he receives a message from Solomon: "Blessed be the Lord this day, who has given to David a wise son to be over this great people" (1 Kings 5.7). When an unknown worshipper comes to express his wonder that he has been saved from death after he had given up all hope of life and thought that God had abandoned him, his praise is expressed in the same way: "Blessed be God who has not turned away from my prayer nor removed his steadfast love from me" (Ps. 66.20). But the most interesting example is found in Genesis 14.19, because it contains two ascriptions to God which became the basic ingredients of all later Jewish berakoth: God as creator and God as deliverer. In the form in which we find it here it is partly God's blessing of a man and partly man's "blessing" of God. "Blessed be Abram by God Most High, maker of heaven and earth; and blessed be God Most High, who has delivered your enemies into your hand!" It will be noticed that all of these berakoth consist simply of a blessing of God together with the reason for which God is blessed: "Blessed be God who has done this or that."

At some point in Israel's history this form of prayer began to be used in public worship. Our difficulty here is that a great deal of the history of the development of Jewish worship is unknown to us and therefore we cannot give even an approximate date. It may be significant that Solomon's prayer at the dedication of the temple (1 Kings 8.14–61) is a developed form of the individual blessings mentioned above. The main difference is that instead of a gracious act toward one person as in the case of Abraham's servant or Abraham himself, it is now the remembrance of what God has done for Israel in fulfilling the promises that he made.

> Blessed be the Lord, the God of Israel, who with his hand has fulfilled what he promised with his mouth to David my father, saying, "Since the day that I brought my people Israel out of Egypt, I chose no city in all the tribes of Israel in which to build a house, that my name might be there; but I chose David to be over my people Israel".

Then follows a series of intercessions for various states and needs, and at the end a form corresponding to the beginning: "Blessed be the Lord who has given rest to his people Israel, according to all that he promised." A more developed form of this liturgical berakah is found in Nehemiah 9. It begins with an invitation to worship (said or sung) by the Levites (v. 5): "Stand up and bless the Lord your God from everlasting to everlasting. Blessed be thy glorious name which is exalted above all blessing and praise." Then Ezra continues with praise for the work of creation, for the covenant made with Abraham, for deliverance from Egypt, for the gift of the Law at Sinai and the guidance through the wilderness, and for the entrance into the Promised Land. There follows in the concluding verses a confession of the corporate sin of the nation (vv. 32–7). The whole historical retrospect of this prayer is an expression of wonder at the goodness of God to a people who did not deserve it:

> Thou art the Lord, the God who didst choose Abram ... and thou didst see the affliction of our fathers ... and didst perform signs and wonders ... and thou didst divide the sea ... Thou didst come down upon Mount Sinai. ... Thou didst give them bread from heaven ... But they and our fathers acted presumptuously ... and did not obey thy commandments ... but thou in thy great mercies didst not forsake them ... And thou didst give them kingdoms and peoples. ... Nevertheless they were disobedient and rebelled against thee ... yet in thy great mercies thou didst not make an end of them or forsake them; for thou art a gracious and merciful God.

Here we have on a grand scale the liturgical use of the shape of the individual prayer of blessing.

Some of the Psalms follow the same pattern, in that they begin with a blessing, continue with a recalling of the "wonderful works of God" in creation or redemption—sometimes both—and end with another blessing or doxology. Psalm 105 is a good example of this. Verses 1-4 give us an elaborate form of introductory blessing, verses 5-45 the remembrance of God's word in redemption, while the conclusion is a simple "Praise the Lord!" Psalm 106 differs from this only in having a much more expanded form of doxology; "Blessed be the Lord, the God of Israel, from everlasting to everlasting! And let all the people say, 'Amen!'" Psalm 104 has as its central section the praise of God in creation, while Psalm 111 deals with both themes. The former begins simply with "Bless the Lord"; the latter ends just as simply: "His praise endures for ever!" The five books into which the Psalter is divided all end with elaborate doxologies (Ps. 106 is one of these).

It is in the berakoth of the synagogue that this pattern is given its clearest expression, for by this time the doxology had become an integral part of the prayer. A few quotations will show this. All are regarded by competent scholars as having come from the first century.

1. THE YOTZER
   (One of the berakoth before the Shema)

   Blessed art thou, O Lord our God, King of the Universe,

   who formest light and createst darkness; who makest
   peace and createst all things; who givest light in
   mercy to the earth and to those who live thereon, and
   in goodness renewest every day continually the work
   of creation. Be thou blessed, O Lord our God, for the
   excellency of the work of thy hands, and for the bright
   luminaries which thou hast made; let them glorify thee.

   Blessed art thou, O Lord, who formest the luminaries.

2. BENEDICTION 3 OF THE AMIDAH

   Holy art thou, and holy is thy name.
   And holy ones praise thee every day.
   Blessed art thou, O Lord, the Holy God.

To this was added at an early date, the Kedushah:

   And one cried unto another, and said, Holy,
   Holy, Holy is the Lord of hosts; the whole

earth is full of his glory. Blessed be the
glory of the Lord from his place.

3. BENEDICTION 7
Look upon our affliction, and plead our cause,
and haste to redeem us;
For thou art God, Mighty Redeemer.
Blessed art thou, O Lord, the Redeemer of
Israel.

4. THE KADDISH
(A doxology said after Scripture reading and at other times)

Magnified and hallowed be his great Name in
the world which he created.
May he establish his Kingdom in your lifetime,
and in your days, and in the lifetime of all
the house of Israel speedily and in a near time.
And say ye, Amen.
May his great name be blessed for ever and to
the ages of ages.

5. THE ALENU
(This prayer is one of the oldest of all, and was used by a proselyte
when he was admitted to Israel.[80] Part of it is given here.)

It is meet for us to praise the Lord of all;
To ascribe greatness to him
Who formed the world in the beginning;
He made us not as other nations,
Nor placed us like other families of the earth.
He has not assigned us a portion like to them,
Nor our lot like all their multitude. . . .
We bow our knees before the King of the kings
of kings. . . .
He is our God and there is none beside;
Truly our King, and there is none but he. . . .
For the Kingdom is thine, and thou shalt
reign in glory
Unto the ages of the ages.

To each of these berakoth the congregation was expected to
reply "Amen". So important was this response considered, that in
a large synagogue in Alexandria where it was difficult for some to
hear, an official stood on a raised platform and waved a scarf as a
sign to the congregation to reply.[81]

One further berakah needs to be quoted, not only because it is a good example of this type of prayer, but also because it was used in the home or at private gatherings over the wine cup. It begins with the host saying, "Let us bless our God" (if a hundred are present he says "the Lord our God"), and after they have assented by a bow of the head, he continues:

Blessed art thou, O Lord our God, King of the universe, who feedest the whole world with thy goodness, with grace, with lovingkindness and tender mercy; thou givest food to all flesh, for thy lovingkindness endureth for ever. Through thy goodness food has never failed us; may it not fail us for ever and ever for thy great name's sake, since thou feedest and sustainest all beings, and doest good unto all, and providest food for all thy creatures whom thou hast created. Blessed art thou, O Lord, who givest food unto all. We bless thee, O Lord our God, because thou didst give as an heritage unto our fathers a desirable good and ample land, and because thou didst bring us forth, O Lord our God, from the land of Egypt, and didst deliver us from the house of bondage; as well as for thy covenant which thou hast sealed in our flesh, thy law which thou hast taught us, thy statutes which thou hast made known to us, the life, grace and lovingkindness which thou hast vouchsafed to us, and for the food wherewith thou dost constantly feed us on every day, in every season, at every hour. For all this, O Lord our God, we bless thee; blessed be thy name by the mouth of all living continually and for ever, as it is written, And thou shalt eat and be satisfied, and thou shalt bless the Lord thy God for the good which he hath given thee. Blessed art thou, O Lord, for the land and for the food.[82]

One further point may be noted. When a berakah ends with a doxology, the doxology is never in the second person but always in the third. "The Lord thy God, O Zion, shall be king for evermore and unto the ages of ages" (Ps. 146.10). "Blessed be his glorious name for ever, and let the whole earth be filled with his glory. Amen and Amen" (Ps. 72.19). "Praised be his name whose glorious kingdom is for ever and ever" (synagogue liturgy). It is a curious fact that while this doxological form tended to disappear from the synagogue services, it became a more dominant element in the developing Christian liturgies; the daughter at this point stayed closer than the mother to the old ways, still retaining in many instances, though not always, the third person: "Glory be to the Father and to the Son and to the Holy Ghost."

B. *The Reading of Scripture and Sermon*

The nucleus of the Sabbath liturgy, as distinct from the daily services, was the public reading of Scripture and comment on it. Since the synagogue had probably begun as a house of instruction, rather than as a house of worship, the reading of Scripture and the study of what had been read would naturally become a part of worship when the synagogue began to be used for the latter purpose also. In the Old Testament itself the reading of the Law at appointed times is ascribed to Moses (Deut. 31.10–12), while in Nehemiah 8.7–8, it is ascribed to Ezra, which probably means that it is an ancient custom. In the preface to Ecclesiasticus (second century B.C.) we are told that the public reading of the Law was a regular part of the life of Egyptian Jewry, and H. St John Thackeray makes the interesting suggestion that the origin of the Septuagint lies in the lectionary need of Greek-speaking Jews.[83] Josephus in the first century A.D. says that Moses ordered the people "to assemble together for the hearing of the Law, not once or twice or oftener, but every week" (*contra Apionem* II.18). A. Büchler, collating the evidence that has come down to us in the rabbinic literature, thinks that the custom arose out of disputes with Samaritans over the dates and meanings of the festivals; the part of the Law pertaining to a particular festival was read when that festival came round, and then by an extension of custom a portion of the Law was read on each Sabbath. He believes this to have taken place by 200 B.C. on the ground that the Alexandrian Jews would have imitated Palestinian usage.[84] Aileen Guilding would go further still and say that the Pentateuch took its present form at a time when the needs of the worshipping community were of primary importance.[85] In this she follows a suggestion of S. H. Hooke.[86] Be that as it may, by the time of the New Testament the public reading of Scripture is regarded as an immemorial part of synagogue worship: "For from early generations Moses has had in every city those who preach him, for he is read every Sabbath in the synagogues" (Acts 15.21).

At what point a reading from the prophets became a regular part of Sabbath worship, it is impossible to say. Acts 13.15 tells us that both the Law and the Prophets were read in the synagogue at Antioch in Pisidia when Paul preached there. When Jesus preached in the synagogue at Nazareth, he first read a portion from Isaiah.

I. Abrahams tried to show that the wording of the Lucan account (Luke 4.16 ff) indicates that the lesson was not Jesus' own choice, but that it was the regular lesson for the day. The prophet from which he read was not his own choice, for the book was given to him and he was not free to choose the passage but opened (ἀνοίξας) the book at the place where it had been marked. When he had finished he rolled up (πτύξας) the scroll.[87] Büchler comes to the same conclusion for slightly different reasons. The rule for the prophetic lection was that it should be similar in content to the reading from the Law, and he does not think it likely that the choice of passage would be left to the discretion of the reader but would be marked beforehand by the rulers of the synagogue. Jesus "found" the place that had been marked for him. This does not mean that there was a set lectionary at that time, but that on any given Sabbath the reader did not have a free choice.[88] Büchler goes on to say that the prophetic lections also arose out of controversy with the Samaritans. Since the Samaritans did not accept the prophetic canon, the reading from them in the synagogue would have strengthened the hand of those orthodox leaders who insisted that the prophets were "Scripture". Readings from them began on special Sabbaths and were extended in the same way that the reading of the Law had been extended. We may add that even if Luke has deliberately placed the beginning of Jesus' ministry at Nazareth and put this particular lection in his mouth, the way in which the incident is described shows that in Luke's experience the Haftorah was not left to the choice of the reader. Büchler thinks that there was a prophetic lectionary in Palestine before the end of the first century A.D. Werner would go further. He says that certain marks on the prophetic scrolls that have been discovered at Qumran indicate the beginnings and endings of prophetic pericopes.[89] This would indicate that regular reading from the prophets is pre-Christian. Thackeray agrees because of certain Septuagintal readings. In some Hebrew scrolls a key word from the Law lection was written in the margin of the prophetic scroll in order to indicate that this portion of the prophet went with the particular Torah lection that the word indicated. Some of these key words were incorporated into the Septuagint when the prophets were translated. Thackeray would therefore put the reading of prophetic lessons, at least on the great feasts, back to 200 B.C. or even earlier.[90]

The way in which the Law was read through differed in the Palestinian and Babylonian synagogues. In the Babylonian synagogues the Law was read in its entirety in one year beginning at Tishri 1; in the Palestinian synagogues the reading occupied three years and began in Nisan.[91] In such a triennial cycle, the first year readings would be from Genesis 1 to Exodus 11, the second year from Exodus 12 to Numbers 6.21 and the third year from Numbers 6.22 to Deuteronomy 34. The lections would not necessarily be the same in length in any triennium as the number of Sabbaths could vary from 147 to 161. (The Hebrew Pentateuch at the present time is divided into 154 sections.) The main reasons for believing that this triennial cycle existed are as follows:

1. The dates given in the Pentateuch coincide with the day on which the lessons were read. Genesis 1 would be read on the first Sabbath in Nisan, the day which the Mishna gives as the Day of Creation (Rosh Hashanah, 10b), Exodus 12 on the same date a year later, where the month is explicitly stated, while in the third year, a second institution of the Passover is described in a passage (Num. 9) which is out of time sequence. (Numbers begins in the second month but in chapter 9 it goes back to the first month.) In the first year the story for Passover is that of Cain and Abel; the reason for the association of this story with Passover must be that it was read as a lesson.[92] The story of the flood would fall in the second month, the month in which it took place, according to Genesis. The death of Moses, in Jewish tradition, took place on Adar 7, which is the day on which the account of his death would be read, in the triennial cycle. In short, nearly all the dates mentioned in the Pentateuch coincide with the days of the year when they would be mentioned in the synagogue.

2. In the Mishna (Rosh Hashanah, 1), it is said that there are four New Year's days every year: Nisan 1, Elul 1, Tishri 1, and Shebat 15. These are the days on which the first chapters of the five books would be read—Exodus and Numbers both would begin on the same day of the year, Shebat 15.

3. The recurrence of the same themes at the same time of the year: the death of Jacob and the death of Moses occur on the same day in the first and third years respectively.

Lest we should seem to be straying far from the subject of this book, it may be noted that our purpose here is to show that the tradition which connected the Law-giving with Pentecost may have arisen out of a triennial cycle of readings, for the reading at Pentecost in the second year of the cycle would be Exodus 19, 20 and for the third year Numbers 17, 18—the covenant with Aaron and his sons. Scholars are not agreed on the *Seder* for the first year; some would say that it was Genesis 11, the tower of Babel, while others would give Genesis 14, Abraham and Melchizedek. It may be that the irregular number of Sabbaths in a triennium would account for this discrepancy. The chapters of Genesis at this point are short, and shiftings of the beginnings and endings of the *Sedarim* would have to be made to adjust to the calendar.

There is also evidence which leads some scholars to conclude that the Psalter was read through in a triennial cycle on Sabbath afternoons, to correspond with the cycle of the Law in the mornings.[93] The evidence may be summarized as follows: the comparison that is made in the Midrash Tehillim (1.1) between the five books of the Law and the five books of the Psalter; the number of the Psalms is approximately the same as the number of Sabbaths in a three-year cycle; the repetition of the same ideas in Psalms which would be read at the same time of the year, for example Psalm 47 and Psalm 96; the Midrash on the Psalms, some of which is very old,[94] often reflects, either in language or ideas, the *Seder* from the Law which would be read on the same Sabbath. To this Snaith adds that Psalm 1, a psalm in praise of the student of the Law, is placed at the beginning of the Psalter because those responsible for the final arrangement of the Psalter had the triennial lectionary in mind and put this psalm at the beginning to link Law and Psalter.[95] This does not mean that the Psalms were written to order, but they were arranged, where possible, to fit the lectionary.

The sermon or homily as part of synagogue worship is in the Old Testament traced back to the time of Ezra. When the Law was read, it was read "with interpretation; and they gave the sense so that the people understood the reading" (Neh. 8.8). The many volumes of Midrashim that have been preserved from ancient times give us an idea of what these sermons were like. For the most part they were exegeses of Scripture that had been read (according to Acts 13.15, the sermon followed immediately after the prophetic lection), often fanciful in finding connections between one part of Scripture and another, filled with much speculation and legend,

and having a strong tendency to moralize. For many centuries before the codification of the Halakah in the Mishna, they were the
chief medium for the expression of Jewish thought and teaching.
According to Mann,[96] the Law, the Prophets, and the Psalms for a
given Sabbath were the main source of the sermon, and one of its
purposes was to relate the old words to new situations and new
times. One example of this may be given. In Midrash on Deuteronomy 20.3, the word "enemies" is interpreted to mean non-
Israelites, and 2 Chronicles 28.15 is quoted to show that in a war
between Israel and Judah, the prisoners had been sent home after
being clothed and fed. There is no distinction in Deuteronomy
between different kinds of enemies, but later times and customs demanded the interpretation given in Midrash. By the time of Christ
a whole series of these interpretations had grown up, and sermons
frequently quoted lists of authorities of the past. It is not surprising that the preaching of Jesus was received with astonishment
when he taught them on his own authority and not on the authority
of the past; when he quoted Scripture, it was usually to give his
own interpretation. The sermons that are put in the mouths of
others in Acts are more along traditional Jewish lines.

C. *The Beth Midrash Prayers and the Qumran Hodayoth*

One other type of Jewish prayer, not strictly connected with the
service of the synagogue, must be mentioned briefly. The berakoth
of the synagogue, as we have seen above, always begin in the
second person: "Blessed art thou, O Lord", followed by a descriptive clause; and this is repeated at the end. For the most part,
they are in the second person throughout, though occasionally the
descriptive clause is in the third person. The Beth Midrash
prayers, however, are invariably in the third person. They were
used before and after the reading and exposition of Scripture,
when this took place outside the context of worship; they were
usually short and mainly consisted of praise and thanksgiving and
requests for enlightenment in the understanding of the Law:
"Blessed be the name of the Holy One, who has chosen Israel and
given to us the Torah"; "May the great name of the Holy be
blessed for ever and for ever and ever"; "May his will be before us,

which we will place in our hearts to do." Some of these prayers eventually found their way into the synagogue service and were used before and after the lections, still retaining their third person form. One of the longer forms, the *Alenu*, ultimately became the concluding prayer at all morning services. Since the *Alenu* contains no request for the coming of the Kingdom, expresses more strongly than any other prayer the belief in God as Creator, speaks of bowing the knee, and of the glory of God as being in the heavens rather than in the Temple, some have thought that it was composed while the Temple was still standing and that it was part of the Temple synagogue service. (The emphasis on creation stems from the fact that part of the creation story in Genesis 1 was read at the daily service in the Temple synagogue).[97]

The Hodayoth from Qumran are of interest to us because of their form as well as their content. Many of them begin with the words, "I will give thanks to thee, O Lord". Hence they are called the "Thanksgiving Hymns". This is, strictly speaking, a misnomer, for some of them also begin, "Blessed art thou, O Lord". They belong therefore to the berakah type of prayer, since, as we have seen, the Septuagint carefully avoids using the Greek word for thanksgiving when it translates the Hebrew *yadah*. Most of the Hodayoth are in the second person throughout whether they begin with *yadah* or *barûk*. But in the books of the Septuagint which are also found in the Hebrew canon there are only two instances (1 Chron. 29.10; Ps. 119.12) where "Blessed" is addressed to God directly[98] (there are many instances in the other Septuagint books). It would appear therefore that at some point in the last two centuries before Christ, the form of the berakoth prayers changed from the third to the second person, since both the Synagogue and Qumran adopted it. In the canonical books of the non-Greek-speaking Jews there does not seem to have been any hesitation over addressing God with the verb *yadah*. Why the distinction was drawn between the two words at first and later blurred, we have no means of knowing. The New Testament follows the distinction in never using εὐλογέω when addressing God directly.

The content of the Hodayoth, like the content of all berakoth, is largely concerned with the marvel of the lovingkindness of God in his mercy toward sinful man. Over and over again these hymns express amazement at the fact that God has condescended to grant his knowledge and grace to a "creature of clay". (It is true that

there are also passages which can only be described as coming from
those "who trust in themselves that they are righteous and despise
others"; but the note of wonder is a very prominent one.)

How can man say aught to account for his sins?
How argue in excuse for his misdeeds?
How can he enter reply to any just sentence upon him?
Thine, O God of all knowledge,
Are all works of righteousness
And the secret of truth;
While man's is but thraldom to wrongdoing,
And works of deceit. . . .
But thou in thy mercy and thy great loving kindness
Hast strengthened the spirit of man to face his afflictions,
And hast cleansed it of the taint of multifarious wrongdoing,
To the end that thy wonders may be shown forth
In the sight of all thy works   (1QH, 1)

For lo, thou hast taken a spirit distorted by sin,
And purged it of the taint of much transgression,
And given it a place in the host of holy beings,
And brought it into communion with the sons of heaven.
Thou hast made a mere man to share
The lot of the Spirits of knowledge
To praise thy name in their chorus
And rehearse thy wondrous deeds before all thy works   (1QH, 3)

Blessed art thou, O Lord,
Who hast given unto man the insight of knowledge,
To understand thy wonders,
To tell forth thine abundant mercies.   (1QH, 11)

Blessed art thou, O Lord, creator of all things,
Mighty in deed, by whom all things are wrought.
Behold, thou hast granted mercy to thy servant,
And shed upon him in thy grace thine ever-compassionate Spirit
And the splendour of thy glory.
Nevertheless I know that no man can be righteous without thy help.
Wherefore I entreat thee through the spirit thou hast put within me,
To bring unto completion
The mercies thou hast shown unto thy servant,
Cleansing him with thy Holy Spirit,
Drawing him to thee in thy good pleasure
Granting to him that place of favour

Which thou hast chosen for them that love thee
And observe thy commandments,
That they may stand in thy presence for ever.   (1QH, 16)[99]

The evidence which we have given from the Old Testament, the Synagogue, Qumran, and the "Bible Class", if we may so translate Beth Midrash, shows that the berakah form of prayer not only had a long history before the time of Christ, but was also a living form in the first century.[100]

D. *Pentecost in Worship and Tradition*

We have seen that in the Qumran community the Feast of Pentecost was the great feast of the year and that in the Book of Jubilees all the covenants were made on that day. In the triennial cycle of Torah readings, the lessons for Pentecost were Genesis 11 or 14, Exodus 19, 20, and Numbers 18. The Psalms that would have been read on Sabbath afternoons in a triennial cycle are 9, 58, and 110. In the Megilla, the Law lessons were Deuteronomy 16.9–12 and Exodus 19, the prophetic lessons Ezekiel 1 and Habakkuk 3, while the Psalms for the day were 29 and 68. The Megilla represents the tradition which had replaced the triennial cycle, retaining only one of the lessons, but the Deuteronomy 16.9–12 lesson is an extra lesson, stating the reason for the feast, and it was probably read even when the triennial cycle was read, as an extra lesson. The other feast days also had the short passages from Leviticus 23 which were the warrant for observing them. The common theme which runs through the special psalms and the prophetic lections is the majesty and glory of God, and the word pictures that they give us have a great deal in common with the picture of the theophany at Sinai in Exodus 19; this is probably the reason why they were chosen. "God came from Teman. . . . His glory covered the heavens, and the earth was full of his praise. His brightness was like the light . . . he looked and shook the nations. . . . Thou wentest forth for the salvation of thy people, for the salvation of thy anointed" (Hab. 3). "A stormy wind came out of the north, and a great cloud, with brightness round it, and fire flashing forth continually. . . . Such was the appearance of the likeness of the glory of the Lord" (Ezek. 1). "O God, when thou didst go forth before thy people, the earth quaked at the presence of God. . . .

Sinai quaked at the presence of God, the God of Israel. . . . Sing praises . . . to him who rides in the heavens . . . he who sends forth his voice, his mighty voice" (Ps. 68). "The voice of the Lord is upon the waters; the God of glory thunders. . . . The voice of the Lord is powerful, the voice of the Lord is full of majesty. . . . The voice of the Lord flashes forth flames of fire" (Ps. 29).

In the psalms for the triennial cycle, the Midrash on Psalm 110 gives the explanation of the psalm in terms of Genesis 14, and, indeed, quotes the chapter in several instances where it has no apparent connection with the psalm; from this we may conclude that the passages must have been associated in worship for the rabbis to explain one by the other. The other two psalms of the cycle are imprecatory psalms; according to Büchler, part of the liturgy for Pentecost was the recital of the cursings from Leviticus 26 and Deuteronomy 28 [101] (we have seen that the recital of blessings and curses was part of the ceremony of entering the covenant on the Day of Pentecost in Qumran). Psalm 29 ends with a reference to the flood, "Yahweh sat enthroned at the Flood". In the Book of Jubilees (6.15), we are told that the covenant with Noah was made at the Feast of Pentecost. The flood was therefore associated with Pentecost well before the first century B.C., and the use of this psalm, though its main theme is a theophany, may be partly due to this subsidiary reference. Various other subsidiary references are to be found in Psalm 68. "His name is Yahweh and exult before him. Father of the fatherless and protector of widows is God in his holy habitation. God gives the desolate a home to dwell in; he leads out the prisoners to prosperity" (4–6), is but a comment on Deuteronomy 16.11–12: "You shall rejoice before the Lord your God, you and your son and your daughter, your manservant and your maidservant, the sojourner, the fatherless, and the widow who are among you, at the place which the Lord your God will choose, to make his name to dwell there. You shall remember that you were a slave in Egypt." The Targum on this psalm changes verse 18 from "Thou didst ascend the high mount, leading captives in thy train, and receiving gifts among men", to "Thou ascendest to the firmament, O prophet Moses, thou didst take a captivity captive, thou didst teach the words of the Law, thou gavest gifts to the sons of men". [102] The same interpretation is found in the Midrash on the psalm. This interpretation would never have been given if Psalm 68 and Exodus 19 had not been associated in the

Pentecost liturgy, but when they had been associated, the exegetical ingenuity of the rabbis was bound to do the rest. The main theme of worship on that particular day had to be found in all the scriptural passages associated with it, even if the text had to be changed to do so.

One further tradition is associated with Pentecost. One of the pictures of the relationship of God with Israel that we find in the prophetic books is the picture of a marriage. Hosea appears to have been the first prophet to use it. After speaking of the wickedness of Israel under the image of adultery, he says that God will take Israel back into the wilderness for a new courtship and win her back with tender words. Then, says Yahweh, "I will betroth you to me for ever; I will betroth you to me in righteousness and in justice, in steadfast love, and in tender mercy. I will betroth you to me in faithfulness" (Hos. 2.19–20). Deutero–Isaiah gives even more explicit expression to it: "For your Maker is your husband, the Lord of hosts is his name" (Isa. 54.5; cf. Isa. 62.4–5; Ezek. 16.8–14). We need not be concerned with the origin of this imagery, or the source from which Israel borrowed it, for the thought of a divine-human marriage is found all over the ancient world, often in the most realistic terms. The Old Testament itself shows that it must have been part of the religion that Israel found in Canaan; the prophets, at the risk of being misunderstood, took the symbol and used it (Ezekiel, in the passage referred to above, is especially daring in this respect).

At some time before the middle of the second century A.D., the rabbis carried this symbolism a step further and said that the wedding-day of Israel was the day when she received the Law and God made a covenant with her at Sinai. Rabbi Simeon b. Gamaliel (c. 140) said that Yahweh came to Sinai as a bridegroom coming to meet his bride. Rabbi Akiba, still earlier, interpreted the bride in the Song of Songs as Israel, the bride of God. The Mekilta on Exodus 19.10 changes the text from "Go to the people and consecrate them today and tomorrow", to "Go to the people and betroth them today and tomorrow". The conceit that the Law is a marriage contract, that Moses is the best man, and that God and Israel are the contracting parties may be older still, for Paul uses a similar picture in 2 Corinthians 11.2: "I feel a divine jealousy for you, for I betrothed you to Christ to present you as a pure bride to her one husband".[103] If 2 Corinthians was written about the time of Pentecost,[104] there would be more here than just coincidence. Paul's comparing of himself to Moses is not surprising, for in another of his letters to the same church, he says that any Christian is greater than Moses (2 Cor. 3.12).

We have now completed our survey of the liturgical traditions of Israel. But before we consider Ephesians we must take a more cursory look at the other books of the New Testament which seem to have some bearing on the subject under discussion. To them we now turn.

3

THE JEWISH
LITURGY AND THE
NEW TESTAMENT

In the first century A.D., Judaism was a highly complex religion. While there were certain basic "dogmas" which every Jew believed, and which may be summarized as "There is one God, who has chosen Israel for himself, who has given her the Law and who has provided a glorious future for her", everything beyond them could be, and was, a matter of hot and often acrimonious debate. Pharisees, Sadducees, Essenes, Therapeutae, to mention only four "parties", all differed in their interpretation of the Law. The mutual hatred of the Pharisees and the Sadducees can be seen in the New Testament and the Mishnah, while the hostility of the Essenes to all who were not of their number is written all across the pages of the Qumran literature. It was not until after the destruction of Jerusalem that the Pharisees captured Judaism, and in the course of a few decades practically remade it after their own image. In the early years of Christianity these parties existed side by side in an uneasy peace and joined together only when a common enemy attacked them all. The Book of Acts describes the Christians as followers of "the Way", but to the non-Christian Jew they are another Halakah in Judaism, and the same word is used to describe them—αἵρεσις—as Luke uses to describe any Jewish party. The gospel preached in Jerusalem, with the possible exception of Stephen's speech, is preached in order to show that Christianity is the true Judaism, and even Stephen's speech is shot through with Old Testament references and quotations. The followers of this Halakah still attend the Temple services (Acts 2.46; 3.1) and gather in the Temple synagogue (Acts 5.12). While it is true, as T. W. Manson points out,[105] that the total life of the Jerusalem church was much more closely knit than that of the Pharisees or

8—E.B.P.

Sadducees—in this closely resembling the Essenes—it did not cut itself off from the rest of Judaism as the Essenes did. When the break with Judaism finally came, and it did not come suddenly, but over a period of time, the Church still regarded itself as the heir of the divine promises, still clung tenaciously to the Jewish Scriptures which it eventually called the old covenant, and refused to accept the teaching of Marcion that "the living God" of the Israelite was not "the God and Father of our Lord Jesus Christ". The old terms in which the predominantly Jewish–Christian Church of the first generation had expressed its faith inevitably came to have different nuances of meaning when Christianity became a Gentile faith, but the Gentile Church never ceased to remember that its roots were in Judaism. Jesus the Messiah became Jesus Christ or Christ Jesus—the title became a proper name—but he still remained Jesus of Nazareth, in spite of all that the Gnostics tried to say or do. The Christian Eucharist centred on the words and actions of a meal that a young Jew had had with his friends the night before he died; the Gnostics, strangely enough, followed the Jewish pattern of words here more closely than the orthodox, if we may use that word of the Church in the first two centuries,[106] before doctrine had been defined. Yet to put it in this way is to give only one side of the story. The old Jewish ideas of Messiahship were transformed even among Jewish Christians themselves before they became the possession of the Gentiles and, while the God of the Old Testament is still the Christian's God, to call him "The God and Father of our Lord Jesus Christ" is to say something new about him. The gospel changed the outlook and attitude of all who accepted it wholeheartedly, and it would be extremely difficult for a Gentile Christian of the second generation who had been a "God-fearer" before his conversion to tell from what source some of his ideas of God had been received, Synagogue or Church.[107] What he lived by and died in was "The Gospel".

But when this necessary caveat has been made, there still remains the fact that the first Christians, when they prayed and worshipped, and this after all is the heart of any faith, turned naturally to the form of words with which they were familiar, unless they were among those who turned "to God from idols, to serve a living and true God, and to wait for his Son from heaven" (1 Thess. 1.9). The fact that the "Liturgy of the Word" never ceased to be an integral part of Christian worship shows that the synagogue form of worship was never repudiated, and the central prayer of Christianity stems from the berakah which was said at Jewish meals. Of necessity, this prayer had now to include the "valorous deeds" of God which he had wrought in Christ, but it speaks of them in the language of Jewish prayer, of redemption and forgiveness, of the kingdom and the power and the glory, of election and inheritance, of lovingkindness and grace. So much is this tradition taken for granted, that although there is a great deal about prayer in the New Testament, forms of prayer are seldom given. Here again the Jewish influence is seen, for the rabbis taught that prayer should not be written down: "He who writes down prayers sins as though he had burned the Torah." [108] The few that we do find are therefore worthy of study. We confine ourselves to the "blessing" type of prayer.

A. New Testament Berakoth

In the Gospels we are told that Jesus spent a great deal of time in prayer, but we are given few of his prayers. Of the type of prayer with which we are concerned, only one example is given in the Synoptic Gospels and one in the Fourth Gospel, and both of these are regarded by many scholars as not being sayings of Jesus, the former (Matt. 11.25–6, the parallel of Luke 10.21) because of its content, and the latter (John 11.41–2) because it occurs in the Lazarus story. Whether this is so or not need not concern us here. Even if Jesus did not say them, the form that is put in his mouth is such as the tradition believes he would have said. [109] This form of prayer was therefore used in the early Christian communities. Since Matthew and Luke give us identical forms, there is no problem here of differing traditions. The prayer is as follows:

> I thank (ἐξομολογέομαι) thee, Father,
>   Lord of heaven and earth,
> That thou hast hidden these things from
>   the wise and understanding
> And revealed them to babes;
> Yea, Father, for such was thy gracious will.

As we have seen, εὐλογέω and ἐξομολογέομαι are closely related in the Septuagint, and by New Testament times εὐχαριστέω has a meaning similar to these when it is addressed to God. This prayer is therefore of the berakah type, an expression of praise to God at the marvellous new thing that he has done. It is not the leaders of the nation who have seen the breaking in of the Kingdom in the ministry of Jesus, but the fishermen and tax collectors and harlots. Since they would not have seen it unless God had revealed it to them, this must mean that all previous understanding of what would happen when the Kingdom came was quite wrong, and since the kind of being God is, is revealed in what he does, Jesus breaks into a "spontaneous" outburst of praise at this wonderful act of God in revealing a new side of his character. The name of God is therefore being proclaimed anew, in the Jewish sense of the word "name". The attributive clause, "Lord of heaven and earth", is a normal accompaniment of prayers of this type.

The prayer in John 11 uses εὐχαριστέω:

Father, I thank thee, that thou hast heard me. I knew that thou hearest me always, but I have said this on account of the people standing by, that they may believe that thou didst send me (John 11.42).

The Christology of John is plainly evident here but the wonder of "life" as John understands it is also evident. And the purpose of the "sign" of the raising of Lazarus is that others may also come to believe and so praise God by confessing his name.

The other passages where εὐλογέω and εὐχαριστέω are to be found are in the feeding of the multitude and at the Last Supper (Matt. 14.19; 15.36; 26.26–9; Mark 6.41; 8.6–7; 14.22–5; Luke 9.16; 22.19–20; John 6.11. Matthew uses εὐλογέω in the case of the 5000, εὐχαριστέω in the case of the 4000; at the Last Supper he uses both; Mark uses εὐλογέω with the 5000, both at the 4000 and at the Last Supper; Luke uses εὐλογέω with the 5000, εὐχαριστέω at the Last Supper and εὐλογέω in the Emmaus story. John uses εὐχαριστέω). The indiscriminate use of both words in all these instances, except John, must mean that for the Evangelists they have the same significance. Though the words that Jesus used are not told us, it would be natural to assume that he used a berakah prayer such as is normally used at Jewish meals to this day. But the form at that time had not become fixed, and the attributive clause may well have varied with the circumstances. It does not follow that he used exactly the same form at both the meals in the wilderness and the meal in the upper room. Audet suggests, and there is much to be said for his suggestion, that the central section of the prayer, which he calls the "anamnesis", may well have been a glorifying of God for the "wonder" of what was happening in his ministry, at the meal in the wilderness, and for the "wonder" of what he believed would happen through his death, at the Last Supper.[110] When Paul tells the Corinthians that whenever they eat the bread and drink the cup, they proclaim the death of the Lord until he comes (1 Cor. 11.26), it may well be that in the berakah that was said when the bread and wine are blessed—strictly speaking it is not the material things that are blessed, but God who is blessed for them—there is proclamation of the death and the resurrection of the Lord; resurrection, because it is only after his resurrection and exaltation that Jesus receives the title "Lord", and the death and resurrection of the Lord are never two separate events in Paul's thought. Certainly the early liturgies never separate them, even though they change the berakah form into a form of thanksgiving in the Greek sense of the word.

If, without going into all the critical problems involved, it may be said that the Emmaus story is a dramatization of early Christian worship—the reading and exposition of Scripture followed by the Eucharist—the same holds true as in the case of Paul. It is the Christ spoken of in symbol and figure in the Old Testament Scriptures who is now made known in the breaking of the bread, for it is in the prayer said when the bread is broken that the marvellous deeds of God through him are explicitly mentioned. It is in the words of this prayer that he is recognized as God's servant, his agent, through whom these deeds have been done. This praise of God is also the confession of the Church's faith.

Like the prayers of the Lord, the prayers of Paul are seldom given us in their actual form. He tells us what the content of his prayers is: thanksgiving or blessing, intercession, and petition. We may note that these are never divorced from each other, and that, like the prayers of the synagogue, requests for himself or others are made against a background of thanksgiving. "I thank my God through Jesus Christ for all of you . . . without ceasing I make mention of you in my prayers, asking that somehow by God's will I may now at last succeed in coming to you" (Rom. 1.8–10). "I thank my God in all my remembrance of you, always in every prayer of mine for you all making my prayer with joy, thankful for your partnership in the Gospel" (Phil. 1.3–5). "We always thank God, the Father of our Lord Jesus Christ, when we pray for you"

(Col. 1.3). Even if Paul is following a pious custom at the beginning of his letters,[111] his advice to his converts about their prayers shows that his own prayers were made in the context of a *eucharistia*. "Continue steadfastly in prayer, being watchful in it with thanksgiving" (Col. 4.2). "In everything by prayer and supplication with thanksgiving let your requests be made known to God" (Phil. 4.6). The only time that he gives us a prayer in his own words, he follows the pattern of a berakah.

> Blessed be the God and Father of our Lord Jesus Christ, the Father of mercies and God of all comfort, who comforts us in all our affliction, so that we may be able to comfort those who are in any affliction, with the comfort with which we ourselves are comforted by God (2 Cor. 1.3-4).

Here the old Jewish form has been taken over and "baptized". Any pious Jew could have used a prayer like this, except for one phrase, when great difficulties by which he was surrounded had suddenly been removed. He could naturally call God, "the Father of mercies and God of all comfort" (Ps. 103.13, 17; Isa. 51.12, etc.), and would, again naturally, go on with a descriptive clause. The only phrase in this prayer that he could not have used is "the God and Father of our Lord Jesus Christ".

Nor are we told very much in the early chapters of Acts about the prayers of the Jerusalem church. "The prayers" are one of the activities of the community (Acts 2.47), but again, except in one instance, we are not told what words were actually said. In the Pentecost story in Acts 2.1-13, the crowd hears the community "telling in our tongues the mighty works of God". It is while they are worshipping together that the Spirit comes,[112] and the state of ecstasy into which they are thrown causes them to break out spontaneously into declaring τὰ μεγαλεῖα τοῦ Θεοῦ. Since the normal content of a berakah is exactly this, and the mood that essentially belongs to it is a mood of wonder, awe, and thanksgiving, we may not be far wrong in saying that it is this type of prayer that the author of Acts has in mind when he describes "the prayer" in this way, particularly when it also has overtones of "confessing" before men. This is borne out by the words of the prayer that is given in Acts 4.24-30, which falls naturally into three divisions:

1. Address to God.
2. Adoration of what he has done in creation, of what he has said

through David and the Holy Spirit, of what he has predestined and is now performing through Christ.

3. The request that the strength be given to "confess" with boldness and also that God continue his "signs and wonders".

A prayer of the same type as that at the first Pentecost is found at the "Gentile Pentecost" in Acts 10.44 ff: "They heard them speaking in tongues and extolling God (μεγαλυνόντων τὸν Θεόν)". In Acts 16.25, Paul and Silas are said to have been "singing hymns to God while they prayed". Here too, intercession is not made without adoration.

A good example of a liturgical berakah is given to us in 1 Peter 1.3–12, or, more probably, 1.3—2.10. It is not always easy to discern the limits of the prayer *per se* in any of the "liturgies" that we find in the Scriptures. The psalms which are most clearly berakoth vary back and forth from direct address to God in the second person, to speaking of him in the third person, to speaking to the worshippers in order to stir up in them the mood of praise. Psalm 106, for example, goes from "O give thanks to the Lord" to "Remember me, O Lord", to "He saved them for his name's sake", to "Save us, O Lord, our God", to "Blessed be the Lord, the God of Israel". We need not therefore expect a consistent sequence of persons or a prayer in the style of later Christian times when the logical mind of the Greek or the precise mind of the Roman created liturgical prayers. The thread on which this section of 1 Peter is strung is the "ἀρεταί" of God, and the author tells his readers that they have been chosen to make these "valorous deeds" known (2.9). It is the mercy of God which has brought about the resurrection, and in so doing, has given those who believe "a living hope", an everlasting inheritance, made them "the people of God", ransomed them from futility, caused their rebirth, and assured them of salvation. These, of course, are all different ways of saying the same thing, and the whole tone of the passage is suffused with exultant gladness that God has acted in the way that he has and brought to those who believe such unexpected good things. Though the word itself is not used, the section under consideration stammers with Alleluias. And in so pouring out its admiration and wonder, it becomes the means by which faith is "confessed" to God before men.

The connection between praise and "confession" is made even

more explicit in Hebrews 13.15. It is frequently said that there is no reference to the Eucharist in Hebrews, and some have gone so far as to say that the argument of this epistle "allows no logical place for the repetition of the Supper".[113] Is the worship which Hebrews has in mind when the author urges his readers "not to forsake the assembling of yourselves together" (10.25), a type of worship fashioned after the synagogue alone? The verse under discussion, especially when it is coupled with the following verse, would seem to deny this. "Through him then let us continually offer up a sacrifice of praise to God, that is, the fruit of lips that confess his name. Do not neglect well-doing and *koinōnia*, for such sacrifices are pleasing to God" (13.15–16). "Sacrifice of praise" is the Septuagint trans-lation of "a sacrifice of thanksgiving", that is, a sacrifice offered with a berakah or psalm of thanksgiving, a psalm which at the same time declares God's goodness before men.[114] What Hebrews may well mean here is that while "there is no more offering for sin" (Heb. 10.18), there is a peace offering which celebrates the name of God by stating before him and before men what he has done for the good of man; the "fruit of lips" is from Hosea 14.2 and describes an act of true and acceptable worship. The true wor-ship is then the *eucharistia*. This exegesis is strengthened by the next verse which speaks of *koinōnia*. As T. W. Manson points out,[115] this word is partly connected with worship and partly with acts of kindness. Now one of the purposes of the eucharist–agape was the sharing of the resources of the Christian community, those who were rich bringing to the "meal-in-the-context-of-worship" more than they needed in order that "those who had nothing" (1 Cor. 11.12) might be fed (the great prominence of the feeding miracles in the Gospels must also be attributed to the centrality of the eucharist–agape in the life of the Church). By an extension of this idea, all sharing of material things is described in liturgical and sacrificial language (2 Cor. 9.11–13; Phil. 4.18). In other words, the application of this kind of language to acts of sharing is read out of the eucharist–agape, not the other way round. The tradition which is manifested in the varying early liturgies in the central prayer cannot be better described than in these words of Hebrews: "The sacrifice of praise, the fruit of lips which confess his name". Affirmations of faith in credal form are a later innovation, because "the Prayer" was expected to praise and confess. Hebrews is not an innovator here, for it does not give us any actual word of prayer.

The fact that it gives such an apt description must mean that at this point, at any rate, it stands in the main stream of the liturgical tradition.

It is generally recognized that the Apocalypse contains a great deal of liturgical material, but for our purposes we are concerned at this point only with the form and contents of the parts of it which are clearly doxological in character. There are five of these doxologies in chapters 4 and 5, two in chapter 7, one in chapter 11, one in chapter 15, one in chapter 16, and two in chapter 19. The vision of the future which the author sees is in the context of worship (4.1), and the first doxology is an acclamation of God himself as one who is from everlasting to everlasting (4.8); the second is similar in content to the Yotzer of the synagogue, the main difference being that the Yotzer is specific in speaking of creation while the Apocalypse speaks in a quite general way (4.11). The third is a hymn of adoration to Christ as redeemer, which may be compared and contrasted with the Avodah, the second benediction before the Shema, which praises God for his choice of Israel out of all the peoples of the earth. The Apocalypse places the theme of redemption immediately after the theme of creation, thus following the Jewish order, but of course the scope of redemption is much wider, even if it is expressed in Old Testament terms: "thou didst ransom men for God from every tribe and tongue and people and nation, and hast made them a kingdom and priests to our God" (5.9). It is addressed to Christ as worthy of worship, by the side of God. The fourth (5.12), which is more correctly a response to the third, is an elaborated and Christianized form of a synagogue doxology, which was frequently used as a response in the Temple as well. "Worthy is the Lamb who was slain, to receive power and wealth and wisdom and might and honour and glory and blessing!" The fifth (5.13, 14) combines praise to God and to the Lamb in the third person and to this the living creatures give the traditional synagogue response, "Amen" (Ps. 106.48). The first doxology in chapter 7 (v. 10), is the shout associated in the Jewish liturgy with the Feast of Tabernacles, this time partly translated as well as Christianized: "Salvation [the Greek equivalent of "Hosanna"] belongs to our God who sits upon the throne, and to the Lamb". The second (7.12) is like the acclamations found in the previous chapters, except that it begins and ends with "Amen". The others need not detain us, for they follow a similar pattern of praise and adoration except at one significant point. The significant point is that the doxology in 16.5–7 repeats the first line as a response at the end after the manner of the berakah in the Shemoneh Esreh; "Just art thou in thy judgments, thou who art and wast, O Holy One . . . And I heard the altar cry, 'Yea, Lord God the Almighty, true and just are thy judgments'". Whether these "blessings" are the composition of the author for inclusion in his prophecy, or whether he has incorporated them from other sources, we need not hesitate to say that his idea of the worship of heaven must to a certain extent have been shaped by his own experience of worship on earth, and that, therefore, hymns of this type were included in the life of the Christian community from which he was exiled.

This cursory survey of the prayers of the New Testament shows us that, though they are thoroughly Christian in outlook, they are not without the influence, either in form or in part of the content, of the worshipping community from which Christianity came.

B. *Scripture in New Testament Worship*

There are some modern scholars who have seriously doubted whether the Old Testament was read in the Gentile churches of the first century. Boeckh quotes with approval an opinion of G. Kunze[116] that the Gentile Christians were not influenced by the synagogue in their form of worship and did not read the Old Testament as part of that worship. Kunze bases his opinion on the absence of quotations from the Old Testament in 1 and 2 Thessalonians, Philippians, Colossians, and Philemon, and the presence of only one quotation in Ephesians; further, he says, Justin is the first to tell us explicitly that the "writings of the prophets" were read at worship (*Apol.* I. 67), and since he gives these as an alternative to the "memoirs of the apostles", he must have known of services where the Old Testament was not read. But even apart from the error of fact about Ephesians—there are three direct quotations (Gen. 2.24; Exod. 20.12; Ps. 68.18)—there are several allusions to the Old Testament in all the letters mentioned above, except Philemon.[117] And what about the large number of quotations and allusions in the other letters? If we leave Romans aside, on the ground that the church there may have had a large number of Jewish–Christians among its membership, the Corinthian correspondence and Galatians show that for Paul and for his readers the Old Testament was authoritative because it contained a genuine revelation of God, albeit incomplete. The Israelites of old are "our fathers" (1 Cor. 10.1) and their experiences "were written down for our instruction" (v. 11). The real meaning of Israel's Scriptures is known only to those who have looked at them with Christian eyes (2 Cor. 3.12–16). Since it is highly unlikely that very many of the members of the church in Corinth could read (1 Cor. 1.26), the only place where they could have come to know the Old Testament was at worship, where it must have been read to them. Paul's letters were read publicly (Col. 4.16), and there is no need to posit another method for the Old Testament.[118] There can be doubt that the Old Testament was Scripture for the Church of the second century, and in view of the antagonism which developed rapidly between the Church and the Synagogue during the last decades of the first century and the beginning of the second, and which is so vividly described for us in Justin's *Dialogue with Trypho*, it is inconceivable that at some time during that period the early Church should have adopted for itself the very writings whose interpretation was at the heart of the controversy. It is much more probable that they were used in the Church from the beginning. By Justin's time there is an official reader; public reading of Scripture, probably followed by preaching on it, is part of the worship of the church of the pastorals (1 Tim. 4.13), although here both appear to be done by one and the same person. The seer of the Apocalypse expects his vision to be read, and since, as we have seen, the whole book is written in the context of worship, it would be natural to assume that he expected his book to be read at worship too. "Blessed is he who reads aloud the words of the prophecy, and blessed are those who hear, and who keep what is written therein" (Rev. 1.3). It has been suggested that the scroll of chapter 5 in the Apocalypse is either the Torah or the Old Testament,[119] which is a sealed book until it is opened (that is, its meaning made plain) by Christ. He, and he only, is able to do this. This point of view is widely held in the early Church. Paul, as we have seen above, teaches it to the Corinthians, but we find it also in Luke and Acts (Luke 24.45; Acts 17.2–3), in John (5.39–46), and in many of the second-century writings. O. A. Piper[120] thinks that the open book of Revelation 10.8–11, as contrasted with the closed book, is one of the Gospels, and the inference he draws is that in the seer's time reading from the Gospel, as well as reading from the Old Testament, was part of worship on the Lord's day.

If we may refer back to Justin's remark, that "the memoirs of the apostles or the writings of the prophets are read", this may be interpreted in a way different from that of Kunze. It may mean that both were read if time permitted, or if they were read as alternates, then both the Old Testament and the Gospels are on the same level, or, at least, that both are regarded as important. We cannot therefore deduce from this that the Church of the second century neglected the Old Testament, or that it did not use it regularly at worship. What is true of the second century is equally true of the first. Whatever the historical value of the Emmaus pericope (Luke 24.13-35) may be, the form in which it is told is so close to the form of worship which is given us from Justin's time onwards that we may justifiably conclude that it is Luke's own experience of worship which has caused him to tell this story in this particular way. Incidentally, one of Luke's peculiarities in his use of the Old Testament is to refer to it by way of inference and allusion unless it is quoted by some speaker directly. Is this because he is so firmly convinced that the Old Testament was not rightly understood until after the resurrection, for only in its light could the Scriptures be opened?

The reading of the Old Testament, then, was part of Christian worship from the beginning and it did not cease to be read even in churches to which it was as new as the gospel itself. The question to which we must turn is the manner in which it was read, that is, whether it was read according to a set pattern or simply according to the choice of the leader of the worship. Justin is not precise enough for us to learn anything from him. It may be that the lessons were read "at random", or the reader may have begun on any given Sunday where he had left off the previous week. We may gather from the writings of some of the later Fathers that a *lectio continua* was the normal custom, for their commentaries on the books of the Old and New Testaments were in the first place given as liturgical sermons. Space does not permit us to go into the very complicated problem of lectionaries or the time at which special lessons were chosen for the annual festivals. The connections between the many lectionaries of the Church and the Synagogue lectionary have been thoroughly investigated by Werner,[121] and he comes to the conclusion that in a great many cases the Synagogue traditions were preserved in most of the churches. But whether this is a revival in the fourth century and later it is impossible to say, for the earliest Christian lectionaries that have been discovered date from the early Middle Ages. Our only source for information is the New Testament itself and this does not give us any direct statement on the matter. Just as we probably would have had no knowledge of the Eucharist in the Pauline churches but for the bad behaviour of the Corinthians, so the reading of Scripture is not discussed because it never became a matter of debate.

It was said at the beginning of this section that some modern students of the New Testament have tried to explain the background of some of its books by relating them to the Old Testament and to Jewish ways of worship.[122] One or two of their works must be dealt with at this point, as they have some bearing on our subject.

In *The Primitive Christian Calendar*, Carrington claims that 1 and 2 Corinthians are full of "rich liturgical material" and that Paul in some of his Old Testament references is following a Christian Midrash on Exodus–Numbers which was composed after the manner of the Jewish Mekilta on Exodus.[123] The Mekilta, which contains some old material, and which was mainly used for purposes of instruction, develops the idea of Israel turning to God from idolatry and becoming the son of God by passing through the Red Sea; it then goes on to deal with the events which lead up to Sinai and to the making of the covenant. W. D. Davies thinks that Carrington is far too sweeping in this statement,[124] because so few traces of the Mekilta appear in Paul's Corinthian letters. It is clear from 1 Corinthians 10.10 that Paul has taken the events which are described in Exodus 13–17 and Numbers 10–15, together with one or two instances outside these passages, in order to warn the church in Corinth against moral foolhardiness. But what practical value would this warning have if these events were unknown to the people for whom the letter was written? The way in which he alludes to them shows that he expects his readers to be able to recall them without much difficulty. Now, in a triennial cycle of readings from the Old Testament, most of these events would make up the lessons for the period from immediately after Passover to Pentecost. Other references in 1 Corinthians show that Paul has Passover in mind when he wrote this letter. In 1 Corinthians 16.8 he says that he is staying at Ephesus until Pentecost. Is it possible that what Paul has in mind when he writes this letter, shortly before Passover, is that some of these stories will be read in full at the time when the Corinthians will be reading his letter?

Again in 2 Corinthians 3 a contrast is drawn between the old and the new covenants. Carrington thinks that the contrast is brought to Paul's mind because the letter was written near the Feast of Pentecost. "The mysticism of chapters 3–6 is inspired by the giving of the Law and the shining of Moses' face."[125] But the passage to which Paul refers at this point (Exod. 34.29–35), while it is found in a chapter which describes the making of a covenant, would be read some ten weeks later than Pentecost. Between the writing of 1 Corinthians and this portion of 2 Corinthians enough time needs to have elapsed for Paul to have had a report from Corinth, made a brief visit there, written a severe letter, and travelled to Troas and beyond to meet Titus (2 Cor. 2.12–13). While it may be possible for this to have happened in a short period of seven weeks, it is far more likely to have taken a longer time. We are persuaded that at this point Paul is much more under the influence of the lectionary than of the Feast of Pentecost. Chapter 34 explicitly refers to the tables of stone upon which the commandments were written (vv. 4, 28) and to the covenant made by God (v. 10). The following chapters describe the construction of the "earthly tabernacle" which gives Paul the picture that he uses in 2 Corinthians 5. W. L. Knox thinks that Paul at this point is making use of Hellenistic modes of thought,[126] but there is no need to look beyond the last chapters of Exodus to discover the sources of his imagery. T. W. Manson would connect 2 Corinthians with New Year and Tabernacles. Philo had associated the Lawgiving with New Year, and Tabernacles comes shortly after. But there is no proof that Palestinian Judaism or Hellenistic Judaism outside Egypt had made this connection, and the relationship to the lectionary appears to us to be much more plausible.

Aileen Guilding, in *The Fourth Gospel and Jewish Worship*, attempts to show that the great discourses of the Lord in this Gospel are actual sermons which Jesus preached in the course of his ministry and which were based on the Synagogue lectionary. "The Fourth Evangelist seems to have preserved a tradition of Jesus' sermons which has not found a place in the Synoptic Gospels, and he has arranged these sermons against the background of the Jewish liturgical year."[127] Indeed, one of the purposes of the

Fourth Gospel is to preserve them for liturgical use in the churches. Miss Guilding has argued her case with a great deal of persuasiveness, and with a wide knowledge of the Jewish liturgy, but her extreme conservatism in holding that most of the discourses of this Gospel are *ipsissima verba* of Jesus vitiates her argument from the beginning. It is extremely difficult to see how the claims that John puts on the lips of the Lord could ever have been made by the historical Jesus; certainly, the omniscience which Jesus has even in the most minute details of life (1.48; 6.6) comes very close to destroying the reality of the incarnation, and the immediacy with which he is recognized by "believers" is an extreme foreshortening of history. If this book had attempted to show that what the Fourth Gospel gives us is a liturgical meditation on the life of Jesus of Nazareth in the light of what he meant to the author of the Gospel, it would have been on much safer ground, for there can be no doubt that the Jewish festivals are the pivots on which the Gospel swings. Jesus is the true Paschal Lamb who fulfills the Passover, the true manna which gives genuine life, the true light and true water which fulfil what Tabernacles could only portray in ceremony. If recent suggestions that the *locus* of the Fourth Gospel is to be found in the Synagogue of the Diaspora and that its purpose was to persuade God-fearers that Jesus was the true Messiah of Israel[128] have any validity, then it may well be that the lectionary of the Synagogue had a part to play in the formation of the discourses. While we have enough direct evidence to show that there was a triennial cycle for the reading of the Torah, and most scholars who have investigated the matter are agreed on this point, the same is not at all true about the choice of the haftoroth upon which so much of Miss Guilding's argument depends. Some of them have come down to us from ancient sources, but how many of the *sedarim* of the Law had a set haftorah in the first century, it is impossible to say. The passages from the prophets which are woven into the Johannine discourses may be nothing more than the author's own choice rather than a choice that had been made by some authority. The same cannot be said about the references to the Torah, for the feasts themselves are associated with certain passages in the Torah, and one would naturally turn to these passages when considering the meaning of the feasts. The main flaws in the whole argument of this book are that Miss Guilding attempts to prove far too much on too little evidence, and that occasionally

her exegesis borders on the point of fantasy. One example of this
may be given: the name of the servant whose ear is cut off in
Gethsemane is Malchus (John 18.10), because the haftorah for the
period just before was Zechariah 11.4–6 which contains the words,
"I will deliver the men every one into his neighbour's hand and
into the hand of his king (*Malko*)".

Two other parts of the New Testament may have been shaped
by their authors' knowledge of the lectionary: the Pentecost story
in Acts 2, and the Epistle to the Hebrews. Luke's account of the
coming of the Spirit shows clear reminiscences of the lections and
psalms which were appointed for that day (Exod. 19; Hab. 3;
Ezek. 1; Pss. 29; 68). The wind, the mighty voice, the flame of
fire, the mighty works of God are all associated with Pentecost
by the lectonary. The picture that Acts 2 gives us is all the more
striking if we compare it with Philo's description of the same
event:[129]

> I should suppose that God wrought on this occasion a miracle of a
> truly holy kind by bidding an *invisible sound* to be created in the air
> more marvellous than all instruments and fitted with perfect har-
> monies, not soulless, nor yet composed of body and soul like a living
> creature, but a rational soul full of clearness and distinctness, which
> giving shape and tension to the air and changing it to flaming fire,
> sounded forth like *the breath* through a trumpet *an articulate* voice so
> loud that it could be heard by those far away as well as those who were
> near. . . . And a voice sounded forth from out of the midst of *the fire
> which had flowed from heaven*, a marvellous and awful voice, the flame
> being endowed with articulate speech in *a language familiar to the
> hearers*, which expressed its words with such clearness and distinct-
> ness that it seemed to be seen rather than heard.

For Luke, the outpouring of the Spirit was the beginning of the
new dispensation and was marked by the same sort of phenomena
that had accompanied the old dispensation of the Law. W. L. Knox
thinks that Luke deliberately altered the place where Jesus gave his
sermon (Luke 6.20–49) from the mountain to the plain, because he
wishes to reserve the giving of the new Torah for the day of
Pentecost.[130]

For the way in which the crowd reacts to the apostles' expression
of their experience of the Spirit, Luke turns to the story of the
tower of Babel (Gen. 11.1–9). In the Babel story God says, "Let
us go down and confuse (συγχέω) their speech (γλῶσσα), so that

each may not understand the voice (φωνή) of his neighbour "(v. 7). In Acts, the apostles speak with other tongues (γλῶσσαι), and at the voice (φωνή) the multitude come together and are confused (συγχέω), but none the less each member of it understands what is being said. As sinful men had been separated by a diversity of tongues, now the cloven tongues of the Spirit draw all men into a new unity, for they are all able to hear of the mighty acts of God, irrespective of race or tongue. The contrast between Acts and the Babel story is even more remarkable if Luke knew the version of the Babel story that is found in the Book of Jubilees (10.18–27). There we read that the Lord sent a mighty wind which overthrew the Tower of Babel. In Acts the mighty wind comes for constructive, not destructive, purposes.

The connection between Babel and Pentecost was pointed out by E. G. King as long ago as 1904.[131] He thought that Luke had made use of this passage because it was the lection for Pentecost in the first year of the triennial cycle. We cannot be sure of this, for except for certain fixed *sedarim*, there would be slight changes from one triennium to another depending on the number of Sabbaths in the cycle, but the passage would have been read about that time. Peter's sermon quotes Psalm 110, which would have been the psalm for the afternoon of Pentecost, in a triennial cycle.

A recent commentator on Acts 2 interprets the speaking with tongues in a completely different way.[132] He says that γλῶσσαι in this chapter does not mean "languages" but "interpretations"; it is a term applied to any piece of literature which requires explanation, and then to the interpretation itself (comparable to our word "gloss"). Speaking with other tongues does not mean speaking in different languages, but reading aloud passages of Scripture which are not in accordance with the traditional passages read at Pentecost and then giving the passages a new interpretation. The confusion in the crowd arises because the apostles are reading the wrong pericopae, and reading them in the different Aramaic dialects which were spoken in different countries by the Jews living there. The crowd not only expected them to speak with a Galilean accent, but to read the traditional passages and give them the traditional interpretation. He bases this view on two facts: Luke's word for languages is διάλεκτος and Peter's sermon is not the speech of a man possessed. He gives an inspired prophetic sermon, interprets the Scriptures in a new and convincing way, and does it with such power that thousands are converted.

This is a very far-fetched interpretation. In the two other instances in which Luke uses the phrase "speaking with tongues" (Acts 10.46 and 19.6), there would not appear to have been an ordered reading of Scripture for anybody to misunderstand. Luke does not draw a distinction between prophecy and speaking with tongues, at least when he mentions the two phenomena together, in the way that Paul does in 1 Corinthians 12 and 14. There is no apparent difference between "They heard them speaking with tongues and extolling God" (Acts 10.46), and "They spoke with tongues and prophesied" (Acts 19.6). An inspired person was capable of both at the same time when he was caught up into an experience of the Spirit.

The main theme associated with Pentecost in Acts, then, is the giving of the Spirit as a result of the exaltation of Jesus (v. 33). With this is associated the giving to Jesus of a share in the divine sovereignty—he sits at the right hand of God and is given the title of Lord (v. 34), the drawing together of all races to hear about the mighty deeds of God (vv. 6–11), and the extension to mankind of the promise made to Israel (v. 39). The contrast is implied, though not openly drawn, between the gift of the Law to Israel and the gift of the Spirit to the new Israel. Is it possible that Luke also has in mind the harvest theme of Pentecost, the gathering in of all "whom the Lord our God calls to him"?[133]

Turning now to the Epistle to the Hebrews, our main concern is not with the problem of authorship or destination, but with the parts of Scripture which the author uses. His purpose in writing is to arouse his readers out of the spiritual sleep into which they have fallen and to urge them to take advantage of the great benefits that have come to them through the gospel. They are not to be content with their present state of spiritual childhood (5.12—6.3). To stand still is to fall back, perhaps even into apostasy (6.4–8). The key word in his argument is "covenant", and he uses it to show that the old covenant was not only inadequate, but also confessed its own inadequacy. If the old covenant had been adequate, Jeremiah would never have looked forward to a new one (8.8–12); if the sacrifices that were an integral part of it had truly taken away sin and brought those who offered them to spiritual maturity, the time would have come when they would have ceased (10.1–3); if the priests who offered them had been able to fulfil the true functions of priesthood in their own lives, they would not have had to offer sacrifices for their own sins (7.27–8; 9.7). As it was, the priest could enter only into a man-made sanctuary, not into the presence of God, offering a sacrifice which could not break down the barrier between men and God, on the authority of a covenant which, though ordained by God, was not God's final word to man.

We have seen that in the Book of Jubilees the Feast of Pentecost is primarily the feast of covenants and that all the covenants of the past were made on that day. We have seen also that in a triennial cycle, the lections for Pentecost would probably be Genesis 14, Exodus 19, 20, and Numbers 18.[134] It is curious that in Jubilees 13, Genesis 14 and Numbers 18 are associated (according to Charles there is an anacolouthon here in the text, so that the sudden change from Genesis 14 to Numbers 18 may not have been so abrupt). The text, as it is, reads: "And Abram armed his household servants . . . for Abram and his seed, a tenth of the first-fruits to the Lord, and the Lord ordained it as an ordinance for ever that they should possess it for ever" (Jub. 13.24–5). But even if there is a break here, this does not alter the fact that the next event described is taken from Genesis 15, so that the association must still be present in the mind of the author of Jubilees. Can it be sheer coincidence that Genesis 14 and Numbers 18 are also associated in Hebrews together with Psalm 110, which may also have been read on the afternoon of Pentecost? The two chapters and the psalm are woven together as follows:

Hebrews 5.1, 3	Numbers 18.1
Hebrews 5.4	Numbers 18.7
Hebrews 5.6	Psalm 110.4

(At this point there comes an admonition)

Hebrews 7.1–2	Genesis 14.17–20
Hebrews 7.5	Numbers 18.21
Hebrews 7.16	Numbers 18.23
Hebrews 7.17	Psalm 110.4
Hebrews 7.21	Numbers 18.7
Hebrews 7.21	Psalm 110.4
Hebrews 7.27	Numbers 18.1

It is true that Psalm 110 was one of the key passages of the Old Testament for the early Christians and that Genesis 14 would naturally come to any person's mind when reading the psalm. There are also other passages in the Law which refer to the duties and privileges of the Aaronic priesthood, but nowhere are these duties and privileges coupled together in the way that they are in Numbers and Hebrews. There are no explicit references in this section of the Epistle to the other Pentecost lection, Exodus 19, 20. Our author reserves this for the great peroration which comes almost at the end of the Epistle (12.18–24), where he contrasts in magnificent language Sinai and Mount Zion. The main point of the contrast is that whereas the people of the old covenant could not come near Sinai, that is, they could not come near to God, the people of the new covenant have already come to the heavenly Jerusalem; but there are other subsidiary contrasts. Moses is the antitype of Jesus (see Heb. 3.3–6), the Israelites are the antitype of the new Israel, the old covenant under Moses is the antitype of the new covenant under Jesus. T. W. Manson's suggestion that Hebrews is connected with the Day of Atonement does not seem to be a valid one, for the main contrast is not between the high priest entering the holy of holies once a year (9.7 ff) and Jesus entering the presence of God once for all, but between the many sacrifices of the many priests and the one sacrifice of the one priest. Hebrews uses "priest" and "high priest" indiscriminately both in the case of the Aaronic priesthood (7.2; 8.3), and in its references to Jesus (5.10; 7.11).

There are many other Old Testament references in Hebrews, but they also are concerned with the theme of incompleteness. Man has not yet had everything put under him, the sabbath rest has not yet come, the worthies of old knew that they had not yet reached their own true native land. But the main point is the incompleteness of the old covenant, which takes up the central section of the Epistle (4.14—10.25).

Our argument is not meant to imply that Hebrews is a Megillah for the Feast of Pentecost, but only that the author was familiar with a triennial reading of the Pentateuch and that the main passages on which he bases his argument were already associated before he used them for his own purposes.

Our survey of the New Testament evidence is now complete. A

great deal of it has necessarily been inferential, except in the case of some of the prayers, but the cumulation of it does give us grounds for a liturgical approach to Ephesians, especially when many scholars are agreed that liturgical language is one of the outstanding characteristics of this letter.

PART THREE

Ephesians
Baptism and Pentecost

EPHESIANS
AND THE JEWISH
TRADITIONS OF WORSHIP

The racial origin of the author of Ephesians is still a matter of debate. For those who accept the Pauline authorship, this is of course a closed question, but those who claim that he was a pseudonymous writer of the late first century cannot agree as to whether he was a Gentile or a Jew. Goodspeed and John Knox think that they have been able to remove the veil of pseudonymity and have identified him with Onesimus.[1] Mitton hesitates to go as far as this. He thinks that the author's knowledge of Paul was confined to his letters and that Tychicus had given his blessing to the undertaking.[2] W. L. Knox, though generally agreeing with Goodspeed's thesis that Ephesians was written as an introduction to the Pauline corpus, is content to call the author "the Ephesian Continuator"; he infers that he was a Gentile and possibly a companion of Paul, because of his knowledge of Jewish exegetical method. It may have been Tychicus himself.[3] Masson makes no attempt at identification.[4] Beare says that he is a Jew and a close friend of the Apostle, partly because of the Semitic flavour of the style and the knowledge of rabbinical methods of exegesis which the letter displays (2.13–17; 4.9–10), partly because he does not think that a Gentile would speak of his fellow-Gentiles in the way that Ephesians 2.11–12 does.[5] Käsemann also thinks that Ephesians was written by a Jewish–Christian working with material that had come from the Synagogue and Qumran.[6]

In the face of this sharp cleavage of opinion, it must first of all be said that not all the arguments which are put forward by both sides have equal weight. When Goodspeed argues[7] that the author is a Gentile because he does not make a distinction between the sins of Jew and Gentile in the way that Paul does in Romans 1 and 2, he fails to note that Paul in Romans 2.21–2 accuses the Jew of sins of the flesh, and in Romans 3.22–3 says that "all have sinned and fall short of the glory of God". If the Church has now become a completely Gentile community, why does the author place so much stress on the unity of Jew and Gentile in Christ, and use the picture of the breaking down of the "dividing wall" in the Temple as the most telling way of describing the new situation? (This is his own metaphor; he does not copy it from Paul.) Were Goodspeed to argue that a Gnostic myth is being used at this point,[8] rather than the Temple wall, his case might be much stronger, but he does not mention it. Goodspeed has given us a very weak case for Gentile authorship; it is not strengthened by saying that a Jew would not have spoken as disparagingly about circumcision as Ephesians does,[9] for Paul himself does so in Philippians 3.2. Beare appears to be on much safer ground when he appeals to a knowledge of rabbinic methods of exegesis, and acquaintance with interpretations of certain passages as indications that the author was a Jew, but it now looks as if certain phrases which he calls "Semitisms" may not be Semitisms at all. "Works of darkness", "children of light", "sons of disobedience", may have been good Greek usage as well.[10] It is also natural to assume that only a Jew would have thought of the state of Gentiles before their conversion in the terms given us in Ephesians 2.12, but this may be nothing more than an attempt to give verisimilitude to the letter. The arguments on either side do not appear to be strong enough to settle the question. Our further discussion may shed more light on this subject.

A. The Form and Language of Ephesians

Strictly speaking, Ephesians is not a letter at all, but a prayer and a discourse thrown into the form of a letter. If we omit the salutation (1.1–2), the closing greetings (6.21–4), and a few other passages, the omission of which does not destroy the coherence of what remains, we can see how superficial the epistolary form of Ephesians is (these passages will be dealt with later). As has frequently been pointed out, it divides easily into two parts: 1—3 a prayer, and 4—6 parenetic material.

The prayer, both in language and in form, is patterned after the Jewish berakoth. It begins with a blessing of God, continues with an "anamnesis", and ends with a doxology. In this it bears some resemblance to 1 Peter except that in the latter the doxology comes at the end of the parenetic section, not at the end of the berakah proper. Ephesians therefore has closer affinities with the tradition than 1 Peter has.

Many scholars are agreed that the first section (1.3–14) is poetic material, though here agreement seems to end. Lohmeyer[11] appears to have been the first to argue that these verses are poetic in character and can be divided into four stanzas: 3–4, 5–8, 9–12, 13–14. Dibelius,[12] while he agreed that Lohmeyer had established the liturgical character of the passage and the Semitic influence upon the manner of its formation, doubted whether it could be as symmetrical as Lohmeyer claimed; he would divide it into four sections, but under topics rather than under form: verse 3, introduction; verses 4–6, election; verses 7–10, redemption; verses 11–14, Jewish and Gentile Christians have both received the blessings of election and redemption. C. Maurer,[13] who is more interested in the content of this section than in the form, holds that it was composed by the author as an introduction to his epistle and that it contains within itself in miniature all the teachings of the Epistle. Masson makes the suggestion that the whole section was originally a chant, composed throughout in the first person. The author took it over and turned the first half of the last strophe into the second person, in order to use it as a transition point for the rest of the letter. "The structure of the hymn is ruled by parallelism, parallelism of the number of syllables and assonance of the first and last syllables. The verses are grouped in six strophes of two stanzas each, and each strophe is dominated by one idea."[14] Schille maintains that the poetic section extends only to verse 12a, and that the author added verses 13 and 14 as a corrective to the thorough-going eschatology of the Hellenistic Church. The poem itself expresses a completely realized eschatology, and the last two verses are added to bring the community down to earth. The inheritance is not received in full as yet, but only the first instalment of it.[15] Dahl makes still another analysis of what he calls a "Briefeingangs-Eulogie" which incidentally he believes to have been composed for the occasion, though the pattern of it is older: verse 3, praise to God who has blessed us in Christ; verses 4–6a, the gracious eternal counsel of God; verses 6b–7, grace as forgiveness; verses 8–9a, grace as revelation; verses 9b–10, universality of salvation; verses 11–12, Christians have been given this salvation; verses 13–

14, the whole thought of the poem applied to the Gentile Christians who will receive the letter.

The number of different divisions which scholars have seen in this short passage means that it cannot be easily or logically divided; the ideas tumble over one another as the author tries to express for himself the magnificence of the act of God in Christ. Clearly the passage is written in what we may call a state of controlled ecstasy. The origin of it is also disputed, some saying that it is the author's own, others that he copied it. The grammatical and syntactical construction is carried on through the whole letter, which would argue for common authorship, but the author of Ephesians may have attempted to imitate the style of a "liturgy" with which he was familiar. Schille would appear to be wrong in saying that parts of Ephesians were written to correct the eschatology of the Gentile Church, for the tension between the "now" and the "not yet" is found in more than one place in the New Testament. To say that our author starts with a belief accepted by the community or communities to which the letter was addressed as a sort of *captatio benevolentiae*, and then goes on to correct it, is to say that there were two different eschatologies in the first generations of Christianity. The Greek mind may have been confused by this unfamiliar concept, but to say that it accepted one side of the paradox and not the other is to forget that the sense of expectant waiting did not die out in the Church till a much later time, as 2 Peter bears witness. If the Gentiles had lost sight of this altogether in the last quarter of the first century, why is it still alive in the middle of the second? In the case of the passage before us, the last two verses cannot be separated from the others, as Schille would have it. Formally, they are an integral part of the passage and cannot be cut off from it without doing violence to both the text and the meaning.

A very attractive suggestion about the form of this passage is the suggestion of Masson, who sets it out in a more logical, and at the same time more poetic, way than any of the others we have mentioned. He also best explains the transition from the first to the second person in the last verse but one.[16] But whatever the form, the tone of wonder and awe which runs through the whole passage, the slow meditative style, the solemnity of the language, the repetition of the phrase, "to the praise of his glory", which is the main purpose of all berakoth, show us the origin of this way of approaching God. Thoroughly Christian in content—though many of the ideas have been taken over from Judaism they have been baptized into Christ—it is yet thoroughly Jewish in attitude. Beginning with a "Blessing" of God, it continues to the end with a recounting of his "noble acts", his "spiritual blessings", which are enumerated as election, adoption, redemption and forgiveness, revelation, and the gifts of the Spirit to those who have heard and believed.

After the prayer in 1.15–19, there is a return in 20–3 to what God "accomplished in Christ". The second chapter continues with what God has accomplished in believers. This chapter, which divides easily into two sections, 1–10 and 11–22, is nothing more than a duplication of what is said in 1.3–14, looked at from two different points of view: those who were dead have been made alive, and those who were alienated have been reconciled. Other ideas are drawn in, some of them expressions of doctrine, but again the dominant note is one of wonder at what God has done. Though men were living lives that should have brought the wrath of God upon them, God in his mercy and in his love rescued them from a living death (in the second section their situation is described as one of alienation from God and from God's people), lifted them up to reign with Christ, made them fellow-citizens with "the saints", members of God's family, stones in a living temple which is God's own habitation. They are exhorted to "remember" (2.11), not lest they should forget that they were once alienated from God, for the word does not necessarily imply "a well advanced stage of Christian development"[17] nor "a long retrospect"[18], but in order that their "remembering" may be material for praise. After a long parenthesis (3.1–13), the author resumes his berakah with a brief "Trinitarian" prayer (14–19), in which he prays that his readers may have the strength of the Spirit, the indwelling of Christ, and the fulness of God. He closes his prayer with a Christianized form of a Jewish doxology.

It is our contention, then, that 1.3–14 with chapter 2 and 3.14–21 make a coherent whole in that they follow the same themes throughout: what God has done for believers and what he still may do. To put it another way, the first sentence (1.3–14) and the whole of chapter 2 are concerned with God's work in the faithful community, while 3.14–21 is a prayer that the community may enter into an understanding of God's amazing work. It is agreed by many commentators that 3.14 is really the continuation of 2.22,[19] on grounds of grammar and sense. "For this reason" of 3.14 is a repetition of 3.1 where no verb is attached to it and verse 13 does not logically lead into verse 14. The Greek text of verse 13 has puzzled commentators, and two or three different translations have been suggested for it, but in whatever way it is translated, it is clear that it is not the cause for the prayer that follows. When we consider the content of 3.1–13, we find that it is mainly concerned with the place of Paul in the whole work of the Gentile mission, and its purpose is to show the greatness of the Apostle and the divine choice which had rested upon him. Not only is it difficult to imagine the Apostle writing a paragraph in which he at one and the same time boasts of the insight which he has into the whole plan of God, and yet speaks of himself in such abject terms (3.4, 8), it is also noticeable that this passage contains two references to the same verse in Colossians, a verse which cannot be regarded as part of any traditional material. "The stewardship of the grace of God that was given to me for you" (Eph. 3.2) and "The gift of the grace of God that was given me" (Eph. 3.7) are both minor variations from "The stewardship of God that was given to me for you" (Col. 1.25). This "protesting too much" over the place of Paul, together with the fact that it is one of the few places where a phrase from Colossians is copied by Ephesians almost verbatim, strengthens the suggestion that 3.14 is the logical continuation of 2.22. This argument is further strengthened by the following:

1. Paul never says elsewhere that his imprisonment is on behalf of the Gentiles.
2. There is an apparent contradiction between verses 3 and 5; in the former the mystery has been revealed to Paul, while in the latter it is revealed to the holy apostles and prophets.
3. Words and ideas are caught up from the first two chapters and worked into a new paragraph, words such as "mystery" (three times), "apostles and prophets" (once), οἰκονομία (once, with a different meaning); the idea that the Gentiles have the right to belong to the new Israel (3.6; 2.19) and have access to God (3.12; 2.18); the eternal purpose of God which in 1.10 is described as the "summing up" of all things in Christ is in 3.10–11 said to be that the Church should be the agency by which the wisdom of God is made known to the principalities and powers; in 1.9 the mystery of the divine will is made known to all Christians

but in 3.2 it is revealed only to Paul and in 3.5 to the apostles and prophets. This transposition has been very effectively done, but as a whole the passage depends upon what has gone before, with the one exception referred to above—the greatness of Paul.

Attention has been frequently drawn to the fact that the majority of Paul's letters begin with a thanksgiving for the manifestation of the grace of God in the church to which he is writing. The two exceptions are Galatians, which begins with an anathema after the greeting, and 2 Corinthians, which begins with a berakah. Paul never begins with a berakah followed by a thanksgiving, for these are two ways of doing the same thing. Ephesians is unique in the Pauline corpus in that it has both forms. The fact that the thanksgiving is superfluous at this point shows that the author, making a conscious effort to imitate the usual Pauline form, did not wish to omit anything which he considered essential to a genuine Pauline letter.[20] As in 3.1–13, we have another passage, 1.15–17, where phrases which cannot be considered traditional have been copied from Colossians 1.4, 9, 3. "Because I have heard of your faith in the Lord Jesus and toward all the saints [love is omitted in the best texts], I do not cease to give thanks for you, remembering you in my prayers, that the God of our Lord Jesus Christ, the Father of glory may give you" is the author's way of combining, "because we have heard of your faith in Christ Jesus and of the love which you have for all the saints", "we have not ceased to pray for you", and "we always thank God, the Father of our Lord Jesus Christ". In a passage much shorter than the one in chapter 3, we may not expect to find as much repetition, especially when verses 20–3 contain traditional material, but we find it none the less. "A spirit of wisdom and of revelation in the knowledge of him" (v. 17) is an echo of "He has made known to us in all wisdom and insight the mystery of his will" (v. 9); "the riches of the glory of his inheritance" combines 1.8 and 1.14. "Faith" in verse 15 arises out of "believed" in verse 13. None of the Pauline thanksgiving-prayers shades off into doctrinal matter as Ephesians 1.20 does. They are concerned with "the fruits of the Gospel" present in the church to which he is writing and his hopes and prayers for his readers. Clearly what we have in this passage is an attempt to imitate a Pauline thanksgiving which does not quite succeed. Before the author has reached the end of his sentence, which appears to be a deliberate attempt to imitate the long sentence preceding, he has forgotten the purpose of the intercession and returned to the theme of the berakah.

The διὰ τοῦτο κἀγώ (v. 15) is so loosely connected with what precedes and what follows that commentators are divided over whether it goes with one or the other. It may be drawn from Colossians 1.9 where it naturally follows the preceding paragraph, or it may be a general reference to verses 3–14. The passage that follows makes complete sense without it and its redundancy leads us to suspect that, like the τούτου χάριν of 3.1, it is another insertion into a form which the author already has before him. In effect, the parts of chapters 1–3 which we have described as a berakah may be summed up in one sentence: God has done this for all of us, he has done it for you, and I pray that you will come to a deeper understanding of it. As we have seen, this is a very common pattern in the Psalms and is to be found in a slightly different form in 1 Peter. It is at once a blessing of God and a proclamation of the gospel, just as Psalm 106 is a proclamation of the Old Testament "gospel". Psalm 107, a series of thanksgivings for various occasions, has the same clearly delineated form that we find in Ephesians. It begins with an invitation to all who have been redeemed to "confess" to the Lord. Then the various groups take up their own particular cause for thanksgiving, the lost, the prisoner, the sick, the storm-tossed. Each describes how it was in trouble and was redeemed, and utters its praise. The psalm ends with these words: "Whoever is wise, let him give heed to these things; let men consider the steadfast love of the Lord". The form which the berakah takes in Ephesians is as follows:

1.3	Opening blessing (invocation followed by an attributive clause).
1.4–9	Blessings enumerated in general.
1.10–14	The divine plan for the world and the destiny of the "Called".
2.1–10	The dead have been raised to life.
2.11–22	The alien has been enfranchised.
3.14–19	Prayer for deeper understanding of the love of Christ.
3.20–1	Doxology.

The solution we have suggested to the first section of Ephesians is strengthened by the fact that some recent scholars think that the greater part of Ephesians 2 is made up of liturgical material. Schille finds two liturgical passages (2.4–10 and 14–18).[21] W. Nauck believes that 2.19–22 is a *tauflied*.[22] It remains to be added that the passages which we do not think were part of the original material from which Ephesians is drawn are the two passages which are clearly epistolary in form, and one of them makes the definite claim that Paul is the author.[23]

Not only is the form of the basic part of Ephesians 1–3 traditional, the material itself has echoes of some synagogue prayers, as the following comparison shows:

EPHESIANS	SYNAGOGUE
Blessed be the God and Father of our Lord Jesus Christ who . . . (1.3)	Blessed art thou O Lord God, King of the Universe who
He destined us in love to be his sons (1.5)	Blessed art thou, O Lord, who hast chosen thy people Israel in love (Ahabah).
the forgiveness of our trespasses, according to the riches of his grace which he lavished upon us (1.7, 8)	Blessed art thou, O Lord, who art gracious and who dost abundantly forgive (Shemoneh Esreh)
He has made known to us in all wisdom and insight the mystery of his will (1.9)	Thou favourest man with knowledge . . . Grant us knowlege and understanding and insight (Shemoneh Esreh)
God, who is rich in mercy, out of the great love with which he loved us (2.5)	With great love hast thou loved us, O Lord, our God; with great and exceeding mercy hast thou had mercy upon us (Ahabah)
When we were dead through our trespasses, [God] made us alive (2.5)	Blessed art thou, O Lord, who makest the dead to live (Shemoneh Esreh)
[He] made us sit with him in the heavenly places in Christ Jesus (2.6)	The seat of his glory is in the heavens above and the abode of whose might is in the loftiest heights (Alenu)
I bow my knees before the Father, from whom every family in heaven and on earth is named (3.14, 15)	He has not made us like other nations, he has not placed us like families of the earth
	We bow our knees and offer worship and thanks before the King of Kings (Alenu)[24]
Doxology and Amen	Doxology and Amen

These echoes are not always imitations; sometimes they are deliberate "corrections" of the synagogue prayers in the light of the Christian revelation, as, for example, the last one of the list. The Alenu was a prayer used at first in the Temple synagogue; is it brought to the mind of the author because he has just described the Church as a temple? [25] In the Shemoneh Esreh, the reference to giving life to the dead is to physical death, whereas in Ephesians it is to spiritual death. [26] The prayer for knowledge in 1.17–18 is repeated in various ways during the synagogue service, and it cannot be sheer coincidence that the only place where "enlighten your hearts" is found in a prayer is in the blessing at the covenant-renewal service at Qumran (IQS, II, 3), which Vermes connects with the fourth blessing in the Shemoneh Esreh (see above, Eph. 1.9). [27]

When we turn to the parenetic section (4–6), we find that it divides into four exhortations: (a) An appeal to unity (4.1–16); (b) The two ways of darkness and light (4.17—5.20); (c) The *Haustafeln* (5.21—6.9); (d) The peroration (6.10–18). The last few verses, apart from the final blessing (23–4) are borrowed from Colossians 4.3, 4, 7, 8, verses 21 and 22 being almost a direct transcript.

As in the first section, the phrases or sentences which turn this document into a letter can be removed without doing any harm to the sense. There are four of them: "I, the prisoner" (4.1); "assuming that you have heard about him and were taught in him, as the truth is in Jesus" (4.21); 6.19–20; 6.21–2.

The first of these as it now stands is a unique phrase in the Pauline corpus. "I therefore exhort you, I, the prisoner in the Lord". In Philemon 1 and 9 Paul calls himself "a prisoner of Christ Jesus", by which he probably means that he is suffering as a Christian. [28] In Ephesians 3.1 we have the phrase, "a prisoner of Christ Jesus". Why then is this phrase not used here? Probably because the phrase originally read, "I therefore exhort you in the Lord", a construction which we find in 1 Thessalonians 4.1 and 2 Thessalonians 3.12. It has been added here to stress the fact that the "letter" comes from Paul. The second is a parenthesis, as it stands, for the words that come before and after obviously go together. "You have not so learned Christ. . . . Put off your old nature." [29] The third makes a rather lame ending to a magnificent passage and puts a personal ending on a long exhortation which up to this point is highly impersonal, except for "the prisoner in the Lord" at the beginning. Since it is for the most part taken from a personal passage in Colossians 4.3–4, and misused in the taking, we have good grounds for suspecting that this too has been added to give verisimilitude to a pseudonymous writing. The fourth confirms our suspicion because it simply copies Colossians. What we have in the last three chapters, therefore, is an admonition which has been turned into a letter by the use of a few judicious phrases and sentences. The author must have had Colossians before him when he made the finishing touches to his document, for it is extremely unlikely that anyone would have committed to memory the comparatively unimportant news about Tychicus.

The question remains why the rest of Colossians has influenced the letter in the way that it has, with words and phrases from it occurring here and there, but no continuous passages other than the one mentioned above. The thesis of literary dependence is questionable because Ephesians does not follow Colossians either in general outline or in detail. Some "Colossian" parts are separated from each other, others are conflated or joined in new ways. If we take Mitton's table of comparison, we find that there are very few places where he draws upon more than two consecutive verses in Colossians. For the most part, he has to go back and forth from one chapter to another, or back and forth in the same chapter, in order to find words or phrases that will fit into the order of Ephesians. Ephesians 1.22—2.7, for instance, is drawn from Colossians 1.19; 1.24; 2.9–10; 3.11; 2.13; 3.7; 3.6; 2.13; and possibly 3.1 and 3.3.[30] Part of the answer may be that both letters depend to a certain extent upon a body of traditional material which has been used in different ways,[31] but this does not solve the problem of such passages as Ephesians 5.19–21 and Colossians 3.16–17, where we have a clear case of conflation with a change in meaning. The passage in Colossians must have been known to the author of Ephesians, but he did not know it well enough to quote it exactly. Johnston may have provided a clue when he said that this is the sort of trick that our memories may play upon us when we are quoting the Bible.[32] In the passage under consideration, Colossians has, "do all in the name of the Lord Jesus, giving thanks to God the Father through him", while Ephesians has, "giving thanks always for all things in the name of our Lord Jesus Christ to God and the Father". If this admonition had originally been

given orally, this is the kind of "mistake" that would be very likely
to happen. Or it could have happened if the author was composing
his admonition without referring to the actual text of Colossians,
turning to the text only when he came to write the final verses. Our
judgement is that the greater part of Ephesians was originally composed to be spoken. The solemn and sonorous style is better explained in this way than in any other. The theory of Mitton, to
which we have already referred, that Ephesians was written to be
read at worship, is partly true, but there is no reason to think that a
letter, if originally conceived as a letter, would have to be written
in this style. All of Paul's letters were written for public reading, as
the author of Ephesians must have known. The idea of publishing
the material in letter form must have occurred to him after a great
deal of it had been already composed. If the greater part of it had
originally been composed for use in public worship, the style in
which it is written would have been the natural style to use. Our
author would just as naturally have followed the same style when
he turned the material into letter form by the additions which we
have suggested. The style itself may well have been, and probably
was, modelled on that used in the prayers of the Synagogue, for
they are written in the same sonorous style (the Alenu is a good
example). This tradition of style and language for prayer is maintained by Hippolytus in his *Apostolic Tradition*. Here a prayer is
suggested for the bishop's use at the Eucharist if he himself is unable to compose a "sustained and elevated" prayer. Nuances of
style and language are seen by different people in different ways,
but to this observer the long parenthesis (Eph. 3.1–13) does not
reach the same level as the rest of the letter either in matter or
manner.

Hans Lietzmann has suggested that the eucharistic prayer of
Hippolytus, which consists of a thanksgiving for what God has
done through Christ and a petition that the Spirit may enter into
the "oblation" and so pass to those receiving back what they had
offered, has its roots in Pauline thought.[33] He thinks also that
some of the christological hymns embedded in the New Testament were originally parts of thanksgivings said at the Eucharist;
as examples, he cites: Philippians 2.5–11; 1 Timothy 3.16;
1 Peter 3.18–22. He also shows that in the thought of Paul those
who receive the Eucharist receive at the same time an influx of the
Spirit in a quite realistic way. The ideas of the second half of the

Hippolytean *eucharistia* are therefore Pauline, but when Lietzmann goes on to say that "we have no conclusive proof that at the Pauline celebration of the Supper, the *eucharistia* had a christological content", he overlooks the fact that Paul himself says that whenever the bread is eaten and the cup is drunk "the death of the Lord" is proclaimed (1 Cor. 11.26). As has been said previously, this proclamation took place during the berakah or thanksgiving prayer.

Now the berakah form is the form of the prayer in Ephesians as we have suggested it. It proclaims what God has done in Christ and specifically connects the divine action with the death and resurrection of the Lord (2.5, 13, 15), but it remains closer to the Jewish pattern than does Hippolytus by a reference to creation (1.4) and is also more eschatologically centred in that it refers to the new creation which has already taken place (2.15). The prayer (3.14–19) is not only for the strength of the Spirit, but also for the indwelling of Christ and the fulness of God, in order that God may be glorified (3.20–1).[34] The last paragraph of the *eucharistia* of Hippolytus is instructive at this point.

> And we pray thee that thou wilt send thy Holy Spirit upon the oblation of thy holy Church; gather it into one, and grant to all thy saints who partake that they may be filled with thy Holy Spirit, that their faith may be strengthened in truth, in order that we may praise and glorify thee through thy Servant Jesus Christ, through whom to thee be glory and honour with the Holy Spirit in the Holy Church, now and always and unto the ages of the ages. Amen.

There is no direct copying of Ephesians by Hippolytus here, but the two prayers belong to the same general field of ideas (cf. John 6.56). If it be objected that there is no direct reference to the Eucharist in this Ephesian berakah, the reply may be made that there is equally no reference to the sacrifice of thanksgiving in many of the Psalms which are clearly liturgies to be used when a sacrifice of thanksgiving was offered (1 Chron. 16.8–36; Ps. 106); there is only one with a reference (Ps. 107.22). They are accompaniments to it, not explanations of it. As has frequently been said, the Jew did not think it necessary, when making an oblation, to offer it formally with explanatory words and ask God to accept it, nor did he "bless" it or ask God to "bless" it. All this was understood and not formally expressed. It was not until Christianity had

become completely Gentile that all of these ideas had to be expressed in words, for the ideas were foreign to the Gentile mind.
Ephesians marks a stage in the transition from the Jewish berakah
form to the eucharistic form that we find in Hippolytus. It is much
more likely that this happened gradually than suddenly. It is still
the general pattern of Ephesians that is found in Justin Martyr in
the middle of the next century: "We thank God for having created
the world . . . and for delivering us from the evil in which we were
and for completely overthrowing principalities and powers by him
who suffered according to his will" (*Dial. with Trypho*, 41). It is
bread over which thanksgiving has been said that is called
Eucharist (*Apol.* I.66).

Dahl thinks that the opening benediction (1.3–14) is an imitation
of a blessing that was said over the water before baptisms took
place, but we have no direct evidence of this kind of prayer until
the *Apostolic Constitutions* in the late fourth century; there it is
clearly based on the eucharistic prayer (Bk. 7, c. 43).

Our conclusion is that the main part of Ephesians 1–3 is a
berakah for use in public worship, possibly at the Eucharist.

B. *The Exaltation and Sovereignty of Christ: The Spirit*

The Sovereignty of Christ is one of the great themes of our
Epistle, placed at the beginning of both sections of it (1.3 and 4.7).
It is referred to again either directly or indirectly in 1.10, 1.20–2,
2.6, 2.18, and 2.20. But even more than the references, the continual repetition of "in Christ" or "in Christ Jesus", shows how
central this theme is to our author's thought. Indeed, it may be said
that the greater part of the first section is simply an expansion of
1.3. The "spiritual blessings" which we receive are election (1.4),
sonship (1.5), grace (1.6), redemption and forgiveness (1.7),
revelation (1.9), unity (1.10), the Spirit (1.13), and eternal inheritance (1.14), and they are all ours "in Christ". It is through the
resurrection of Christ that we are made alive, and through his
ascension that we too "sit in the heavenly places" (2.5–6).
Through all eternity, as in the beginning, God's lovingkindness
will come to us only in him (2.7). It is through his death that the
enmity between men is abolished, the barriers between Jew and

Gentile are broken down, and the new creation is accomplished (2.12, 16). Access to God is now possible through him (2.18), and he is the corner-stone of the new humanity, the new temple in which God will dwell (2.20–2). The same theme is found in 1.20–2, where it looks as if we have an early Christian confession of faith in poetic form, for another version of it is to be found in 1 Peter 3.21–2, where it is connected with baptism.

One of the Psalms which is quoted in the two passages last mentioned is also found in Peter's pentecostal speech in Acts 2.14–36, namely Psalm 110.1. In Acts it is used to lead up to the great proclamation of the sovereignty of Christ.

> For David did not ascend into the heavens; but he himself says,
> "The Lord said to my Lord, sit at my right hand
> till I make thy enemies a stool for thy feet."
> Let all the house of Israel therefore know assuredly that God has made him both Lord and Christ, this Jesus whom you crucified (Acts 2. 35–6).

We have seen that this is also one of the great themes of Hebrews, which we have associated with Pentecost. Its centrality in Ephesians leads us to suggest that Ephesians also has a connection with Pentecost.

The other great theme of the feast in Acts is the Spirit, and there are no fewer than twelve references to the Spirit in Ephesians; this is a higher percentage per page than any other letter in the Pauline corpus with the possible exception of Romans, which has so many references in chapter 8. The Spirit is the first instalment of our future inheritance (1.13–14), the sphere of our approach to the Father (2.18), the medium of revelation (3.5), the source of strength (3.16), the source of unity (4.3), the one who marks us as Christ's own (4.30), the sphere of our prayer (6.18). But the one passage to which we wish to draw attention is 5.18: "Do not get drunk with wine, for that is debauchery, but be filled with the Spirit." Commentators find it very difficult to put a precise meaning on this verse. Beare would not make this a reference to the Spirit at all. He would translate it "be filled in spirit". "The antithesis is not between wine and spirit but between two states— intoxication with its degrading effects on the one hand; and a progressive fulfilment of the spiritual life on the other." [35] Most others find in it a reference to the Holy Spirit, but are divided as to how it should be understood. E. F. Scott thinks it should be paraphrased, "find your overflow of soul in the rapture which the Spirit will give you",[36] while Masson has, "seek the fulness which the Spirit gives".[37] Dibelius says that the following verse refers to ecstatic singing, under the influence of the Spirit.[38] Of the three main passages where wine is mentioned in the New Testament two use it in a bad sense (Acts 2.13 and Eph. 5.18), and one in a good sense (John 2.1–11). One of the meanings of the sign at Cana is that a religion of legalism is replaced by a religion of Spirit and power. In Acts the inspiration of the Spirit is mistaken for drunkenness, in Ephesians the inspiration of the Spirit is held up as a far better alternative than the "riot" caused by wine. Paul, incidentally, never uses the phrase "be filled with Spirit". Though the two verbs are different (Acts has πίμπλημι, Ephesians πληρόω), the use of the word "wine" in a bad sense, even if there are two different words for wine, would seem to indicate either that the author of Ephesians knew Acts, or, more probably, was aware of the tradition of Pentecost that is found in Acts.[39]

C. *The Church and its Unity*

If two of the great themes of Ephesians are the ascension and the spirit, its distinctive doctrine is surely its doctrine of the Church. The Church not only represents the first step in the fulfilment of the divine plan to gather up all things into Christ (1.10), it also is the means by which the whole creation is to know of that plan (3.10). The proof of this is to be found in the fact that already in the Church the most fundamental division of mankind on earth— the division between Gentile and Jew—has been brought to an end. By the cross of Christ Jew and Gentile have been brought into the new humanity, which is now represented in microcosm by the Church, and this is the guarantee that the whole human race will become one family in God. Of this new humanity Christ is the head, and so close is the connection between it and him, that altogether they make one single personality (4.31–2). This metaphor is balanced by an emphasis on the Church growing up into him (4.15); to transpose a phrase of Anderson Scott into another key, "the Church is a body which is becoming what she is",[40] and all the members have a part to play in that growth (4.16). The gifts of ministry—apostles, prophets, evangelists, pastors, and teachers (4.11)—have been bestowed by Christ for that purpose.

So central is this to the thought of the epistle that all the moral exhortations are directed towards it. The members are to speak the truth because they belong to each other (4.25); they are to work honestly, not simply "to earn their own living" (2 Thess. 3.12), but so that they may be able to share what they earn with the needy members (4.28); the only kind of talk that is permitted is conversation that helps to build up the life of the community (4.29); the divisive sins of anger and backbiting are to be replaced by kindness and willingness to forgive, because obviously the former would shatter the life of the beloved community (4.31); sexual sins of word or deed have no place in the holy community, and the covetous have no place in the final goal of the community—"the kingdom of Christ and of God" (5.3–5); joyful comradeship is one of the marks of the new family's life and the ecstatic gifts of the Spirit, which cause those who possess them to break forth into song, and so make others cheerful, are to be encouraged (5.19). Our author cannot get away from this emphasis on the social nature of the new life even when he comes to speak about what we may call the natural relationships of life. As soon as he begins to speak about the husband–wife relationship, he is reminded of the relationship between Christ and the Church (5.22–3), and all other relationships are "in the Lord" (6.1–4). The social relationship of slave to master and master to slave is not said to be "in the Lord", but it is lived out in his sight (6.6, 9). If we compare this with Colossians, we see how different the approach is. "Husbands, love your wives and do not be harsh with them. Children, obey your parents in everything, for this pleases the Lord. Fathers, do not provoke your children, lest they be discouraged" (Col. 3.19–21). All these admonitions are given a social direction because the goal of the community is the maturity of the new man, the Christ (4.13), and this maturity will not come about unless all are "eager to maintain the unity of the Spirit in the bond of peace" (4.3). We may almost say that the ethical admonitions throughout these three chapters are an expansion of that one phrase, for all the sins that are mentioned destroy unity in one way or another. Nor can the unity be maintained without "separateness", even though the final goal of the divine purpose is that all men are to be one in Christ. The community cannot associate with those who belong to "darkness" and whose works are the works of darkness (5.7, 11).

The question that arises here is why Ephesians is so controlled by the theme of unity, why the positive aspect of its ethical section is concerned with everything that will maintain and deepen unity, and its negative against everything that would destroy it. It is not enough to say with Goodspeed that it is because sects are beginning to appear,[41] for there is only a passing reference (4.14) to the acceptance of new doctrine, and here the warning appears to be against instability on the part of the membership—tossed to and fro like a ship without a rudder—rather than against a definite body of teaching which would be one of the marks of a sect. Another aspect of this letter which is indirectly connected with the unity theme is its apparent unconcern about those who do not belong to the community. The only explicit reference to them is that they are to be avoided (5.7); not a clear word is said about their conversion. There may be a veiled reference to conversion in the extremely difficult and obscure passage found in verses 11 and 13: "Take no part in the unfruitful works of darkness, but instead expose them . . . but when everything is exposed by the light it becomes visible, for anything that becomes visible is light."[42] But a thought that is so obscurely expressed can hardly be called a positive approach to the outsider. When we compare this with the fact that every facet of the community's own ethical life is touched on, we may safely say that the people addressed in Ephesians are a closely knit enclave which must at all costs retain its closeness, but which has no social duties whatever outside itself. Most of Paul's ethical admonitions are of an *ad hoc* nature, but when he does range over a wide field, as he does in Romans, for example, we are made aware of a much wider world. The same is true of the ethical section of 1 Peter. Closest to Ephesians in this respect is Hebrews 13, which also seems to have been addressed to a group with few outside interests.[43] In spite of the lofty doctrine and the great claims that it makes for the gospel, in spite of the vision of a unified mankind that we find in chapters 1–3, it would not be very difficult for a group that practised the ethical teaching of Ephesians, and nothing beyond it, to degenerate into a mutual admiration society with little or no responsibility to or for the world around it.

Käsemann points out that there are a great many contacts in

Ephesians with the ideas and the terminology of Qumran: the community's view of itself, the enlightenment which both possess about the divine plan of salvation, the heavenly inheritance, the eschatological understanding of the present, the dualistic approach to ethics—truth and obedience are described as light and their opposites as darkness, the eschatological army of God, and the angelology; [44] to these may be added the emphasis on unity and the introverted nature of the community's ethical life. In a very real sense the greater part of Ephesians 4—6 may be called "A Manual of Discipline for Christian Communities", for though it does not go into details in the way that the Qumran document does, nor lay down rules with penalties attached, it clearly expects that all who belong to the community will submit themselves to the community's way of life. They will be expected to give to the needy, for example, and the language used leaves little choice in the matter. The discipline may not be strict, and the approach is quite different from the legalism of Qumran, but the communal emphasis is found in both. Käsemann also believes that a great deal of the parenetic material comes out of the synagogues of the Diaspora; it has been taken and slanted in a Christian direction. Ephesians, for him, stands at the confluence of three streams of thought: Pauline Christian, non-Palestinian Jewish, and Essene. This is not to say that the author is aware of the three and has made a conscious effort to combine them, but only that Christianity as it has come to him is the result of the interaction of all three.

We have already referred to the hypothesis of Dahl, that Ephesians was written by Paul to remind churches that were unknown to him, but which were in his missionary territory, of the privileges and responsibilities of their baptism; and to that of G. Kretschmar, that the Jerusalem church held an annual ceremony on the Feast of Pentecost, at which the covenant was renewed. Both of these we have rejected, the former on the ground that a letter of this nature would have been detailed in its instruction on worship and conduct, the latter because there is no proof in Acts that there ever was such a ceremony in the church at Jerusalem, and very little evidence on which to build an hypothesis. But there is a combination of these two hypotheses which may carry more weight, at least as far as Ephesians is concerned, for the material in Ephesians, without its epistolary references, would be extremely suitable for a renewal of the Christian covenant. There is no evidence for any such ceremony in later Christian history, although it may be said that by the beginning of the third century, and perhaps a great deal earlier, Easter was not only the main day for baptism, but also the time when all who had previously been baptized relived their "passing over" from death to life. What is striking about the way in which Ephesians is composed is that it follows in a general way the covenant renewal service as it is described in the Qumran Manual of Discipline. This does not rule out our suggestion above that the berakah of Ephesians 1—3 could have been used at the Eucharist, for there is no reason to suppose that a form of prayer used at one time for one purpose could not have been used at another for a slightly different purpose, or even that the Eucharist would not have been part of a service such as we are considering. The Qumran service (1QS, I, 21-3) begins with a recounting of the righteous acts of God in his mighty works, and all the acts of his steadfast love and mercy upon Israel; there follow a confession of sin and then the recital of the blessings and curses. No better words could be found to describe Ephesians 1—3 than the first half of the preceding sentence. The confession of sin is not used because the Christian community already knows the forgiveness of sins; confession of sins as part of an act of Christian worship is not found in any Christian liturgical document until the Middle Ages. The remaining section of Ephesians is an exhortation to remain faithful in unity—one of the great words of Qumran— and to live as sons of light, having no fellowship with "the unfruitful works of darkness" (5.11). The exhortation ends with a call to the holy war. "From henceforth [not "finally"], be strengthened in the Lord and in the strength of his might" (6.10). Scholars are not agreed as to whether "the evil day" (6.13) is the last battle of the war, or any evil day (cf. 5.16), but the whole tone of this passage and especially the demonology makes it highly probable that "the last and fiercest strife" is meant.[45] We need not expect our author to be completely consistent, particularly when he is building up an imaginative picture such as this. While it is true that Ephesians says nothing about the parousia, this does not mean that it has no eschatology.

Dahl, in our opinion, is right in saying that Ephesians is intimately connected with baptism, but not in the way that he connects it. The baptism of those to whom Ephesians is addressed has taken place at some time previous to the letter, but there is no evidence which enables us to decide whether it was a long or short time. "You were sealed" (1.13), "you were made alive" (2.5), "you were brought near" (2.13), "you were called" (4.1), "you did not so learn Christ" (4.20), are all aorists. What has happened must continually be renewed. "Put off the old man and put on the new" (4.22, 24), though this has already been done. The way of light has been chosen and they are children of light; they must therefore have nothing to do with the way of darkness, nor give the devil an opportunity to lead them into it. The so-called "code of subordination", which probably came into the Church by way of the Synagogue, may have been added to the admonition on the "Way of Light and of Darkness", because it probably formed part of the ethical teaching connected with baptism.[46] There is nothing like it in Qumran literature; here we have only the subordination of the members to their superiors.[47]

Our main difficulty in defending an hypothesis such as this is the lack of definite knowledge about forms of worship in the first century. But the form of the letter, the style, and the content do fit the pattern of Qumran's service. If there was such a service it was probably held on the Feast of Pentecost. We have already made some connections between Ephesians and that festival, but this has been made from Christian literature. Any evidence of connections between Ephesians and the Jewish traditions of Pentecost would strengthen the hypothesis outlined above.

D. *Ephesians and the Jewish Pentecost*

We may recall that, in the Jewish tradition, probably going back into the first century, Pentecost was the feast of Lawgiving, and the day on which Yahweh took Israel for his bride.[48] The Psalms for the day were 29 and 68, and the Lessons from the Torah, Genesis 14, Exodus 19 and 20, and Numbers 18. We have also seen that, in Jubilees, Pentecost was the day when all the covenants of the past were made. Direct references to some of these passages or reflections of them are to be found in Ephesians.

Psalm 68 is quoted directly in Ephesians 4.8, and the manner in which it is quoted is very striking. It is not strictly relevant to the subject under discussion, but is almost an aside. The text could read equally well without it: "But grace was given to each of us according to the measure of Christ's gift. . . . And his gifts were that some should be apostles . . ." (4.7, 11). The only apparent reason why the quotation should have been brought in here is that the ascension of Christ and the gift of the Spirit must have been in the author's mind. For the interpretation which he gives to the verse is a Christianization of a piece of rabbinic exegesis. The Psalm itself celebrates the triumph of God over his enemies and in the original it reads: "Thou didst ascend the high mount, leading captives in thy train, and receiving gifts among men" (v. 18). The rabbis had interpreted this verse as referring to Moses who had ascended Mount Sinai (Exod. 19), to receive gifts *for* men, that is, to receive the Torah. One of the Targums translated it, "gave gifts to men".[49] Our author simply takes over the tradition and replaces Moses by Christ. The polemic is caused by the Jewish interpretation of the Psalm. That this Psalm was connected with Pentecost in Acts is shown by W. L. Knox:

> The Targum on that Psalm interpreted the verse "The Lord gave the word; great was the company of preachers" by rendering it "Thou by thy word gavest thy word unto thy servants the prophets". So Jesus, having been exalted to the right hand of God, received from the Father the promised Spirit and has poured it out on the Apostles.[50]

He thinks that it is only in the light of this rabbinic view that any sense can be made of Acts 2.33, for no reason is given in Acts why the ascension should have been followed by the gift of the Spirit. In a similar way, the author of Ephesians brings in Psalm 68.18 to show that the ascended Jesus gave gifts to men. In 4.7, the grace is given to each individual to fit him for his function in the Church, but in 4.11 the gifts are different orders of ministry. In Numbers 18, which describes the covenant of God with Aaron and the priests and Levites, it is said that the Levites are given to Aaron as a gift, for the service of the Tabernacle, but God himself gives Aaron his priesthood as a gift (vv. 6, 7). Has the change from the gift of the Spirit to the gifts of ministry been made because of the influence of this chapter in Numbers?

There may be another reference to this Psalm in chapter 2. Those outside the Church are called the "sons of disobedience" (v. 2), while those within are said to be a "dwelling place of God in the Spirit" (v. 22). The continuation of verse 18 of the Psalm in the Septuagint is "even among the disobedient that the Lord God may dwell among them".[51]

E. *Psalm* 29

One of the words which has caused some scholars to think that Ephesians is non-Pauline is the use of the title Ἠγαπημένος for Christ (1.6), because it is never found in Paul, but was coming into popular use by the second century. Dibelius gives instances of it from 1 Clement, the Epistle of Barnabas, Hermas, and Ignatius;[52] he finds its source in Isaiah 44.2, but gives no reason for this. Masson finds it there also but gives no reason.[53] To say that it is late because it is found in second-century writers means nothing, for all of them may have found the title in Ephesians. Beare says that the word is used to mark the thought that Christ is the supreme object of the love of God, but says nothing about its derivation.[54] In Psalm 29.6 the Hebrew has, "He makes Lebanon to skip like a calf and Sirion like a young wild ox"; in the Septuagint we find, "He pulverizes Lebanon like a calf, and the beloved shall be as the son of an unicorn". What has caused the Hebrew and Greek texts to differ so much at this point is impossible to say; the Greek translators may have had *Jeshurun* in their Hebrew text at this point, for they always translate this rare word with the Greek participle ἠγαπημένος. This Psalm is the only place in the Septuagint where "beloved" is associated with words or symbols denoting majesty or exaltation. Since the whole passage in Ephesians (1.3–14) is centred upon the acts of God in the exalted Christ, there is some possibility that the author borrowed the word here, especially as the Psalm is a paean of praise in the presence of the power and majesty of God and its highpoint is the line, "In his temple all cry 'Glory'" (cf. "The praise of his glory" in Eph. 1.6, 12, 14).

F. *Exodus* 19–20

This passage has already been referred to in connection with Psalm 68, where we saw that the author must have known of the connection between the two passages. A passage is quoted directly from Exodus 20 in Ephesians 6.2, "Honour your father and mother" (this is the first commandment with a promise), "that it may be well with you and that you may live long on the earth". But in Ephesians 4.25–31 we are given a Christian explanation of some of the Ten Commandments. "Be angry but do not sin", is based on the sixth commandment; "Let the thief no longer steal", comes from the eighth; "Let no evil talk come out of your mouths", from the ninth; while verse 31 expands what has been said on the sixth and ninth: "Let all bitterness and wrath and anger and clamour and slander be put away from you, with all malice". The other two commandments from the second table—the seventh and the tenth—are referred to in the next chapter. "But immorality and all impurity or covetousness must not even be named among you, as is fitting among saints . . . no immoral or impure man, or one who is covetous (that is, an idolater), has any inheritance in the kingdom of Christ and of God" (5.3, 5). Since this is the only place in any parenetic section of the Pauline corpus where all six of the commandments in the second table of the Law are referred to, the best explanation is that the author had the reading of the Ten Commandments in mind. It may also be possible that there was an oath taken at baptism—so the evidence in Pliny's letter to Trajan has been interpreted by some scholars—and that Ephesians has this too in mind.[55] If this is so, then some sort of renewal ceremony is indicated here, as Ephesians clearly has all its references to baptism in the past tense.

G. *Pentecost and Marriage*

In his learned defence of Paul's authorship of Ephesians, E. Percy tries to show that the extended teaching on marriage in Ephesians (5.22–33), is not incompatible with Pauline authorship, although Colossians has only two verses (3.18–19). He admits that it is very strange that, in two letters written at the same time, one of them should have such a long passage on marriage coupled with an instruction on Christ and the Church, while the other should have two sentences, and concludes that the only hypothesis which helps towards a solution of the difficulty is that of Dahl, that Ephesians is a baptismal letter,[56] though he had earlier in his book rejected it. Goodspeed rightly points out that the writer of Ephesians is not so much interested in the marriage relationship as he is in the union between Christ and the Church, and that he is far more interested in marriage as a symbol than in right relationships in marriage.[57] It may be that his predominating interest in unity has led our author to expatiate on this theme, but it may also be that the "marriage" of God and Israel at Pentecost was in his mind, for in rabbinic thought the day when God would make the new covenant with a restored and purified Israel would be the day of a new and true marriage.[58] One rabbi went so far as to say that there was no sin-offering attached to Pentecost because Israel on that day was without sin.[59] In other words, Pentecost, sinlessness, and marriage are connected in one strand of rabbinic tradition. The allegorical interpretation of the Song of Songs as a description of the mutual love of God and Israel goes back to the first century and many of the connections between Pentecost, Sinai, and marriage are to be found in it. Rabbi Akiba said that no day was greater in the history of Israel than the day when she received the Song of Songs.[60] These ideas may have been discussed in Jewish circles or Jewish–Christian circles before Ephesians was written. It is therefore not far-fetched to say that the marriage symbol comes to the author's mind because he is aware of a pentecostal tradition connected with it. It may also be from here that he draws the idea of a corporate baptism, for the people of Israel are sanctified by Moses before they receive the Law (Exod. 19.14).

There is one minor point to be added, on the use of the word "covenants" in Ephesians 2.12, "strangers to the covenants of promise". There are only two places in the New Testament where "covenant" is found in the plural; here and in Romans 9.4, where the text is doubtful. It must be admitted that while the Jew could think of covenants made with God, the more normal way of speaking was in the singular, the covenant. It is the Book of Jubilees which speaks of the covenants of promise and connects them all with Pentecost. It may be this which causes Ephesians to use the plural.

We have now come to the end of our arguments. We submit that, though each of them would not have much weight when viewed independently, their cumulative strength is such as to show that a high degree of probability attaches itself to our thesis that Ephesians has close connections with Jewish liturgical forms and also with Jewish and Christian traditions of Pentecost in the late first century.

EPHESIANS AND BAPTISM

At several points in this book reference has been made to the connection between Ephesians and the sacrament of baptism, and to the theory of N. A. Dahl that Ephesians has a baptismal orientation. Another theory that has recently been suggested is that Ephesians is a catholicized version of Colossians. An unknown author of the late first century took the material in Colossians, expanded it by the addition of traditional material, together with some ideas of his own, and then recast the whole in such a way that it could be used as a homily at baptism.[61] We have already stated our objections to Dahl's theory in its present form; somewhat similar objections can be raised against this variation of it. Ephesians as it stands is epistolary in form, and can hardly be considered a homily unless the basic material first appeared in the form which we have suggested. A comparison with the homiletic section of 1 Peter shows that Ephesians 1.15–19 and 3.1–13 would have no place in a homily.

We have attempted to show that when the epistolary sections of Ephesians are removed, we are left with a document complete in itself which could be used in an act of worship. We have also suggested that this act of worship may have had a close connection with baptism, though not necessarily with the administration of the sacrament itself. In this chapter we shall discuss the direct and indirect references to baptism that are to be found in Ephesians, together with other related matters.

A. *Direct References to Baptism*

The first of these is found in a sevenfold statement which stresses the theme of unity and connects the unity of the Church to the unity of God. "There is one body and one Spirit, just as you were called to the one hope that belongs to your call, one Lord, one faith, one baptism, one God and Father of all, who is above all and through all and in all" (4.4–6). Dibelius argues that the structure of these verses—the rhythmic parallelism of the lines, the repetition of "one" before each of the nouns, the word-play on the various forms of "one" and the prepositions used, εἶς, μία, ἕν, ἐπί, διά, ἐν—shows that we have a traditional formula here.[62] Whether this is so or not, the passage has clearly influenced the form in which the Eastern churches expressed their faith, the form which was the basis of the so-called Nicene Creed: "I believe in one God . . . and in one Lord . . . and in one Church . . . I confess one Baptism". It also has much in common with Jewish affirmations on unity which had been developed from the basic affirmation of the Shema: "Hear, O Israel: the Lord our God, the Lord is one". Both Josephus and Philo had argued that there could be only one Temple, since there was only one God.[63] The Apocalypse of Baruch made its claim against Christianity on the ground of unity: "We are all one celebrated people; we have received one Law from One" (2 Bar. 48.24). However that may be, the inclusion of baptism in this formula is an indication of its importance in the mind of our author, for in some ways it is the key word around which all the others are grouped. It is by one Spirit that we are baptized into one body (1 Cor. 12.13), it is at baptism that confession of faith in the one Lord is made (Rom. 10.9), and it is the fact of our baptism which gives us the right to call God our Father. (Rom. 8.15: "we cry, 'Abba! Father!'" is probably a reference to liturgical prayer, which could not be shared by the unbaptized.)[64] The connection between baptism and unity is found in Galatians 3.27–8 and 1 Corinthians 12.12–13. This does not necessarily mean that the author of Ephesians is acquainted with these epistles, but only that the ideas he expresses were commonplaces of the preaching and teaching of Paul.

The second reference is found in the passage dealing with the husband–wife relationship.

> Husbands, love your wives, as Christ loved the church and gave himself up for her, that he might sanctify her, having cleansed her by the washing of water with the word, that the church might be presented before him in splendour, without spot or wrinkle or any such thing, that she might be holy and without blemish (5.25–7).

It has been argued that the phrase "having cleansed her by the washing of water with the word", refers to a ceremonial bath taken by a bride before her marriage,[65] but the majority of commentators hold that it refers to baptism, and that "the word" is either a baptismal formula pronounced over the candidate or a confession of faith made by him. In all probability the latter is the right interpretation, for there is no evidence in any of the early liturgies of a sacred form said by the minister of the sacrament while the candidate is immersed in the water. In Hippolytus, for example, the candidate is given a threefold interrogation: "Do you believe in God the Father Almighty? And in Jesus Christ...? And in the Holy Spirit in the Holy Church?" To each of these questions he answers, "I believe", and he is immersed after each answer.

In attempting to bring out the full meaning of baptism the author is not consistent in his use of imagery. Christ as the bridegroom administers the sacramental washing of baptism to the Church and at the same time acts as the one who presents the bride to her husband. The analogy breaks down towards the end of the passage (v. 32), for here Christ and the Church together constitute the new Adam, the bride has become the body.

The experience of the individual candidate in baptism is, in this passage, transferred to the life of the Church as a whole. She passed through death with Christ when he died on the cross for her (cf. 2.16), and the individual member's baptism is an acceptance of that fact. It is also an eschatological fact. What Christ did then was to create the Church and she will be at the end what she was at her beginning. He will present her to himself in glory. It is probably the idea of *Urzeit wird Endzeit* which causes our author to bring in the creation story at this point, for the Genesis myth does not appear to have been used by Jewish scholars as an allegory of the marriage between Yahweh and Israel. For our author the marriage has taken place on the cross. Where Christ created the Church, he also married her and made the new covenant with her.

The same imagery is found in a much more subtle way in the Gospel of John. It has frequently been noted that the Fourth Gospel begins and ends with a sacred week. On the first day of the first week the Baptist points to Jesus as the Lamb of God while on the first day of the last week Jesus is anointed at Bethany, the day being the tenth of Nisan when the paschal lamb was selected in Egypt. On the last day of the first week the marriage takes place at Cana and at the end of the last week Jesus is crucified. Since there is a parallel between the first days of the two weeks, it is natural to assume that John intends an analogy to be drawn between the last days as well. In other words, the crucifixion is a marriage. The water and wine of Cana symbolize the water and the blood of Calvary, and the hour which has not yet come at Cana has come when "the Son of Man is lifted up". It is also the time when the Spirit is given. Since the Spirit is given when Jesus is glorified (John 7.39), and the cross is the glorification, Lightfoot's suggestion that the end of the passion narrative in John should be translated, "He bowed his head and handed over the Spirit" may well be right.[66] For John, the crucifixion, the resurrection, the ascension, and the gift of the Spirit are all different aspects of the glorification of the Lord. For the author of Ephesians, the Spirit is associated with his exaltation, but the other "events" are not far from his mind.

Our third and fourth references may be taken together, for they are both concerned with "the seal of the Spirit". "In him you also, who have *heard* the word of truth, the Gospel of your salvation, and have *believed* in him, were *sealed* with the promised Holy Spirit, which is the guarantee of our inheritance until we acquire possession of it, to the praise of his glory" (1.13-14). "Do not grieve the Holy Spirit of God, in whom you were sealed for the day of redemption" (4.30). Though the word "baptism" does not occur here, both these passages must refer to baptism. The combination of "hearing", "believing", and "baptism" is a frequent one in Acts (8.12; 16.14-15; 18.8); in Ephesians, "sealing" takes the place of "baptism", but that it means the same thing can be shown from the total context of the first passage; presumably therefore the second reference would carry the same meaning. The metaphor of sealing must have been a well-known one or more explanation of it would have been given.

The whole sentence from which the first passage comes is an expansion of one of the phrases found at the beginning of it: "Blessed be the God and Father of our Lord Jesus Christ, who has blessed us in Christ with every spiritual blessing" (1.3). These "spiritual blessings" are election (v. 4), sonship (v. 5), redemption (v. 7), forgiveness (v. 7), knowledge (v. 9), the Spirit (v. 13), and the inheritance (v. 14). These blessings were all given to those addressed when they heard, believed, and were sealed. Since the last three verbs are all aorists, they must refer to events at a definite point of time in the past. Now Paul uses the word "seal" of circumcision in Romans 4.11, where he says of Abraham that "he received circumcision as a sign or seal of the righteousness which he had by faith, while he was still uncircumcised". Here he is using a Jewish metaphor, not coining one of his own. It is found in the berakah that was said at a circumcision: "Blessed art thou . . . who didst sanctify Isaac the well-beloved . . . and seal his offspring with the sign of the holy covenant." [67] From this Jewish usage the metaphor passed over into Christianity and was widely used as a synonym for baptism. Whether it was made to refer to the actual immersion itself or to an anointing which took place afterwards it is impossible to say, for the evidence can be read both ways.[68] It could not have been a cross marked on the forehead with water, for the method of baptism would make this superfluous, but even if it were an anointing with oil, the metaphor is an inappropriate one, since no visible mark would be left. We do not know who was the first to use it, but it was probably Paul, for he refers to baptism as a kind of circumcision in Colossians 2.11; a simple extension of the metaphor would have led him to think of baptism as a sealing. The same metaphor is found in 2 Corinthians 1.22, where it is used in an eschatological context and where the word "anointing" is also used. Since the word "anointing" is applied only to Christ in the rest of the New Testament, and in Acts 10.38 is definitely associated with his baptism, we may reasonably conclude that in the text of Corinthians Paul had baptism in mind. The association of the same ideas in Ephesians leads to the same conclusion. The second passage (4.30) is even more eschatological in tone. In the Spirit believers have been marked as God's very own, so that they will be recognized as such on the day of the final deliverance. Again the aorist marks a definite point in the past, when the invisible presence of "the Holy Spirit of God"—we may note in passing the solemn liturgical phrasing—was given to the believer.

B. *Indirect References to Baptism*

But it is in the indirect references to baptism that we see how much the sacrament dominates the thought of the epistle. Indeed the whole of chapter 2 is little more than a comment on the meaning of it. The heart of the first section, verses 1–10, is found in 4–6: "But God, who is rich in mercy, out of the great love with which he loved us, even when we were dead through our trespasses, made us alive together with Christ (by grace you have been saved), and raised us up with him, and made us sit with him in the heavenly places in Christ Jesus" (here again we have the aorist). What has happened to Christ has happened to those who believe on him; the three verbs, all compounded with συν, stress the thought that Christians even now share in the life of their exalted head, for they were made alive with Christ and rose again with him. We may note here that the normal Pauline metaphor for the baptismal experience is death and resurrection (Rom. 6.4 ff; Col. 2.12; 3.1–3). Only once does he describe the life of believers before their conversion as a "living death". "And you, who were dead in trespasses and the uncircumcision of your flesh, God made alive together with him" (Col. 2.13). It is strange that Ephesians has taken the rarer Pauline metaphor and used it, particularly when the much more vivid one is found in the preceding verse. The answer to this is probably that the "living death" metaphor was much more prominent in the tradition on which Ephesians depends than the symbolism of death and resurrection; Paul takes it for granted that the latter is known to the Romans (the same metaphor is found again in 5.14, which we shall discuss later). It was widely held in Judaism that a Gentile, before he became a proselyte, was spiritually dead, and his conversion was regarded as a passing from death to life. "He who separates himself from the uncircumcision is like him who separates himself from the grave", was a dictum of the school of Hillel in the first century.[69] The parallelism between the two parts of the sentence implies that an actual comparison is to be made between departing from heathenism and rising from the dead. This is stated even more explicitly in a comment on Ecclesiastes 8.10: "I saw the wicked one buried and they came . . .", which is interpreted as a reference to the proselytes, since proselytes are people who have risen from their graves.[70] Though the rabbis did not agree among themselves about the order of the rite for the initiation of a male Gentile, some arguing that baptism should come first, others that the proselyte should first be circumcised, all were agreed that when a man had undergone it, his old life was left completely behind him. So seriously was this taken, that marriage was allowed between a Gentile and one of his relatives within the prohibited degrees, even if both had become members of Israel; their old relationships no longer existed, and they therefore were exempt from any penalty. Towards the end of the first century, Joshua ben

Hananiah stated that baptism alone was sufficient to make a Gentile male into a Jew, on the ground that if it was all that was necessary for a woman, it should be the only necessary rite for a man, although he did not go on to say that the law of circumcision should be abrogated for proselytes. The same rabbi taught that a convert was subject to the law respecting the uncleanness of a dead body, for at his conversion he had risen from the grave. "When he has undergone baptism and come up [i.e., from the grave], he is regarded in all respects as an Israelite." [71] This was held to be as true for a female as a male, though she had only received baptism.

Enough has been said to show that the idea of "making alive" in baptism is not Christian in origin, but was taken over by Christians from Judaism. Naturally, it is filled with a depth of meaning which goes beyond any rabbinic teaching, for the pattern of the death and resurrection of the Lord becomes the Christian initiation pattern. But the material was at hand to be transformed and Ephesians makes use of it even when it goes beyond it. Before they were baptized into Christ both Jew and Gentile were dead while they lived (2.1, 3), but then they were made alive and raised up, and even in this world share in the life of "the heavenly places" with their exalted Lord.

If the emphasis in the first section of this chapter is on the change in the moral condition of those addressed, the second section (vv. 11–22), discusses their change of status from a religio-political point of view. Stylistically, it consists of a very elaborate chiasmus, the second half being antithetically parallel to the first and also in inverted order, as follows:

A. Therefore remember that at one time you Gentiles *in the flesh*,
B. called the uncircumcision by what is called the circumcision, which is *made in the flesh by hands*—
C. that you were at that time *separated from Christ*,
D. *alienated from the commonwealth of Israel*,
E. *strangers* to the covenants of promise,
F. having no hope and *without God* in the world.
G. But now in Christ Jesus you who once were *far off*
H. have been *brought near* in the blood of Christ.
I. For *he is our peace*, who has made us both one,
J. And has broken down the dividing wall of *hostility*,
K. By *destroying in his flesh* the law of commandments and ordinances,

K. that he might *create in himself* one new man in place of two,

J. so making *peace*, and might *reconcile* both in one body to God through the cross,

I. thereby bringing the *hostility* to an end.

H. And he came and preached peace to you who were *far off*

G. and peace to *those* who were *near*;

F. for through *him* we both have access in one *Spirit* to the *Father*.

E. So then you are *no longer strangers* and *foreigners*,

D. but you are *fellow citizens with the saints* and *members of the household of God*,

C. built upon the foundation of the apostles and prophets, *Christ Jesus himself being the chief corner-stone*,

B. in whom the whole structure is joined together and grows into a *holy temple in the Lord*;

A. in whom you also are built into it for a dwelling place of God *in the Spirit*.

It may be noted in this arrangement of the text that, with one exception, the contrast is drawn by the use of contrasting words as well as contrasting ideas. That exception is the second line of the chiasmus where "made in the flesh by hands" is contrasted with the "holy temple in the Lord". This is, of course, the temple made without hands.

The central thought of this passage is that the Gentiles who are in Christ have free access to God on the same terms as the Israelites. All through it the writer is giving us a Christian midrash on Isaiah 57.19: "Peace, peace to the far and to the near, says the Lord, and I will heal him." In the Isaiah passage the prophet is not referring to differences of race or nation, but to the Jews of the Diaspora and to those of Jerusalem; however, some of the rabbis had expanded its meaning to include proselytes. In Midrash Bemidbar Rabba, VIII. 4, the question is asked about proselytes having a share in the building of the Temple, and the answer is, "To inform you that the Holy One, blessed be he, brings near those who are distant and supports the distant just as the nigh. Nay more, he gives peace to the distant sooner than to the nigh; as it says, 'Peace, peace to him that is far off and to him that is near' (Isa. 57.19)". Ephesians has expanded the thought still further to include Gentiles. Since a passage connected with proselytes in the Jewish tradition is here applied to Gentile Christians, it is legitimate to ask whether Jewish thought about proselyte baptism lies in the background also. In the days before the destruction of the Temple, the rite of proselyte initiation included the offering of an expiatory sacrifice in the Temple as well as baptism and circumcision. "The proselyte's atonement is not complete until the blood of his offering has been tossed for him against the base of the Altar."[72] But the blood which flowed when a proselyte was circumcised, or indeed when a Jew was circumcised, was also regarded as sacrificial. Since blood was a normal part of all Old Testament covenants, "the blood of the covenant" at circumcision must have assumed great importance when Temple sacrifices could no longer be offered. G. Vermes[73] has pointed out that in the Targumic and Septuagintal versions of the brief tale in Exodus 4.24–6, in which Moses is saved from death when his son is circumcised, his preservation is due to the sacrificial blood of the circumcision. Vermes thinks that this was the commonly accepted exegesis of this passage during the first century A.D. and earlier, and that it was applied to all circumcisions. Unless "the blood of the covenant" flowed, the rite was not thought to have been validly performed. It was even specified that where there was no foreskin to sever, blood had to flow for the rite to be effective. One of the paraphrases of Leviticus 17.11, "The life of the flesh is in the blood", is "Life is the blood of circumcision". In proselyte initiation, therefore, sacrificial ideas would be intertwined with thoughts of rising to a new life, the idea that was developed in the first part of this chapter. It is on the analogy of the proselyte sacrifice of circumcision blood that the second part develops, for it is not likely that the breaking down of the dividing wall (v. 14) would have been used as a symbol of the end of the division between Jew and Gentile, if the barrier against Gentiles entering the court of Israel were still standing; the sacrificial system of the Temple was probably no longer in operation, and that analogy would not be likely to come to our author's mind. Just as the Gentile is brought near to Israel and made a proselyte by the blood of circumcision, so by the blood of Christ the Gentiles are brought near and made members of God's household, real citizens of Israel. The peace which the prophet had promised to the far and the near had become a reality in the Gentile and the Jew being reconciled in Christ, when the barrier which had separated them from each other and both from God had been done away. The rabbis had taught that "he who brings a Gentile near to God is as though he had created him",[74] but Christ, having first destroyed the cause of their enmity, created out of two warring factions one new man in

himself, and through himself they could approach the Father in the
Spirit. The old temple has now been replaced by the new, and God
who "does not dwell in temples made with hands", has now found
a dwelling-place among those who formerly were "sons of disobedience". If our exegesis of this passage is correct, all that our
author has done is to make use of some of the Jewish teaching on
baptism in his exposition of Christian baptism. The enumeration
of all the privileges which those addressed are said to possess
(vv. 18–22), and which were won for them by Christ on the cross,
would be bound to remind them of their baptism, the time at which
they entered into possession of them.

The thought expressed in the first part of chapter 2 is given a
different form in the admonition in 4.22–4, where the emphasis is
on the new kind of life that must be the result of accepting in faith
the gracious gift of God. "Put off the old man which expressed
itself in your former way of living and which is perishing through
the lusts of deceit, and be continually renewed in the spirit of your
mind, and put on the new man, which is created according to
God's design in righteousness and holiness of the truth." Here
again the contrast is drawn between man under the dominion
of sin, and dying as a result of it, and man under the dominion
of grace through which he has been re-created. By putting on
the "new man" men become what God at creation designed
them to be, and by putting off the "old man" they have escaped
death. "Put off" and "put on" are aorist infinitives, referring to
a change that was made once for all; "be renewed" is a present
infinitive, implying that the Christian life is a paradox. What has
been done once for all must be done over and over again. What
happened at baptism must be a continual experience of the
Christian life.

That this passage refers to baptism has been shown by the writings of Carrington, Selwyn, Davies, Dibelius, and others, which
were touched on in our first section and need not be gone into in
detail here. Suffice it to say that a body of material which is found
in such varied books as 1 Peter, James, Hebrews, and Colossians, as
well as in Ephesians, could not be the result of writers copying
each other. The "form of sound words" must be drawn from a
common storehouse of catechetical material since the key words in
it cannot be regarded as those that the New Testament authors
normally used.[75] Daube too has shown that every part of it can be

found in the instruction that rabbis gave to proselytes before their initiation into Israel.[76]

That this is so, as far as Ephesians is concerned, is proved by the continuation of the admonition (5.8–14), which is best understood as a baptismal passage. It is now generally agreed that the fragment quoted from an unknown source, "Awake, O sleeper, and arise from the dead, and Christ shall give you light" (5.14) is part of a Christian baptismal hymn. Light and enlightenment, which are spoken of here, play an important role in the symbolism of baptism, especially in the writings of the Fathers (in the New Testament, baptism is called enlightenment in Hebrews 6.4, and Ephesians 1.18 may be another reference to it). The period before the conversion of those addressed is in this passage said to be a time when they were living in darkness, and were themselves darkness, but when they came to the Lord (at their baptism), they came to the light and became light. "Once you were darkness, but you are now light in the Lord" (5.8). The light of Christ has enlightened those who believe on him and enabled them not only to partake of his nature, which is light, but also to become a source of illumination to others. The hymn quoted makes use of the double symbolism of sleep and death to describe the situation of men apart from Christ; our author probably quotes it because both symbols are allied with his third symbol, darkness. Since believers have been raised from the dead, they are to walk in the good works which God has prepared for them (2.6, 10) and since they are now light, they are to walk as children of light (5.8). Both indicatives are followed by imperatives, and the hymn-fragment which sums them both up is also followed by the same imperative: "Look carefully then how you walk" (5.15).

Bultmann says that this hymn-fragment is cast in Gnostic terms,[77] but there is no trace here of the metaphysical dualism which is the hall-mark of Gnosticism. A much closer parallel is found in the Qumran literature in which all the members of the community are called sons of light, or sons of righteousness who walk in the ways of light, while all those outside are sons of iniquity, or sons of darkness who walk in the ways of darkness (IQS. III, 20–21). This ethical dualism by which men are divided on the basis of their relationship to God, as the Qumran community sees that relationship to be constituted, is clearly reflected in Ephesians in terms of the Christian community. Similarly the metaphor of sin as death is found in some of the hodayoth, although this of course is found also in Paul. In some of the later Jewish literature we also find the metaphor of sin as sleep (Ps. Solomon 16.1–2). A further connection of Ephesians with Qumran is seen in the call to the saints to arm for the holy war.[78]

We see then, that the theme of baptism runs through the greater part of the berakah of Ephesians 1—3, and that there are at least five references to it in the admonition, 4—6. This bears out our contention in the previous chapter that the sacrament plays an important role in the development of the thought of the epistle.

C. *The Eschatalogy of Ephesians*

One of the reasons frequently given for the non-Pauline authorship of Ephesians is the lack of any reference to the parousia, which occupies a prominent place in 1 and 2 Thessalonians and indeed is found in all the letters generally accepted as Pauline (1 Cor. 7 and 15; 2 Cor. 5; Rom. 13; Phil. 4; Col. 3, to mention only a few instances). The only passages in Ephesians which can be said to refer to it, and not all scholars agree on this, are 4.20 with its reference to the "day of redemption" and the "evil day" (6.13). The note of urgency which we find in 1 Corinthians, or even in Philippians, is completely absent and the author appears to look forward to a gradual building up of the Church (4.14–15). The phrases, "the coming ages" (2.7) and "to all generations" (3.21), which are sometimes used as proofs that Ephesians thinks in terms of a long and indefinite future, may safely be discounted, since they are doxological phrases and to take their time references literally is simply to misunderstand them. It is the whole tone and outlook of the letter, rather than any specific phrase in it, which shows that the author is not interested in "the end of all things" as that phrase or the like is used in the New Testament. His approach to eschatology is along a different path, the path which C. H. Dodd has made familiar to us under the name of "realised eschatology". In this, as in other ways, Ephesians stands closer to the Fourth Gospel than to some of the Pauline epistles.

For Ephesians gives us a realized eschatology of the most thoroughgoing kind. "The now" is emphasized much more strongly and at much greater length than "the not yet", the latter being little more than a concession to the tradition, somewhat in the same way as John uses "the last day". The only references to it are found in 1.14, "the first instalment of our inheritance until we acquire possession of it", 4.30, "the day of redemption", and possibly 6.13, "the evil day". The remaining phrases or sentences which may be classified as eschatological stress the present possession of salvation. The believers are already in the presence of God and enjoy the blessedness of "the heavenly places" (1.3), they have redemption and forgiveness (1.7), all wisdom and insight (1.9), they already possess the knowledge of the divine plan (1.10), and the Spirit (1.13). The same thought is expressed much more strongly in 2.4–8. They have been raised up and even now are sitting in the heavenly places with Christ Jesus. That this is meant to be taken quite literally is shown by the use of the perfect tense in the twice-repeated phrase, "by grace you have been saved" (2.5, 8). Here and now salvation is complete. Pauline as this sounds, with its emphasis on salvation by grace and not by works (2.8–9), it goes far beyond anything that Paul wrote, for as we have seen, Paul never uses σώζω in the perfect and only once does he use it in the aorist. For him salvation is something that has begun but its completion is still to come (Rom. 5.9; 10.9; 1 Cor. 3.15, in the future; 1 Cor. 1.18; 15.2; 2 Cor. 2.15, in the present). In the one place where he uses the aorist, he associates it with "hope", not "faith", and even here the context is one of expectation, not realization: "we wait for adoption, the redemption of our bodies. For in this hope we were saved. . . . But if we hope for what we do not see, we wait for it with patience" (Rom. 8.23–5). In the second half of Ephesians 2 the new creation has already taken place (cf. 2.10); through the cross Christ has created "one new man" (2.15) by reconciling Jew and Gentile. This means not just that the new people of God has appeared in history, but that the new age of the Spirit has come (2.22). While the eschatological outlook is not as prominent in the second part of the Epistle as in the first, when it does appear, it is expressed in the same kind of language: "God in Christ forgave you" (4.32); "No immoral or impure man, or one who is covetous (that is, an idolator), has [present] any inheritance in the Kingdom of Christ and of God" (5.5); "Once you were darkness, but now you are light in the Lord" (5.8). The Church was cleansed and Christ has presented her to himself "without spot or wrinkle or any such thing" (5.26–7).

As we have said, this almost complete swallowing up of "the not yet" by "the now" is not found in any of the extant letters of Paul, who was too conscious of the tension between them, at any rate when he is writing or dictating his letters, to allow one to be over-stressed at the expense of the other. But this does not mean that in the excitement of preaching, or when praying under the influence of the Spirit, he would always have been so careful to maintain this balance. The Thessalonians misunderstood his references to the parousia to such an extent that they were troubled when some of their number died before the Lord came (1 Thess. 4.13–18), and some of them thought that the Day of the Lord had already come (2 Thess. 2.2). The Corinthians believed that they were already reigning with their Lord, and coupled with the belief the thought that since they had arrived at the End, they could behave as they pleased, so that Paul was obliged to write to them, in tones of sar-casm: "Already you are filled! Already you have become rich! Without us you have become kings!" (1 Cor. 4.8). The author of Ephesians is too deeply aware of the moral implications of the Christian Faith ever to degenerate to the Corinthian level, and he is so conscious of the presence of the Lord in the community, or rather of the community being present with its Lord in "the heavenly places", that the future does not have a controlling in-fluence in his thought (there is no word about physical death in this letter). Now it was in worship that the presence of the Lord was most fully realized (1 Cor. 5.4; 14.26; 16.22); or, as the Apocalypse expresses it, the worshippers were caught up into the heavenly places (Rev. 1.10; 4.2); it was also the time when they entered into posses-sion of their inheritance, when past and future met in the present, and this was particularly true during the great fifty days of the Pentecost, when the worshippers thought of themselves as already risen and ascended with their Lord. It is this "liturgical eschato-logy" that we find in Ephesians. With it Paul would have largely agreed, but his own realism, and his sense of living at the point in time when the Ages "overlapped" (1 Cor. 10.11), would have pre-vented him from ever saying that even in worship "the New Age" had completely arrived, that "we have been saved".

Yet Paul's own teaching on baptism, if it were taken out of con-text and one side of it stressed, might easily have led to the teaching of Ephesians. "You also must consider yourselves dead to sin and alive to God in Christ Jesus" (Rom. 6.11); "You were washed, you were sanctified, you were justified, in the name of our Lord

Jesus Christ, and in the Spirit of our God" (1 Cor. 6.11): "If any one is in Christ, he is a new creation; the old has passed away, behold, the new has come" (2 Cor. 5.17); "For as many of you as were baptised into Christ have put on Christ" (Gal. 3.27); "You died, and your life is hid with Christ in God" (Col. 3.3). These passages, taken almost at random from Paul's letters, show how baptism meant for him a real change of status, a topic which he might well have elaborated at a time when a baptism took place, which may have been fairly frequently during his three years at Ephesus, or indeed when he spoke of it on any occasion whatever. The author of our letter is well versed in Pauline thought, but on this point he either misunderstood the Apostle, or laid more emphasis on this aspect of his teaching than Paul himself would have done.

3

THE "LITURGY" BECOMES
A LETTER

It is now clear that we have rejected the Pauline authorship of
Ephesians. Indirectly, we have also rejected the theory held by
Goodspeed, J. Knox, and others, that Ephesians was written by a
Gentile. The knowledge of rabbinic exegetical methods which is
evinced in the treatment of Isaiah 57.19 in 2.12–19 and of Psalm
68.18 in 4.8–9, the application of Jewish ideas on proselyte baptism
to Christian baptism, the awareness of Jewish traditions of worship, the similarities with the outlook of Qumran and the inter-
Testamental literature, the frequent use of Christ as a title (1.10,
13; 2.5, 13; 3.1, 4, 8, 11, 17, 19, to give only a partial list), the importance of Israel in the divine plan of salvation (2.12–14), the use
of the imagery of the Temple barrier, the Semitisms of the style,
and especially the affinities with the style of the Qumran texts—all
this points to a person whose background and training were Jewish
rather than Gentile. The Pauline understanding of Christianity,
which he probably received from Paul himself, has been somewhat
modified by this previous training, by the milieu in which he lived
when he wrote his letter, and by the "raw material" that was at his
disposal.

There are several indications that point to the Ephesian area as
the place of origin of Ephesians. Quite apart from the textual
problem of 1.1, no author who knew Paulinism as well as our
author does would have been ignorant of the fact that Paul had
worked for a longer time in Ephesus than in any other city, and
had used it as a centre from which to preach the gospel in the Province of Asia (Acts 19.10, 26); if he had addressed it to the church
in Ephesus, he would not have written it in such an impersonal
way. The theory that "in Laodicea" was in the original text, and
that this was later changed cannot be maintained either on the
basis of Pauline or non-Pauline authorship, as we have shown. It

will not do to say that the title "To the Ephesians" was invented
by a second-century scribe who combined the references to
Tychicus in Ephesians 6.21–2 and 2 Timothy 4.12.[79] Ephesus was
one of the leading churches in Asia Minor and the traditions of its
founding must have been well known apart from Acts. Tradition
was one of the most important weapons in the fight against heresy
in the second century, as Irenaeus and others bear witness. Our
letter must have been connected with Ephesus in some way or
other, or it would never have received the title "To the Ephesians".

Tradition is almost unanimous that the Fourth Gospel was
written at Ephesus, and some modern scholars have come to the
same conclusion on critical grounds.[80] The resemblance in thought
and outlook between Ephesians and the Johannine Gospels and
Epistles has frequently been noted in modern times. W. Lock went
so far as to say that "It would be a tenable view that the writer was
the author of the Fourth Gospel, writing in the name of Paul".[81]
Moffatt held that "the likelihood is that the unknown *auctor ad
Ephesios* was a Paulinist who breathed the atmosphere in which the
Johannine literature afterwards took shape";[82] but with the growing tendency to place the Fourth Gospel well within the first century, it may be truer to say that both writings come from authors
who are breathing the same atmosphere, an atmosphere which we
have described as Paulinism modified by Essene ideas. Ephesians,
John, and the Scrolls, all speak of the sons of light and darkness, of
truth as light and error as darkness, the main difference here being
that in the Christian literature the victory of light over darkness has
already been decided; all three speak of the necessity for unity, and
of the duty to love all the other members of the community; all are
concerned primarily with the internal life of the group rather than
with the life of the world around them, though Ephesians does
not use such bitter language about outsiders as do John and the
Scrolls; all maintain the doctrine of predestination, speak of the
need for purification and grace, and lay great stress on knowledge.
These and other parallels show that a common stock of ideas can
be found in all this literature, but it cannot be too strongly stressed
that the coming of the Lord has made a tremendous difference to
the way in which the Essene ideas have been modified in the
Christian writers. The uniting of Jew and Gentile through the
death of Christ is a good example of this (Eph. 2.15–16; John 11.52).

Lock finds the most striking similarity in thought between

Ephesians and John in John 17, the great prayer of the Lord before
his arrest and death, where "almost every verse offers a parallel to
this Epistle".[83] Lock makes the rather fanciful suggestion that
Paul heard the prayer from John when he met him in Jerusalem
and that it influenced him when he wrote Ephesians. It is much
more likely that both John 17 and Ephesians stand in the liturgical
tradition of the Ephesian church, for if we substitute the third person pronoun for the first, and vice versa, in John 17 we have an
almost perfect liturgical prayer (note that the first three verses as
they stand would be much more natural on the lips of a Christian
than on those of his Lord; in the remainder of the chapter the pronouns would need to be changed as suggested).

But there are also similarities in language, though they are not as
frequent or as striking as the affinities in thought. "Take no part in
the unfruitful works of darkness, but instead expose them . . . all
things that are exposed by the light are made manifest, for everything that is made manifest is light" (Eph. 5.11, 13). "Everyone
who does evil hates the light and does not come to the light, lest his
deeds should be exposed. But he who does the truth comes to the
light, in order that it may be made manifest that his deeds have
been wrought in God" (John 3.20–1). These passages are similar
both in thought and expression; they are also the only passages
where ἐλέγχω is used with the meaning of "expose". "He who de-
scended is he also who ascended far above all the heavens"
(Eph. 4.10). "No one has ascended into heaven except he who de-
scended from heaven" (John 3.13). "Walk as children of light"
(Eph. 5.8). "Walk while you have the light . . . that you may become sons of light" (John 12.35–6). "Having cleansed her by the
washing of water with the word [ῥῆμα]" (Eph. 5.26). "You are
clean through the word [λόγος] which I have spoken to you"
(John 15.3)—a saying of the Lord in the upper room after the foot-
washing). "Making melody to the Lord with all your heart, always
and for everything giving thanks in the name of our Lord Jesus
Christ to God the Father" (Eph. 5.20). "If you ask anything of the
Father he will give it you in my name. Hitherto you have asked
nothing in my name; ask and you will receive, that your joy may be
full" (John 16.23–4). The language of Ephesians is very close to
that of Colossians at this point, but the idea of approaching God
"in the name of Christ", rather than "through Christ" is found,
not in Colossians, but in John. John is not copying from Ephesians

here, nor vice versa; both authors are copying from the liturgical tradition. "To each of us grace was given according to the measure of the gift of Christ" (Eph. 4.7). "It is not by measure that he gives the Spirit" (John 3.34). Both John 17.24 and Ephesians 1.4 use the same preposition in the phrase, "before the foundation of the world" (πρό). The only other place in the New Testament where this preposition is used in this phrase is 1 Peter 1.20; in other occurrences ἀπό is used.

This leads us to the conclusion that Ephesians was written at, rather than for, Ephesus. Those who have rejected Pauline authorship have given various reasons for its having been written, varying all the way from Goodspeed's theory that it was occasioned by the publishing of Acts, to Beare's idea that there was no special occasion at all; the author wrote it simply because he believed that what he had pondered about so deeply might be of some service to the whole Church, and after it was written it was sent out under the imprimatur of one of the leading churches. If this were true, then Ephesians would not only be unique in form, but also unique in that no external circumstances led to its writing. With the possible exception of James, this cannot be said of any other book in the New Testament.

But this does not solve the problem of the text of 1.1. Beare would have it that the original text read as it does now: "To the saints who are also faithful", because the author wished to make a distinction between the saints of the old Israel and the saints of the new. (Beare's suggestion that τοῖς οὖσιν καὶ πιστοῖς might be translated "who are also believers in Christ Jesus",[84] must be rejected for this would require the participle rather than the adjective.) If we are to judge by the salutation in the other Pauline letters, the text of 1.1 as it now stands must be emended in some way in order to make sense, for when τοῖς οὖσιν was inserted, a place name must have been inserted with it. The circular letter theory must also be rejected for the simple reason that if a letter were sent out with a place name to be inserted the preposition would have been part of the original text.

The hypothesis here put forward for the origin of Ephesians seeks to sum up the conclusion that we have already reached. It seeks to account for certain aspects of this letter which have been noted by modern scholars: its liturgical style, its stress on baptism, the catechetical character of its ethical material and its realized eschatology. So far as we know, the only work extant on the liturgical style of Ephesians is the dissertation of Schille to which we have already referred. He thinks that Ephesians was composed to be a corrective to the liturgical theology of the Hellenistic churches. This may account for the style of the passages which he regards as hymns, but not for the rest of the letter which is written in the same style. (In confining the liturgical material of the second part of Ephesians 2 to verses 14–18, Schille has failed to see that verses 11–22 must have been composed as a whole, for none of it can be omitted without destroying its symmetry. He would have it that verses 11–13 and 19–22 are the work of the author because they are in the second person; verses 14–18, being in the first person, are a confession of the Faith of the community.)

Paul's letters had been written for individual churches, except in the case of Galatians and Colossians, which had been written for churches in a definite area. There is no need to postulate a long period of time before they began to circulate among the churches. Most of them were written to churches within a limited geographical area. Some of the letters were emended before they were put into circulation, notably the Corinthian correspondence, but possibly Philippians as well. When a request came to Ephesus for a copy of their letter or letters from Paul, probably sometime in the seventies, and probably from the church at Corinth, which would have known from its own letters and also from the personal reminiscences of some of its members that Paul had spent a long time at Ephesus, one of the leaders of the Ephesian church who already knew some of the Pauline letters, especially Colossians, decided to supply this lack. He had no hesitation about using the name of Paul, for the letter he planned to write would indeed be a distillation of the thought of the apostle. But he did not sit down and pore over the Pauline letters and then write a mosaic of them; the worshipping tradition of his church went back to the three years when Paul had lived among them and had presided at their worship. None of his prayers had been written down, but the form of them and even some of the phraseology had become familiar over the three-year period, and had been retained by those who had known him and succeeded him in the rule of the church. In the course of time some of the phrases from his letters were incorporated into the service, not necessarily as they were written, but as they were quoted from memory; some of the members of the local church had also composed liturgical pieces, and these too found their way into the community's worship. But the whole had its roots in the Synagogue out of which the Church had come. In what way the influence of Qumran had entered in we do not know, but there can be no doubt that it was there and that it helped to mould the literary style of the prayers, and, to a lesser extent, their content as well.

One of the features of the worship of the church in Ephesus was a Christianized form of the renewal of the covenant; the Ephesian leader decided to use this pentecostal ceremony as the basis of his letter.[85] Though it had been used in one particular community, there was nothing in it which could not apply to all Christians everywhere, and it did sum up in magnificent language both the privileges and responsibilities of the Christian life. In the berakah at the beginning our author simply inserted two paragraphs; the first begins in epistolary form and then develops into a statement of the greatness of Christ, almost in credal form (1.15–23), while the second is a eulogy on the place of Paul in the divine plan (3.1–13). In the admonition, which stressed the need for unity and the moral life demanded of believers, and also gave specific teaching to certain members of the community, he inserted a few phrases and sentences to give added Pauline "colouring" to his letter. The contention of Percy that Ephesians is addressed to a specific group, rather than to a number of churches, may be accounted for in this way. To the whole he added the reference to Tychicus which he copied almost verbatim from Colossians 4.7–8, and then a closing benediction.

But the letter does not go out to a specific church, though a specific church may have asked for it. It is addressed to "the saints and the faithful in Christ Jesus", that is, to the Jewish and to the Gentile Christians. The careful way in which "fellow-citizens with the saints" (2.19) is paralleled with "alienated from the commonwealth of Israel" (2.12), shows that "saints" in the salutation must mean Jewish Christians.[86] The author may have thought that since he was a leader of one of the important churches in Asia Minor, he had the right to address the Church throughout the world in the name of the apostle.

The salutation was changed after the letter arrived at Corinth for a very practical reason. Since the letter would be read at worship, some means would have to be found to differentiate it from the other letters of Paul that were also being read, and the simplest method of doing this would be to add a phrase. The letter was associated with Ephesus and had been written by "Paul"; it was therefore regarded by the Corinthian recipients as the Apostle's own letter to the church at Ephesus and the phrase τοῖς οὖσιν ἐν Ἐφέσῳ was added after the style of Corinthians and Philippians. (Colossians is slightly different in form, so that it probably was not copied here.) The superscription "ΠΡΟΣ ΕΦΕΣΙΟΥΣ" was also added so that the reader would know at a glance what letter he was going to read from. To say with Beare that the title would not have been added until the letters were collected in codex form, is to fail to see that the primary purpose of copying Paul's letters was so that they might be read at worship.[87]

We have no means of knowing how long the letters of Paul circulated singly before they were bound together into a codex. But when they were bound, and a copy reached Ephesus, it was clear at once that the text had been tampered with and ἐν Ἐφέσῳ was dropped out. The superscription was now more necessary than ever and was retained; τοῖς οὖσιν was also retained, probably because the scribe who made the copy of the codex, or, at any rate, the copy of Ephesians which went into it, was defective in the knowledge of what constituted good style. The text, as we now have it, comes from the copy of the codex that was made at Ephesus.[88]

Here we conclude our argument. The enigma of Ephesians remains, chiefly because the first generations of Christians did not think it necessary to hand on to those who came after them a detailed account of the way in which they worshipped and organized the life of their communities. Some of the aspects of their life together in the Body of Christ they simply accepted and handed on in an oral tradition, and this was especially true of their worship. Everybody knew how to pray, so prayers were not written down, particularly as there was a strong tradition against so doing. It is from one point of view surprising that the Lord's Prayer found its way into the Gospels of Matthew and Luke—even here there are two forms of it—but what would we not give for the words of the prayer that Jesus said when he broke the bread in the wilderness, or in the upper room, or that Paul said when he did it at Corinth or Ephesus or Troas! All that we have attempted to do is to take seriously the judgement of competent scholars that Ephesians is written in a liturgical style, and to give an answer to the problem that the style itself raises. The theories that have been advanced and the conclusions that have been drawn will appeal differently to different minds, but our hope is that they have thrown some light on one of the greatest books of the New Testament.

APPENDIX

Notes
Bibliography
Indexes

NOTES

PART ONE

1. J. Jeremias (1935), C. Spicq (1947), and J. N. D. Kelly (1963) in commentaries on these epistles.
2. *NTS* (January 1959), pp. 91–102.
3. *ET* (April 1956), pp. 195–8.
4. P46, S, B, omit it. It was not found in Origen's or Basil's text. Marcion may have had Laodicea in his text or the place-name may have been a conjecture on his part.
5. E. Percy, *Die Probleme der Kolosser-und Epheserbriefe*, pp. 2, 3.
6. C. L. Mitton, *The Epistle to the Ephesians*, pp. 72–4. Cf. Percy, op. cit., pp. 5, 6.
7. *Introduction to the Literature of the New Testament* (3rd edn), p. 157.
8. "The Epistle to the Ephesians", *Expositor's Bible*, p. 11.
9. *Christ the Lord*, p. 102, n. 20. Cf. J. Weiss, *Earliest Christianity*, Vol. I, p. 150.
10. *Der Autor des Epheserbriefs*, TLZ (1957), pp. 326–34.
11. *Liturgisches Gut in Epheserbrief (Lit. Gut)*. A doctoral dissertation, Göttingen University, 1955. The dissertation as a whole has not been published but part of it has now appeared in *Frühchristliche Hymnen* (Berlin 1965).
12. *Lit. Gut*, pp. 2, 3.
13. loc. cit., pp. 89, 94.
14. *TLZ* (1957), p. 334.
15. pp. 69–76.
16. *NTS* (April 1958), pp. 201–7.
17. loc cit., p. 207.
18. Abbott, *The Epistles to the Colossians and Ephesians* (ICC), p. 70, says it is the one generally adopted but his arguments against it appear to me to be conclusive. It has, of course, been adopted by the *New English Bible*.
19. *Lit. Gut*, pp. 109–13. In *Frühchristliche Hymnen*, pp. 15–20, Schille attempts to provide criteria by which liturgical passages or hymns may be discerned. If the analysis of the literary structure of Eph. 2.11–22 given on pp. 156 f, is correct, then his criteria must be rejected, for this is one of the passages that he uses to prove his case.
20. *Ev. Th.* (1955), pp. 362–71.

21. This presupposition has been challenged by G. Zuntz, *The Text of the Epistles*, p. 228, n. 1. "Duplicates of royal letters, identical in content, were actually sent out to various addresses throughout the Hellenistic period; . . . Such copies evidently go back to an original with the address left blank, and it is most probable that the blank in the address of Ephesians goes back to such an original."

22. We have this information about Marcion from Tertullian, *adv. Marc.* V. 11.

23. *Ep. aux Eph.*, p. 140.

24. *Ep. aux Col.*, p. 93. P. Benoit, *DBS*, p. 198, suggests that Colossians was written immediately before Ephesians and then "touched up" with some of the language of its sister letter.

25. *Ep. aux Eph.*, p. 226.

26. *Ep. aux Col.*, p. 140.

27. *Ep. aux Eph.*, p. 162.

28. loc. cit., p. 178.

29. J. A. Robinson, *Ephesians*, p. 238; R. E. Brown, *Biblica* (1959), p. 76.

30. Mitton, op. cit., pp. 86–90; F. W. Beare, *Int. Bib.*, Vol. X, p. 599.

31. *Ep. aux Eph.*, p. 199.

32. loc. cit., p. 189.

33. loc. cit., p. 193.

34. loc. cit., p. 227.

35. So G. Johnston, *Int. Dict.*, article on "Ephesians".

36. *Ep. aux Col.*, p. 107.

37. *Ep. aux Eph.*, p. 227.

38. *TWNT*, Vol. III, p. 314.

39. *Die Probleme der Kolosser und Epheserbriefe* (1946).

40. loc. cit., p. 6.

41. ibid., p. 16.

42. δικαιόω is not found in 1 Thess., 2 Cor., or Phil.

43. ibid., p. 66.

44. p. 136.

45. p. 185.

46. The other two places where this occurs are quotations: 1 Cor. 6.16 and Eph. 5.31.

47. pp. 179–84.

48. pp. 191–9.

49. pp. 200–2.

50. pp. 254–61.

51. p. 266.

52. p. 270.

53. p. 273.

54. *Bemidbar Rabbah*, VIII. 4.
55. He uses it well over one hundred times, though not always with the same meaning. *TWNT*, Vol. II, pp. 537–9.
56. pp. 288–98.
57. pp. 299–303.
58. p. 309.
59. p. 312.
60. p. 315.
61. p. 518, n. 75.
62. p. 335.
63. pp. 342–9.
64. pp. 353–9.
65. p. 356.
66. pp. 360–72.
67. pp. 372–8.
68. p. 409.
69. pp. 392–4.
70. p. 395. On p. 324, Percy has rejected the thesis of N. A. Dahl, "Adresse und Proömium des Eph.", *TZ* 7 (1951), pp. 241–64, that Ephesians was written to give further instruction to new converts on the meaning of their baptism.
71. p. 422.
72. pp. 443–5.
73. K. G. Kuhn, "Der Eph. im Lichte der Qumrantexte", *NTS* 7 (1960–1), pp. 334–46, states that Semitic syntactical phenomena are found four times as often in Ephesians as in the other Pauline epistles.
74. p. 443.
75. *adv.* Marc. IV.5. The problem of pseudonymous writings in the New Testament has again become a subject of discussion, particularly in the English-speaking world. W. G. Kümmel, *Introduction to N.T.*, Eng. trans. of Feine & Behm's 14th rev. edn, p. 256, while admitting that this problem needs more thorough discussion, still maintains that no adequate reason exists "for declaring pseudepigraphy as impossible in respect to primitive Christian literature and as contradictory to truthfulness".
76. Dahl has worked this out in two articles, one in a Scandinavian theological journal which has not been accessible to me. The other has already been referred to.
77. As Masson says, op. cit., p. 150.
78. So von Soden and Ochel.
79. Goodspeed, *The Meaning of Ephesians* (*Meaning*) and *The Key to Ephesians* (*Key*); Mitton, *The Epistle to the Ephesians*.

80. The theory that Ephesians is an introductory letter to the Pauline corpus is not accepted by many who agree with Goodspeed's theory that a great deal of the Ephesian material is drawn from Paul's other letters and especially from Colossians (see below). Perhaps the most damaging criticism of it, as C. F. D. Moule, *The Birth of the New Testament*, pp. 202 ff, and G. Zuntz, *The Text of the Epistles*, pp. 276 f, point out, is that Ephesians never appears at the beginning or end of the lists of Paul's letters. It would indeed be a strange procedure to write an introduction to a collection of letters and then not to place it in the position of an introduction, either as a prologue or possibly as an epilogue. John Knox, *Marcion and the New Testament*, pp. 60 ff, has suggested a way in which Ephesians could have lost its introductory position. In the Muratorian Canon, the Pauline epistles begin with Corinthians and Ephesians; this would have been enough material for one roll. In an earlier roll, Ephesians stood first, but as a result of the rolling up of the roll in the wrong direction, it lost its pride of place. As Knox himself admits, he has given us only a conjecture and as Moule, loc. cit., points out, if the books listed in the Muratorian Canon were in a codex rather than on a roll, Knox's conjecture would be rendered worthless.

81. In essentials the same theory is found in J. Knox, *Philemon among the Letters of Paul*.

82. Even if the Imprisonment Epistles were written in Ephesus (so G. Duncan), Onesimus would have known of them.

83. *Key*, pp. v–viii.

84. *Meaning*, p. 8.

85. ibid., p. 20.

86. ibid., p. 21.

87. *Int. Dict.*, article on "Ephesians".

88. Mitton, op. cit., p. 239.

89. ibid., pp. 101 f.

90. pp. 138 ff.

91. pp. 63 ff.

92. pp. 263 ff.

93. G. Johnston, *The Church in the New Testament*, Detached Note A and *Int. Dict.*, "Ephesians"; Beare, op. cit.

94. Beare, ibid., p. 603.

95. *The Church in the New Testament*, p. 137.

96. Hippolytus in *The Apostolic Tradition* is very careful to distinguish between certain words and phrases which may be used at an *Agapē* and those which are allowed only at the Eucharist. *Apos. Trad.* III. Jewish doxologies which disappeared from the liturgy of

the Synagogue were retained in the Church. On this whole matter, cf. A. Baumstark, *Comparative Liturgy*, pp. 67 ff.

97. op. cit., p. 189.
98. Justin Martyr, *Dialogue with Trypho* 65.
99. Mitton, op. cit., p. 266, n. 1.
100. Cf. Carrington, *The Primitive Christian Catechism*; Selwyn, *The First Epistle of Peter*, Essay II; W. D. Davies, *Paul and Rabbinic Judaism*, ch. 6. When Mitton says (p. 191), that the parenetic section must be "the spontaneous utterance of an inspired writer", because it is difficult to conceive of Paul copying teaching which was already familiar, he fails to take notice of the many places where Paul does repeat the tradition, reminding his readers of what they had been taught either by himself or by others. For examples of his repetition of his own teaching, see 1 Thess. 4.1 ff, 2 Thess. 3.6; for his repetition of others' teaching, Rom. 6.3 ff. In 1 Cor. 15.3 ff, he reminds the Corinthians of the tradition which he had received and which he had handed on to them (cf. 1 Cor. 11.23 ff). This type of ethical teaching runs outside the Pauline tradition in the New Testament and is to be found in such diverse documents as James and Hebrews. Outside the New Testament, similar material is to be found in 1 Clement, Barnabas, and the Didache. To say, as Mitton does, that the ethical teaching in Colossians is addressed to a particular situation is to lose sight of its general import. While the case of Onesimus may have caused the author to expand the section on the relationship between slaves and masters, the whole ethical section of Colossians could be addressed to Christians anywhere. The same may be said of 1 Peter, where the emphasis on the behaviour of slaves is probably for political reasons. That this ethical material may be Hellenistic–Jewish or Hellenistic in origin is suggested by, among others, Wand, *1 Peter*, p. 5, and Hunter, *Paul and his Predecessors*, rev. edn, pp. 52–7 and 128–31. K. G. Kuhn, op. cit., argues that, with the exception of the Haustafel, it originated in Qumran.
101. Beare, op. cit., p. 623.
102. In an article entitled, "Die Absicht des Epheserbriefes", *ZNTW* 51 (1960), pp. 145–54, and in his brief commentary on Ephesians in Peake's (1962) Commentary on the Bible. Kümmel, op. cit., p. 257, sees some validity in Chadwick's first argument but finds that the second is "hardly demonstrable". Chadwick finds the arguments for and against Pauline authorship so delicately balanced that he does not come down on either side.
103. *The Unity of the Church in the New Testament* (1946).
104. op. cit., p. 108.

PART TWO

1. See the remarkable series of papers given at a Liturgical Conference at Strasbourg, and published by The Liturgical Press, Collegeville, Minn., in 1959, under the title, *The Liturgy and the Word of God.*
2. E. J. Goodspeed, *JBL* (1945), pp. 197–8, defends the theory that ancient authors were stimulated to write by the writings of others.
3. *The Origins of the Gospel according to Matthew* (1946).
4. *The Primitive Christian Calendar* (1952). This book was given an extremely unfavourable review by R. P. Casey, *Theology* (1952), and also by W. D. Davies in *The Background of the New Testament and its Eschatology*, ed. Davies & Daube (1956). Carrington answered his critics in a long appendix in *According to Mark* (1960).
5. *The Beginnings of the Gospel Story* (1909), pp. 197–8.
6. "The Earliest Structure of the Gospels", *NTS* (1959), pp. 174–87.
7. *Studies in the Gospels*, ed. Nineham, pp. 37–55.
8. *Early Christian Worship* (1953).
9. *The Fourth Gospel and Jewish Worship* (1960). A vigorous attack on the whole lectionary system and particularly on Miss Guilding's use of it has been made by L. Morris, *The New Testament and the Jewish Lectionaries* (1964). It must be admitted that the overall impression given by Professor Guilding is one of certainty where no certainty is possible at the present time, although her argument is more tentative at times than Morris will allow. But he himself appears to be unduly sceptical about the existence of the Synagogue itself in the first century. If there is very little rabbinic or archaeological evidence for the existence of the Synagogue in Palestine before the destruction of Jerusalem (p. 13)—and the former statement would be disputed by some scholars—the evidence of the Gospels themselves ought to be sufficient. The casual way in which it is mentioned in the traditions behind the Gospels can only mean that it was a fairly old institution then. If it did not exist, why did the tradition invent it? There appears to be no answer to that question.
10. For Bacon, *The Gospel of the Hellenists* (1933), pp. 138–9; for Grant, *The Gospel of John* (1956), I, p. 17.
11. *JTS* (1945), pp. 1–10.
12. op. cit., pp. 42–4.
13. loc. cit., Manson, *The Epistle to the Hebrews*, p. 131.
14. *1 Peter, A Paschal Liturgy* (1954). Cross's thesis is questioned by C. F. D. Moule, "The Nature and Purpose of 1 Peter", NTS 3

(1956–7), pp. 1–11, and by T. C. G. Thornton, "1 Peter, A Paschal Liturgy?" *JTS*, n.s. 12 (1961), pp. 14–26. Moule sees great difficulty in turning a liturgy into a letter and finds the evidence for the Paschal overtones in 1 Peter far from convincing. He argues that there may be two letters in 1 Peter: (*a*) 1.1—4. 11 and 5.12–14 sent to a church for which persecution was a possibility and (*b*) 1.1—2.10 and 4.12—5.14 sent to a community actually suffering from persecution. Thornton takes the same position as Moule but prefers to think that 1 Peter is a unity. Moule has in turn been criticized by F. W. Beare, *The First Epistle of Peter*, 2nd edn, pp. 196 f. Beare's position, with which the present writer is in substantial agreement, is that the main part of 1 Peter (1.3—4.11) is a baptismal homily. In this he follows B. H. Streeter, *The Primitive Church* (1929), and others.

15. *The Paschal Liturgy and the Apocalypse*, 1960.
16. op. cit., p. 10.
17. Masson, op. cit., p. 152, referring to his reconstruction of the "hymn" in Ephesians 1.3–12.
18. Lev. 23.1–25; Exod. 23.14–17.
19. Mark 14.1.
20. N. Snaith, *The Jewish New Year Festival*, pp. 195–204, says that the so-called "Enthronement Psalms" are Sabbath Psalms.
21. E. Werner, *The Sacred Bridge*, p. 13.
22. J. van Goudoever, *Biblical Calendars*, p. 53.
23. *The Septuagint and Jewish Worship*, p. 43n.
24. D. A. Weiser, *Glaube und Geschichte im Alten Testament*, p. 43.
25. van Goudoever, op. cit., p. 60.
26. *Universal Jewish Encyclopaedia*, Vol. 5, p. 416.
27. *Ten Years of Discovery in the Wilderness of Judea*, p. 32.
28. van Goudoever, op. cit., pp. 95–123.
29. Milik, op. cit., p. 109 and note.
30. SB, Vol. 2, p. 601.
31. Pesahim, 68b.
32. Taanith, 4, 6 (Danby's translation, p. 200).
33. *de spec. leg.*, 2.22.
34. See pp. 90–4.
35. The literature on this subject is enormous. A few of the books consulted may be mentioned here: M. Burrows, *The Dead Sea Scrolls* (1955); F. M. Cross, Jr, *The Ancient Library of Qumran and Modern Biblical Studies* (1958); G. Vermes, *Discovery in the Judean Desert* (1956); Milik, op. cit.; A. Jaubert, *La Date de la Cène* (1957).
36. CD, chapters 19 and 20.

37. 1QS. 2.19.
38. op. cit., p. 117.
39. loc. cit., Milik states that this is to be found in the oldest MSS of *CD*.
40. R. Aron, *La Maison Dieu* (April 1961), p. 14. I have been unable to trace the origin of this delightful story.
41. G. B. Caird, *The Apostolic Age*, p. 185, n. 6.
42. G. von Rad, *Studies in Deuteronomy*, p. 23, believes that this section contains very old material.
43. The question was asked four times: by the wise son, the wicked son, the simple son, and by the father, on behalf of the son who does not know how to ask.
44. Gaster, *The Passover*, p. 63.
45. G. F. Moore, *Judaism*, Vol. 2, pp. 242 f.
46. *CJT* (1961), p. 24.
47. Gaster, op. cit., p. 57.
48. A. A. McArthur, *The Evolution of the Christian Year*, pp. 22 ff.
49. Our main source is Eusebius, *Eccl. Hist.*, V. 23–5.
50. op. cit., pp. 77–87.
51. Eusebius, *Eccl. Hist.*, V. 24.
52. The literature that has developed over the dating of the Crucifixion is listed in Jeremias, *The Eucharistic Words of Jesus*, 2nd edn Eng. Trans. (1955), pp. 177–83. He lists four pages of books and articles which affirm that the Last Supper was a Passover meal, and three pages which deny it!
53. *L'Eglise Primitive*, p. 412.
54. Goguel, op. cit., p. 436.
55. *JBLH* (1960), pp. 1–45, *Die Entwicklung der Altkirchlichen Pentekoste*.
56. Jeremias, op. cit., p. 56.
57. Goguel, op. cit., p. 414.
58. A. E. J. Rawlinson, *The Gospel According to St. Mark*, p. 31 and note. V. Taylor, *The Gospel According to St. Mark*, p. 211, believes this to be an authentic saying of Jesus.
59. op. cit., pp. 41 ff.
60. *Int. Dict.*, "Ephesians".
61. G. Dix, *The Shape of the Liturgy*, p. 341.
62. *de Oratione* 23.
63. *de Corona* 3.
64. *de Baptismo* 19
65. Origen, *contra Celsum* VIII. 22; Eusebius, *Life of Constantine* IV. 64.
66. *Apos. Trad.* III. 29.

67. op. cit., p. 10.
68. op. cit., p. 413.
69. *Vocabulary of the Bible*, ed. Allmen, article on "Festivals".
70. *ZKG* (1954–5), pp. 209–53, *Himmelfahrt und Pfingsten*.
71. Dix, op. cit., pp. 347 ff.
72. *The Acts of the Apostles*, p. 82.
73. *The Beginnings of Christianity*, Vol. IV, pp. 16–17.
74. *The Beginnings of Christianity*, Vol. III, pp. ccxliv–v.
75. Werner, op. cit., p. 23.
76. *Tamid.* 5.1 and 7.1.
77. Oesterley, *The Jewish Background of the Christian Liturgy*, pp. 38–83.
78. It is found only in Judith, Wisdom, and 2 Maccabees.
79. I had come to this conclusion independently when, in a conversation with Reverend J. P. Audet, he informed me of his similar conclusions and sent me a copy of his article, "The Normal Form of a Eucharistia in the First Century". This article appears in *Studia Evangelica* (Berlin 1960), pp. 643–62. ἐξομολογέομαι is used for confession of sin only in the later books of the LXX. It also carries overtones of "witness" before men.
80. Werner, op. cit., p. 7.
81. BT, Sukkah, 51b.
82. These prayers are for the most part from Singer's translation of the Jewish Prayer Book.
83. *The Septuagint and Jewish Worship*, p. 41. Thackeray would place the beginnings of a lectionary as early as 300 B.C.
84. *JQR* (1893–4), Vol. V, pp. 420–68, and Vol. VI, pp. 1–73, "The Triennial Reading of the Law and the Prophets".
85. op. cit., p. 26; cf. also *JTS* (1904), pp. 203–13, "The Influence of the Triennial Cycle on the Psalter".
86. *In the Beginning*, p. 35.
87. *Studies in Pharisaism and the Gospels*, Vol. I, p. 8.
88. *JQR*, Vol. VI, pp. 11 ff.
89. op. cit., p. 95, n. 22.
90. op. cit., pp. 45 ff.
91. BT, Meg. 29b. The classical statement in modern times of the case for a Triennial Cycle is to be found in Büchler, op. cit. An Annual Cycle was accepted by all Jewry in the early Middle Ages.
92. King, op. cit., p. 204.
93. The most important articles on this subject are: King, op. cit.; Thackeray, *JTS* (1915), pp. 177–203; L. Rabinowitz, *JQR* (1935–6), pp. 349–68; N. H. Snaith, *ZATW* (1933), pp. 302–7.
94. Rabinowitz, op. cit., p. 351.

95. Snaith, op. cit., p. 305.
96. Quoted in Guilding, op. cit., p. 20. I regret that I have been unable to procure a copy of Dr Mann's book.
97. *JSS* (1960), pp. 264–80, J. Heinemann, *The Beth Midrash Prayers.*
98. This means of course that the LXX has only these two instances as well. *yadah* originally meant to "throw" or "cast" and probably referred to the offering of sacrifice when the confession (of faith?) was made.
99. These extracts are taken from Gaster's *The Scriptures of the Dead Sea Sect.*
100. That the development of berakoth went on after the destruction of the Temple is shown in their codification in the Mishna. Every pious Jew was expected to recite one hundred berakoth every day.
101. op. cit., Vol. V, p. 440. Philo's dating of the Law-giving at New Year may be due to the fact that in a Triennial Cycle, Deuteronomy 5, which is another description of the giving of the Law, would be read on Tishri I in the third year of the cycle.
102. SB, Vol. 3, p. 596.
103. *TWNT*, Vol. 1, p. 653; SB, Vol. 1, pp. 969 f; Vol. 2, p. 393.
104. Carrington, op. cit., p. 43.
105. T. W. Manson, *Ethics and the Gospel*, p. 81, seems to be unaware of the existence of a Temple synagogue, when he says that the first Christians did not go to the synagogue but to the Temple. Manson admits that the forms of worship borrowed a great deal from the synagogue. We may add that the dispute with Stephen arose in the synagogue of the freedmen (Acts 6.9).
106. M. R. James, *The Apocryphal Gospels*, p. 268.
107. G. Dix points this out very forcefully in *Jew and Greek*, pp. 109–12.
108. Oesterley, op. cit., p. 52.
109. I believe this to be an authentic prayer of Jesus, as I have quoted it. The latter part of the saying, "All things are delivered to me by my Father; ...", may be a confession of the Church, but even here "Father" and "Son" may not be metaphysical terms, but a particularly strong expression of a consciousness of vocation.
110. op. cit., pp. 649 ff.
111. P. Schubert, *Form and Function of the Pauline Thanksgivings*, 1939. Dodd, *The Epistle to the Romans*, p. 6, gives several examples from the papyri.
112. ἐπὶ τὸ αὐτό is "a favourite and semi-liturgical expression in Acts, almost meaning 'in church'". C. S. C. Williams, *The Acts of the Apostles*, p. 62.
113. A. C. Purdy in *Int. Bib.*, Vol. 2, p. 157.
114. In the LXX of Aquila it is translated.

115. op. cit., pp. 79–81.
116. op. cit., p. 3. I have been unable to obtain Kunze's article.
117. The list is given in E. Ellis, *Paul's use of the Old Testament*, p. 154.
118. J. A. T. Robinson, *JTS* (1953), pp. 38–41, suggests that the salutations at the end of 1 Corinthians led into the Eucharist. That this passage need not necessarily be eucharistic is maintained by C. F. D. Moule, "A Reconsideration of the Content of *Maranatha*", *NTS*, 6 (1959–60), pp. 307–10.
119. L. Mowry, *JBL* (1952), pp. 75–84, suggests that it is the Torah; O. A. Piper, *CH* (1951), pp. 10–22, thinks that it is the Old Testament or at least the part of it which deals with the future.
120. op. cit., p. 15.
121. op. cit., pp. 50–102.
122. See above, pp. 60 f.
123. pp. 42 f.
124. W. D. Davies, *Paul and Rabbinic Judaism*, p. 107. Davies criticizes the idea from the expression of it that is found in *The Primitive Christian Catechism*, p. 6.
125. loc. cit.
126. *St. Paul and the Church of the Gentiles*, pp. 129 ff.
127. pp. 1 and 53.
128. W. C. van Unnik, *Studia Evangelica*, pp. 382–414. J. A. T. Robinson, *NTS* (1960), pp. 117–31.
129. *de dec.*, IX and XI.
130. *The Acts of the Apostles*, p. 205.
131. op. cit., p. 82.
132. G. J. Sirks, *HTR* (1957), pp. 78–89.
133. A later Jewish sect, the Kairites, used Joel 2.28–32 as the haftorah for Pentecost. There are no traces of it in any synagogue lectionary, nor is it connected with Pentecost by the Qumran Covenanters.
134. Guilding, op. cit., p. 35.

PART THREE

1. *Key*, p. xv; Knox, *Philemon among the Letters of Paul*, pp. 91 ff.
2. op. cit., p. 263.
3. *St. Paul and the Church of the Gentiles*, p. 184. On p. 203, he thinks it may be Tychicus.
4. op. cit., p. 227.
5. op. cit., pp. 600 f.
6. *RGG.*, article on "Ephesians".
7. *Key*, p. v.
8. Some scholars, e.g., Käsemann and Masson, have seen here a Gnostic redemption myth; the Redeemer breaks down the dividing

wall between heaven and earth. But we need not look any further than the Temple barrier for this metaphor.

9. Mitton, op. cit., p. 229.

10. F. W. Danker, *NTS* (1960), p. 94, claims that this is a perfectly good Greek idiom. But this cannot be said of such phrases as "that we should walk in them" (2.10), where the Hebrew use of the relative pronoun has clearly affected the style. Is it likely that any imitator, no matter how good, would have consciously imitated such an idiom? Imitation is usually much more general than this.

11. *ThB* (1926), pp. 120 ff.

12. *HZNT, An die Kolosser, Epheser, an Philemon*, p. 45.

13. *Ev. Th.* (1951), pp. 151–72.

14. op. cit., p. 149.

15. *Lit. Gut.*, pp. 16–25. Frühchristliche Hymnen, pp. 68 f.

16. op. cit., p. 262. Masson's division is disputed by J. Gambier, "La Benediction d'eph", *ZNTW* 54 (1963), pp. 58–104, who adds still another strophic division to the many that have been put forward. When so many divisions can be found, it is clear that the original one, if there were one, has not yet been discovered. This does not detract from our contention that the passage is part of a berakah.

17. Mitton, p. 231.

18. Goodspeed, *Meaning*, p. 35.

19. Beare, op. cit., p. 674; Abbott, *Ephesians* and *Colossians*, p. 93; Armitage Robinson, *The Epistle to the Ephesians*, p. 174; Percy, op. cit., pp. 303 ff.

20. Schubert, op. cit., p. 44; Dahl, op. cit., pp. 362–71, gives three examples of letters which contain a blessing followed by a thanksgiving, but only one of them can be said to have the same form as Ephesians.

21. op. cit., pp. 33 ff.

22. *Ev. Th.* (1953), pp. 362–71. While there are traditional passages in Paul's letters, e.g., 1 Cor. 15.1–7, none of them contains as many passages which are now claimed to be either traditional or liturgical.

23. This is not to say that the Epistle is non-Pauline in outlook and teaching; Pauline forms of prayer may well have been remembered, but Paul's own way of presiding at worship was doubtless influenced by the Synagogue.

24. The idea of families in heaven and on earth is attributed to one of the early rabbis: "He who busies himself with the Law for its own sake causes peace in the upper and lower families" (Montefiore and Loewe, *A Rabbinic Anthology*, p. 277).

25. The normal posture for prayer in the synagogue was standing; in the Temple, the worshippers prostrated themselves.

26. Eph. 2.1, 5, has clear affinities with Col. 2.13, but this is one of the difficult passages in Colossians. The Pauline doctrine of baptism is stated clearly in Col. 2.12; 2.20; and 3.1. If you are dead already how can you die in baptism? This passage may be nothing more than a description of the pre-Christian life of the Colossians, but the juxtaposition of the two ideas makes us appreciate the view of those who hold that Colossians, as we now have it, is non-Pauline.

27. *Discoveries in the Judaean Desert*, p. 114.

28. Allen, *NTS* (1958), pp. 54–61; Beare, *Epistle to the Philippians*, p. 56.

29. The ellipsis in this sentence may make the infinitives epexegetic, or they may come after "affirm" in v. 17.

30. op. cit., p. 287.

31. Käsemann, op. cit., p. 519.

32. *Int. Dict.*, article on "Ephesians".

33. *Messe und Herrenmahl*, pp. 178 ff; Eng. trans. by Dorothea Reeve, pp. 145 ff.

34. cf. John 6.56 and 14.23.

35. op. cit., p. 714.

36. *The Epistles to Colossians, Philemon and Ephesians*, p. 234.

37. op. cit., p. 209.

38. op. cit., p. 271.

39. A Guilding, op. cit., pp. 180 f.

40. Anderson Scott, *Footnotes to St. Paul*, p. 40.

41. *Key*, p. vi.

42. So Beare, op. cit., p. 710; Abbott, op. cit., p. 155.

43. Hebrews does not speak about avoiding outsiders; it simply ignores them.

44. In article cited above, p. 519.

45. Dibelius, op. cit., p. 75; *contra*, Beare, op. cit., p. 739; Masson, op. cit., p. 220; Abbott, op. cit., p. 184.

46. The works of Carrington, Selwyn, and Davies have already been cited (Part I) in this connection.

47. Frequently in IQS.

48. W. L. Knox is quite definite on this point. Pentecost had become the Feast of Lawgiving between Philo and Luke.

49. SB, Vol. 3, p. 96.

50. *The Acts of the Apostles*, p. 85.

51. B. Lindars, New Testament Apologetic, p. 253: "The value of this [i.e. Ps. 68.18] verse lies in the combination of the ideas of the Ascension and of the gift of the Spirit in a single quasi-prophetic verse." Cf. pp. 51–9 of the same book. Abbott is one of the few modern exegetes who interprets Eph. 4.9 as a reference to the

ascension and the gifts of the Spirit (op. cit., pp. 114 ff), most others explaining it as the descent of Christ into Hades. Strong support for Abbott's position may now be found in a paper of G. B. Caird: "The descent of Christ in Eph. 4.7–11", *Texte und Untersuchungen*, 88, pp. 535–45. W. Lock, *The Epistle to the Ephesians* (West. Comm.), pp. 11 f, finds in Ephesians the following reminiscences of Ps. 68: v. 16, Eph. 2.22, and 3.17; v. 9, Eph. 1.18; v. 10, Eph. 2.7; vv. 4 and 32, Eph. 5.19; vv. 28 and 35, Eph. 3.16 and 6.10.

52. op. cit., p. 48.

53. op. cit., p. 143.

54. op. cit., p. 617.

55. "They bind themselves with an oath not to commit thefts, robberies, or adulteries, not to perjure themselves, nor to refuse, when called upon, to make a deposit." This looks very much as if it were based on the last four of the Ten Commandments. R. M. Grant, *The Decalogue in Early Christianity*, HTR (1947), pp. 1–18.

56. op. cit., pp. 395 f.

57. *Meaning*, pp. 60–2.

58. *TWNT*, Vol. I, pp. 651 ff.

59. *Midrash on the Song of Songs*, IV, 4.1.

60. M. Jastrow, *The Song of Songs*, p. 70.

61. R. R. Williams, *Studies in Ephesians* (ed. F. L. Cross), p. 96.

62. op. cit., p. 60.

63. Josephus, *contra Apionem* II. 193; Philo, *de. spec. leg.* I. 67.

64. F. J. Leenhardt, *The Epistle to the Romans*, p. 214.

65. Armitage Robinson, op. cit., pp. 206 f, discusses this idea and rejects it. It may be that this passage refers to the preaching of the word, which is a necessary prelude to baptism. Cf. 6.17: "The sword of the Spirit, which is the word of God".

66. *St. John's Gospel*, p. 319; C. H. Dodd, *The Fourth Gospel*, pp. 428, 442 n.

67. Jewish Prayer Book (Singer's translation), p. 305.

68. G. W. H. Lampe, *The Seal of the Spirit*, argues that the seal refers to water; L. S. Thornton, *Confirmation: its place in the Baptismal Mystery*, argues that it is an anointing.

69. D. Daube, *The New Testament and Rabbinic Judaism*, pp. 109 ff. I am indebted to Dr Daube for some of the ideas in the paragraph.

70. Eccles. Rabba, 8.10.

71. *Bab. Yebamoth*, 47b.

72. *The Mishna* (Danby's translation), pp. 564–5.

73. Baptism and Jewish Exegesis, *NTS* (1958), pp. 309–18. A footnote in O. Cullmann's *Baptism in the New Testament*, p. 56, draws attention to an article by H. Sahlin in a Swedish theological journal; he

appears to have worked out an exegesis of this passage along the lines suggested here, but it has not been possible to obtain this article.

74. Gen. Rabba, XXXIX. 14.

75. Carrington, *The Primitive Christian Catechism*, pp. 47–57.

76. op. cit., pp. 106–40.

77. *The Theology of the New Testament* Vol. I, p. 175.

78. *TWNT* Vol. V., pp. 297 ff.

79. Beare, op. cit., p. 602.

80. W. C. van Unnik, "The Purpose of St. John's Gospel", *Texte und Untersuchungen* 73, pp. 382–411.

81. *HDB*, Vol. I, p. 717.

82. *Introduction to the New Testament*, p. 385.

83. op. cit., p. 716.

84. So Abbott, op. cit., p. 3.

85. The careful way in which 1.3–14 and 2.11–22 have been constructed makes it highly likely that these passages had been written before our author wrote his letter. The pattern of 2.1–10 is not so easy to discern, but that its author has taken great care in its construction can be seen because: (*a*) the passage begins with "dead in your *trespasses* and sins in which you *walked*" (2.1), and ends "for *goods works* which God prepared beforehand that we should *walk* in them" (2.10); (*b*) the repetition of "in Christ Jesus" in vv. 6, 7, 10; (*c*) the ascending number of important words in v. 2: the αἰών of this world (2), the prince of the power of the air (3), the Spirit now working in the sons of disobedience (4); (*d*) "sons of disobedience" and "children of wrath" are clearly meant to parallel each other in vv. 2 and 3; (*e*) the repetition of "by grace you have been saved" in vv. 6 and 8.

It may be added that vv. 4–7 are said to be a liturgical fragment in *Monumenta eccl. liturg.* 1.31 (I owe this reference to Schille's Dissertation, p. 10).

86. Paul uses "saints" with the meaning of Jewish Christians in Rom. 15.26, 1 Cor. 16.1, and 2 Cor. 9.1, but he can also use it of Gentile Christians, e.g., Rom. 1.7, 1 Cor. 1.2. Dr Johnston has drawn my attention to the idea of Karl Holl in *Gesammelte Aufsatze auf. Kirchengeschichte*, Vol. 2, pp. 44–67, that "saints" is a technical term for the members of the Jerusalem church, and that the collection made by Paul for its relief fund was not a voluntary offering, but akin to the Temple tax. Holl is followed in this by Schweitzer in *The Mysticism of Paul the Apostle*, pp. 31 and 156. But Paul's attempt to make the collection as large as possible hardly agrees with the idea of a tax, and "saint" in the New Testament does not mean only a

member of the Jewish–Christian community, though there are places where it does have this narrower meaning. I believe that Eph. 1.1 and 2.19 are two of these places.

87. op cit., p. 601. It may be added here that one of the great difficulties in accepting the theory of Goodspeed, Mitton, Beare, Johnston, and others, that Colossians provides the model for Ephesians, is the almost complete absence of any teaching on the Holy Spirit in Colossians. The Spirit is mentioned only once in Colossians (Col. 1.8), while there are twelve references in Ephesians (1.13; 2.18,22; 3.5,16; 4.3,4,30; 5.9,18; 6.17,18).

88. The problem raised by Romans 16 may be dealt with briefly here, as this chapter of Romans is thought by many scholars to be a letter or part of a letter to the church at Ephesus. That a letter consisting of greetings only would be sent by anybody in the ancient world is hardly likely, as C. H. Dodd says (*Epistle to the Romans*, p. xix). T. W. Manson has suggested that Romans was sent not only to Rome, but also to other places; this would account for the omission of "in Rome" in some of our MSS and also for the omission of chapter 16 in P 46. The copy that went to Ephesus had chapter 16 attached to it. But if Paul sent this letter to Ephesus, he must have sent it shortly after he left there, and there would be no need to tell the Ephesians details about the lives of people whom they knew well, for it is highly probable that there were no large Christian congregations in any city. Again, why would a letter meant for Ephesus be finally attached to the Roman copy of the circular letter, if there was a circular letter? (Rom. 1.13 could hardly be written to a church which Paul himself had founded.)

If some of the Christians had gone to Rome from Asia Minor, Paul might naturally tell the Roman church about them, but again, it is hardly likely that so many people whom Paul knew intimately had moved to Rome. The warning against divisions in Rom. 16.17 ff is so unlike the rest of Romans in tone and content that it does not seem to fit Rome either. Neither the Ephesian nor Roman hypotheses are free from difficulty.

The third hypothesis, that Romans 16 was written in the second century in order to strengthen the hand of the Roman church in its fight against heresy, may at first sight have much to commend it, and vv. 17 ff would certainly fit this situation. But again, why the list of names? The Pastorals, which belong to this period, contain warnings such as we find here, but they do not contain personal greetings to this extent. The origin of Romans 16 must still be regarded as a mystery.

BIBLIOGRAPHY

COMMENTARIES ON EPHESIANS

Abbott, T. K., *Ephesians and Colossians* (ICC), New York, Scribner's, 1897.

Beare, F. W., Ephesians (*The Interpreter's Bible*), Vol. 10, pp. 597–749, New York & Nashville, Abingdon–Cokesbury, 1953.

Dibelius, M. *An die Kolosser, Epheser, an Philemon* (HZNI), 2nd rev. edn, Tubingen, Mohr, 1927.

Lock, W., *The Epistle to the Ephesians*, London, Methuen, 1929.

Masson, C., *L'Epître de Saint Paul aux Ephésiens*, Neuchatel & Paris, Delachaux & Niéstle, 1953.

Robinson, J. A., *St. Paul's Epistle to the Ephesians*, London, Macmillan, 1922.

Scott, E. F., *The Epistles to the Colossians, to Philemon and to the Ephesians* (MNC), London, Hodder & Stoughton, 1930.

Synge, F. C., *St. Paul's Epistle to the Ephesians*, London, S.P.C.K., 1941.

OTHER BOOKS ON EPHESIANS

Cross, F. L. (ed.), *Studies in Ephesians*, London, Mowbray, 1956.

Goodspeed, E. J., *The Meaning of Ephesians*, Chicago, University of Chicago Press, 1933.

—— *The Key to Ephesians*, Chicago, University of Chicago Press, 1956.

Mitton, C. L., *The Epistle to the Ephesians*, Oxford, Clarendon Press, 1951.

Percy, E., *Die Probleme der Kolosser- und Epheserbriefe*, Lund, Gleerup, 1946.

Schille, G., *Liturgische Gut im Epheserbrief* (Microfilm of Dissertation), University of Göttingen, 1955.

—— *Frühchristliche Hymnen*, Berlin 1965.

REFERENCE BOOKS

Black, M. and Rowley, H. H., *Peake's Commentary on the Bible*, London 1962.

Cazelles, H. and Feuillet, A., *Supplément au Dictionnaire de la Bible*, Paris 1960.

Hastings, J. (ed.), *Dictionary of the Bible*, New York and Edinburgh 1901–4.

Kittel, G. (ed.), *Theologisches Worterbuch zum Neuen Testament*, Stuttgart 1933.
Richardson, A. (ed.), *A Theological Wordbook of the New Testament*, London 1950.
Strack, H. and Billerbeck, P., *Kommentar zum Neuen Testament aus Talmud und Midrasch*, Munich, Beck, 1926.
von Campenhausen (ed.), *Die Religion in Geschichte und Gegenwart*, 3rd edn, Tubingen 1957.
von Allmen, A. (ed.), *Vocabulary of the Bible*, London, Lutterworth, 1956.

OTHER BOOKS CONSULTED

Bacon, B. W., *Beginnings of Gospel Story*, New Haven 1935.
—— *The Gospel of the Hellenists*, (ed. C. H. Kraeling), New York n.d.
Baumstark, A., *Comparative Liturgy* (Eng. trans. by F. L. Cross), London 1958.
Beare, F. W., *The Epistle to the Philippians*, London, A. & C. Black, 1959.
Bultmann, R., *The Theology of the New Testament* (Eng. trans. by K. Grobel), New York 1954.
Burrows, M., *The Dead Sea Scrolls*, New York, Viking Press, 1955.
Caird, G. B., *The Apostolic Age*, London, Duckworth, 1955.
Carrington, P., *The Primitive Christian Catechism*, Cambridge University Press, 1940.
—— *The Primitive Christian Calendar*, Cambridge University Press, 1952.
Cross, F. L., *1 Peter, A Paschal Liturgy*, London, Mowbray, 1954.
Cross, F. L., and others, *Studia Evangelica*, Berlin, Akademie-Verlag, 1959.
Cross, F. M. Jr, *The Ancient Library of Qumran and Modern Biblical Studies*, New York, Doubleday, 1958.
Cullmann, O., *Baptism in the New Testament* (Eng. trans. by J. K. S. Reid), London, S.C.M. Press, 1950.
—— *Early Christian Worship* (Eng. trans. by Todd and Torrence), London, S.C.M. Press, 1953.
Daube, D., *The New Testament and Rabbinic Judaism*, London, Athlone Press, 1956.
Davies, W. D., *Paul and Rabbinic Judaism*, 2nd edn, London, S.P.C.K., 1955.
Davies, W. D. and Daube, D. (ed.), *The Background of the New Testament and its Eschatology*, Cambridge University Press, 1956.
Dix, G., *The Shape of the Liturgy*, Westminster, Dacre Press, n.d.
—— *Jew and Greek*, Westminster, Dacre Press, 1953.

Edersheim, A., *The Temple*, London, James Clarke, 1959 edn.

Ellis, E. E., *Paul's Use of the Old Testament*, Edinburgh, Oliver & Boyd, 1957.

Gaster, T., *The Scriptures of the Dead Sea Sect*, London, Secker & Warburg, 1957.

—— *Passover, its History and Traditions*, New York, Schuman, 1949.

Goguel, M., *L'Eglise Primitive*, Paris, Payot, 1947.

Grant, F. C., *Ancient Judaism and the New Testament*, New York, Macmillan, 1959.

Guilding, A., *The Fourth Gospel and Jewish Worship*, Oxford, Clarendon Press, 1960.

Hanson, S., *The Unity of the Church in the New Testament*, Uppsala 1946.

Hooke, S. H., *In the Beginning*, Oxford, Clarendon Press, 1947.

—— (ed.), *Myth and Ritual*, Oxford University Press, 1933.

Jackson, F., and Lake, K. (ed.), *The Beginnings of Christianity*, London, Macmillan, 5 vols., 1930–3.

James, M. R., *The Apocryphal New Testament*, Oxford, Clarendon Press, 1924.

Jaubert, A., *La Date de la Cène*, Paris, Gabalda et Cie., 1957.

Jeremias, J., *The Eucharistic Words of Jesus* (Eng. trans. by A. Ehrhardt), Oxford, Blackwell, 1955.

Johnston, G., *The Church in the New Testament*, Cambridge University Press, 1943.

Kilpatrick, G. D., *The Origins of the Gospel according to St Matthew*, Oxford, Clarendon Press, 1946.

Knox, J., *Philemon among the Letters of Paul*, 2nd rev edn, New York and Nashville, Abingdon 1959.

Knox, W. L., *The Acts of the Apostles*, Cambridge University Press, 1948.

—— *St. Paul and the Church of the Gentiles*, Cambridge University Press, 1939.

Kümmel, W. G. (ed.), *Introduction to the New Testament* (Eng. trans. of the 14th edn of Feine and Behm), Nashville and New York 1966.

Lampe, G. W. H., *The Seal of the Spirit*, S.P.C.K., London 1967.

Leenhardt, F. J., *The Epistle to the Romans* (Eng. trans. by H. Knight), London, Lutterworth, 1961.

Lietzmann, H., *Messe und Herremahl* (Eng. trans. by D. Reeve), 7 fascicles, 5 published, Leiden, Brill, n.d.

Lindars, B., *New Testament Apologetic*, London 1961.

Manson, T. W. *Ethcis and the Gospel*, London, S.C.M. Press, 1960.

Manson, W., *The Epistle to the Hebrews*, London, Hodder and Stoughton, 1951.

McArthur, A. A., *The Evolution of the Christian Year*, London, S.C.M. Press, 1953.

McNeile, A. H., *Introduction to the New Testament*, 2nd rev. edn, C. S. C. Williams, Oxford, Clarendon Press, 1953.

Milik, J. T., *Ten Years of Discovery in the Wilderness of Judaea* (Eng. trans. by J. Strugnell), London, S.C.M. Press, 1959.

Moffatt, J., *Introduction to the Literature of the New Testament*, 3rd rev. edn, Edinburgh, T. and T. Clark, 1918.

Montefiore, C., *The Synoptic Gospels*, London, Macmillan, 2 vols., 1909–27.

Montefiore, C., and Loewe, H., *A Rabbinic Anthology*, London, Macmillan, 1938.

Moore, G. F., *Judaism*, Cambridge, Massachusetts, Harvard, 3 vols., 1927–30.

Morris, L., *The New Testament and the Jewish Lectionaries*, London 1964.

Moule, C. F. D., *The Birth of the New Testament*, Edinburgh 1962.

Nineham, D. (ed.), *Studies in the Synoptic Gospels*, Oxford, Blackwell, 1955.

Oesterley, W. O. E., *The Jewish Background of the Christian Liturgy*, Oxford, Clarendon Press, 1925.

Rawlinson, A. E. J., *The Gospel According to St. Mark*, London, Methuen, 1925.

Schubert, P., *Form and Function of the Pauline Thanksgiving*, Berlin, Topelmann, 1939.

Selwyn, E. G., *The First Epistle of St. Peter*, 2nd edn, London, Macmillan, 1947.

Shepherd, M. H., *The Paschal Liturgy and the Apocalypse*, London, Lutterworth, 1960.

Snaith, N. H., *The Jewish New Year Festival*, London, S.P.C.K., 1947.

Stendahl, K. (ed.), *The Scrolls and the New Testament*, New York, Harpers, 1957.

Taylor, V., *The Gospel According to St. Mark*, London, Macmillan, 1952.

Thackeray, H. St. J., *The Septuagint and Jewish Worship*, London, Humphrey Milford, 1921.

Thornton, L. S., *The Common Life in the Body of Christ*, Westminster Dacre Press, n.d.;

—— *Confirmation: Its Place in the Baptismal Mystery*, Westminster Dacre Press, 1954.

van Goudoever, J., *Biblical Calendars*, Leiden, Brill, 1959.

Vermes, G., *Discovery in the Judean Desert*, New York, Desclee Co., 1956.

von Rad, G., *Studies in Deuteronomy* (Eng. trans. by D. Stalker), London, S.C.M. Press, 1948.

Weiser, D. A., *Glaube und Geschichte im Alten Testament*, Stuttgart, Kohlhammer, 1931.

Weiss, J., *Earliest Christianity*, New York, Harper Torchbooks, 2 vols., 1959.

Werner, E., *The Sacred Bridge*, New York, Columbia University Press, 1959.

Williams, C. S. C., *The Acts of the Apostles*, London, A. & C. Black, 1957.

Zuntz, G., *The Text of the Epistles*, Oxford 1953.

ARTICLES

Allan, J. A., "The 'in Christ' Formula in Ephesians", *NTS* (1958–9), pp. 54–62.

Aron, R., "Réflexions sur la notion de temps dans la liturgie juive", *La Maison Dieu* (1961), pp. 12–20.

Boeckh, J., "Die Entwicklung der Altkirchlichen Pentekoste", *JBLH* (1960), pp. 1–45.

Büchler, A., "The Triennial Reading of the Law and the Prophets", *JQR* (1894–5), pp. 420–68 and (1895–6), pp. 1–73.

Cadbury, H. J., "The Dilemma of Ephesians", *NTS* (1958–9), pp. 91–102.

Coutts, J., "Ephesians 1:3–14 and 1 Peter 1:3–12", *NTS* (1956–7), pp. 115–27;

—— "The Relationship of Ephesians and Colossians", *NTS* (1957–8), pp. 201–7.

Dahl, N. A., "Addresse und Pröomium des Epheserbriefes", *TZ* (1951), pp. 241–64;

—— "Anamnesis", *Stud. Theol.* (1948–9), pp. 68–95.

Danker, F. W., "The υἱός Phrases in the New Testament", *NTS* (1960–1), p. 94.

Daube, D., "The Earliest Structure of the Gospels", *NTS* (1958–9), pp. 174–87.

Frost, S. B., "Towards a Biblical Doctrine of the Holy Communion", *CJT* (1961).

Gambier, J., "La Bénédiction d'Eph.", *ZNTW* (1963), pp. 58–104.

Grant, R. M., "The Decalogue in Early Christianity", *HTR* (1947), pp. 1–18.

Heinemann, J., "The Beth Midrash Prayers", *JSS* (1960), pp. 261–80.

Käsemann, E., "Christus, das All und die Kirche", *TLZ* (1956), pp. 585–90.

King, E. G., "The Influence of the Triennial Cycle on the Psalter", *JTS* (1904), pp. 203–13.

Kretschmar, G., "Himmelfahrt und Pfingsten", *ZKG* (1954–5), pp. 209–53.

Kuhn, K. G., "Der Epheserbrief im Lichte der Qumrantext", *NTS* (1960–1).

Manson, T. W., "ἱλαστήριον", *JTS* (1954), pp. 1–10.

Maurer, C., "Der Hymnus von Epheser 1 als Schlüssel zum ganzen Briefe", *Ev. Th.* (1951–2), pp. 151–72.

Mitton, C. L., "Important Hypothesis Reconsidered: Ephesians", *ET* (1956), pp. 195–8.

Moule, C. F. D., "The Nature and Purpose of 1 Peter", *NTS*, 3 (1956–1957), pp. 1–11;

—— "A Reconsideration of the Contents of 'Maranatha'", *NTS*, 6 (1959–60), pp. 307–10.

Mowry, L., "Rev. 4–5 and Early Christian Liturgical Usage", *JBL* (1952), pp. 75–84.

Nauck, W., "Eph. 2:19–22—Ein Tauflied", *Ev. Th.* (1953), pp. 362–71.

Piper, O. A., "The Apocalypse of John and the Liturgy of the Ancient Church", *CH* (1951), pp. 10–22.

Rabinowitz, L., "Does Midrash Tillim reflect the Triennial Cycle of the Psalms?" *JQR* (1935–6), pp. 349–68.

Robinson, J. A. T., "Traces of a Liturgical Usage in 1 Cor. 16:20–4", *JTS* (1953), pp. 38–40;

—— "The Destination and Purpose of St. John's Gospel", *NTS* (1960), pp. 117–31.

Schille, G., "Der Autor des Epheserbriefes", *TLZ* (1957), pp. 326–34.

Sirks, G. J., "The Cinderella of Theology", *HTR* (1957), pp. 78–89.

Snaith, N. H., "The Triennial Cycle and the Psalter", *ZATW* (1933), pp. 302–07.

Thackeray, H. St. J., "The Song of Hannah and other Lessons and Psalms for the Jewish New Year's Day", *JTS* (1915), pp. 177–204.

Thornton, T. C. G., "1 Peter, A Paschal Liturgy?", *JTS*, N.S. 12 (1961), pp. 14–26.

Vermes, G., "Baptism and Jewish Exegesis", *NTS* (1957–8), pp. 309–318.

Williams, R. R., "Logic versus Experience in the Order of Credal Formulae", *NTS* (1954–5), pp. 42–4.

INDEX OF NAMES

Abrahams, I., 91

Bacon, B. W., 60, 61, 77
Beare, F. W., 49ff, 54, 125, 168, 171
Boeckh, J., 76, 80, 110
Büchler, A., 90f

Cadbury, H. J., 3, 82
Carrington, P., 60, 113f
Chadwick, H., 54f
Coutts, J., 8f
Cross, F. L., 61
Cullmann, O., 60

Dahl, N. A., 40–4, 127, 143f, 148, 150
Daube, D., 60
de Wette, W., 4
Dibelius, M., 140
Dodd, C. H., 161

Evans, C. F., 60

Findlay, G. G., 5
Frost, S. B., 71

Goguel, M., 76, 80f
Goodspeed, E. J., 44–7, 52, 125, 142
Grant, F. C., 61
Guilding, A., 60, 90, 114ff

Hippolytus, 79, 136f, 152
Holtzmann, H. J., 4f
Hooke, S. H., 90

Jeremias, J., 77
Johnston, G., 47, 49, 53, 78
Josephus, 90, 151
Justin Martyr, 74, 110, 138

Käsemann, E., 56, 125, 142f
King, E. G., 117

Kilpatrick, G. D., 60
Knox, J., 5
Knox, W. L., 82, 114, 116, 125, 146
Kretschmar, G., 81, 143
Kunze, G., 110

Lake, K., 82
Lietzmann, H., 136
Lightfoot, R. H., 153
Lohmeyer, E., 127

Manson, T. W., 61, 114, 120
Manson, W., 61
Marcion, 10, 43
Masson, C., 9–18, 127, 140
Maurer, C., 127
McArthur, A. A., 75
Milik, J. T., 68
Mitton, C. L., 3, 47ff, 51ff, 125
Moffatt, J., 5

Nauck, W., 9

Percy, E., 18–40
Philo, 116, 151

Ropes, J. H., 82

Sarapion, 52
Schille, G., 5ff
Schmidt, K. L., 17
Scott, C. A. A., 140
Scott, E. F., 140
Shepherd, M. H., 61, 78
Synge, F. C., 7

Tertullian, 77, 79
Thackeray, H. St J., 90f

Ussher, Abp, 3

Werner, E., 91, 112

INDEX OF BIBLICAL REFERENCES

OLD TESTAMENT

Genesis

1	92, 95
2.24	110
11	93, 97
11.1–9	116
14	93, 97, 119, 145
14.19	85

Exodus

4.24–6	158
11	92
12	92
12.27	63
13—17	113
13.3	63
8	70
14	64
18.10	85
19.1	64
10	99
14	149
16	72
19, 20	93, 97, 119, 120, 145, 147
20.12	110
34.4, 10, 28, 29–35	114

Leviticus

17.11	158
23.15–17	67
26	98

Numbers

6.21, 22	92
24–6	83
10—15	113
7, 18	93

18	97, 119, 145
18.6, 7	146

Deuteronomy

16.9–12	97
11, 12	98
20.3	94
26.1–11	69
27.11–26	69
28	98
31.10–12	90

Joshua

24.1–28	70

1 Kings

5.7	85

1 Chronicles

16.8–36	137
29.10	95

2 Chronicles

5.3	62
10	63
8.12f	62
15.8–11	63
28.15	94
30.8	62
35	62

Ezra

3.4	62
6.22	62

Nehemiah

8.7–8	90
8	93
16–17	63
9	86

Job

1.6	62

Psalms

9	97
29	97, 98, 145, 147
29.6	147
47	93
58	97
66.20	85
68	97, 98, 145
68.18	110, 146, 165
72.19	89
89.27ff	72
96	93
98.1–2, 7–9a	71
103.13	106
105	87
106	107
106.48	109
107.22	137
110	97, 119, 120
110.1	139
119.12	95
146.10	89

Ecclesiastes

8.10	155

Song of Songs	149

Isaiah

2.3	72

4.5	72
14.24–7	72
28.16	30
51.12	106
54.5	99
57.19	25, 157, 165
60.1–4	72
62.4–5	99

Jeremiah

23.24	28
31.31–4	72

Ezekiel

1	97
16.8–14	99
37.1–14	73
45.21–5	63

Hosea

2.8	64
19–20	99
14.2	108

Joel

2.28	73

Amos

5	71

Habakkuk

3	97

Zechariah

3.1	22
11.4–6	116
14.9	72

NEW TESTAMENT

Matthew

11.25–6	103
14.19	104
15.36	104
26.26–9	104

Mark

2.20	77
6.41	104
8.6–7	104
12.13–37	60
13.35	77
14.22–5	104
15.25, 33, 34	77

Luke

6.20–49	116
9.16	104
10.21	103
22.19–20	104
24.13–35	112
45	111

John

1.48	115
2.1–11	140
21	74
3.13	167
20–1	167
34	168
5.39–46	111
6.6	115
11	104
56	137
7.39	153
10.22	62
11.41–2	103
42	104
52	166
12.35–6	167
14.1–7	60
15.3	167
16	23

16.23–4	167
17	167
17.24	168
18.10	116

Acts

2.1	80
1–11	81, 106
6–11	118
13	140
14–36	139
33	118, 146
34	118
39	118
47	106
4.24–30	106
6.14	73
8.12	153
10.38	154
44ff	107
46	118
11.27	32
13.1–3	32
15	90, 93
15.21	90
32	32
16.14–15	153
17.2–3	111
18.8	153
19.6	118
10, 26	165
20.7–11	73
16	80, 81

Romans

1.8	48
8–10	105
8–15	40
2.21–2	126
3.1–3	8
22–3	126
30	25
4.11	154
5.1, 10	24

Romans—continued

5.2	24
5, 8	23
9	26,162
19–20	26
20	23
6.3–5	12, 25
4ff	155
5	13
11	13, 103
7.13–25	26
25	48
8	27, 139
8.15	24, 26, 27, 151
18–25	11
23	26
23–5	162
24	26
28	23
38–9	23
9.4	149
23	23
10.9	151, 162
11.17	25
25	13
12.3	15
3–5	29
4–6	14
14	78
14.17	28
19	29
14, 15	40
15.7	28
7, 9	23
14	27
16	11
16.7	31

I Corinthians

1.18	26, 162
26	111
27	23
2.1, 4	13
6	13
6–8	19, 22
7	23
7–10	14
2.10–12	27
3.10–11	30
11	9
15	26, 162
4.1	13
8	163
9	19, 22
12	53
20	28
5.4	163
5	17
6–8	76
6.11	24, 26, 164
14	24
7	33
8	27
8.11	30
16	28
9	31
10	77
10.1, 11	111
11	163
17	44
20–1	22
32	17
11.2	108
26	105, 137
12.2	23
4–6	14
7	29
7–9	15
12–13	151
12–14	28
13	27
28	17, 29, 31, 32
13	27
14	31
14.26	163
15.1–11	6
2	162
9	7, 17, 33
19	26
20	77
25, 27	28
51	13
16.2	73
8	77, 80, 113
22	163

2 Corinthians

1.3	54
3–4	106
11	23
14	33
21–2	54
22	27, 154
2.12–13	114
15	26, 162
3—6	114
3.12	100
12–16	111
18	27
4.4	22
10–12	24
15	23
5	114
5.5	27
17	25, 164
18–21	23
6.16	17
8.7	27
9.11–13	108
11.2	17, 24, 30, 99
6	27
31	54
12.7	17, 22, 23

Galatians

1	6
1.1	31
13	17
2	6
2.5	13
12	78
14	13
20	28
3.14	25
22	23
26–8	25
27	164
27–8	151
4.3	78
4	53
6	24, 27
10	78

4.21–3	25
5.5	26
16–18	27
6.15	25

Ephesians

1.1	3, 9, 31, 43, 165, 168
3–12	6
3–13	12
3–14	41, 127, 129, 138, 147
3—2.22	34
3	133, 138, 162
4	23, 48, 137, 138, 168
5	21, 24, 133, 138
6	138, 147
7	24, 138, 162
7–8	133
8	131
9	33, 48, 129, 133, 134, 138, 162
9–10	14
10	53, 129, 138, 140, 162, 165
12–13	8
13	11, 21, 27, 138, 145, 162, 165
13–14	139, 153
14	27, 40, 131, 162
15	6, 131, 132
15–16	34, 48
15–17	129
15–19	129, 150
15–23	170
17	131
17–18	27, 134
18	11
19	24
20	131
20–2	138, 139
20–3	6, 131
21	21
22	14, 26, 29
23	26, 28
2.1	12, 156
1–2	34
1–10	129
2	46, 146

Ephesians—continued

2.3	23, 156
4	21
4–6	154
4–8	162
4–10	5, 6, 132
5	12, 26, 133, 145, 165
5–6	138
5–7	28
5, 13, 15	137
6	25, 133, 160
7	138, 161
8	26
8–9	162
10	160, 162
11	23, 46, 129
11–21	24
11–22	33, 129, 156, 169
12	21, 26, 35, 40, 126, 149, 170
12–14	7, 165
12–19	165
12, 16	139
13	9, 145, 165
13–16	14
13–17	125
14	158
14–16	25
14–18	6, 24, 132
15	9, 30, 137, 162
15–16	166
16	9, 24, 152
18	24, 130, 138, 139
19	130, 170
19–22	9, 133
20	4, 9, 15, 16, 31, 34, 46, 138
20–2	30, 139
21	74
21–2	42
22	129, 146, 162
3.1	38, 129, 132, 134, 165
1–6	34
1–13	31, 32, 33, 129, 136, 150, 170
2	50, 129
3.3	14, 33, 46, 47

3.4	13, 130, 165
4–6	8
5	4, 9, 14, 16, 27, 31, 34, 46, 129, 139
6	14, 129
7	129
7ff	55
8	7, 14, 130, 165
10	140
10–11	129
11	165
12	24, 129
14	129
14–15	133
14–19	27, 129, 137
16	26, 35, 139
16–17	34
17	165
18	31
19	26, 165
20–1	137
21	161
4—6	134, 143
4.1	134, 145
1–6	15
2–6	34
3	21, 27, 35, 44, 139, 141
3–6	46
4	14
4–6	151
5	40
7	15, 29, 138, 146, 168
7–9	29
7–16	33
8	145
8–10	47
8–19	165
9–10	46, 125
10	28, 167
11	29, 31, 141, 146
11–12	15
11–16	14
12	16
13	8, 21, 141
13–14	30
14	27, 46, 142
14–15	161
14–16	29

Ephesians—continued

4.15	14, 29, 140
15b–16	8
16	29, 140
17	50
18	35
20	145, 161
21	134
22	26, 145
22–4	159
24	26, 145
25	17, 141
25–8	34
25–9	33
25–31	147f
28	53, 141
29	141
30	27, 40, 47, 139, 153, 154, 162
30–1	17
31	141
31–2	140
32	162
5.2	24, 53
3	148
3–5	141
5	28, 148, 162
7	142
8	40, 162, 167
11	142, 144, 167
13	142, 167
14	47, 155
14, 19	46
15	160
15, 19	34
16	144
18	27, 139, 140
19–20	48
19–21	135
20	36, 39, 40, 167
21	36
21–5a	21
22–3	36, 37, 141
22–32	39
22–33	148
25–7	151
25–33	34

5.26	24, 40, 167
26–7	162
29–30	28
32	152
6.1–4	141
1–9	21
2	147
4	39, 46
5–9	39
6	141
8	36
9	8, 141
10	21, 144
10–12	26
13	144, 161, 162
17	21
18	27, 31, 139
19	36
19–20	134
21	42, 43, 51
21–2	34, 48, 134, 166

Philippians

1.3–5	105
9	27
19	26
2.5–11	136
10	28
11	23
3.2	126
6	17
10	24
4.6	106
7	28
18	24, 53, 108

Colossians

1.3	105, 131
3–7	11
4	34, 131
4–14	26
5	8
9	34, 131, 132
11	35
13	28
16–20	28

Colossians—continued

1.18	8
20	9, 22
21	7, 35
23–7	34
24	19, 33
25	32, 129
26	22, 31
26–7	13
28	8
2.2	8, 13
4—3.4	6
8–16	40
11	154
12	12, 25, 155
12b–13	12
13	12, 34, 155
13–15	5
16–17	78
19	8, 29
20	12, 78
3.1	12, 25
1–2	12
1–3	155
3	12, 164
5–8	34
7	34
12–15	34
14	19, 35
16–17	48, 135
17	36, 39
18	36
18—4.11	19
18–19	36, 148
19–21	141
21	39
22—4.1	39
24–5	36
25	8
4.2	106
3	13, 36
3–4	135
3, 4, 7, 8	134
5	34
7	51
7–8	34, 48, 170
7–14	40

4.10–18	7
13	44
15	10
16	10, 111
18	37

1 Thessalonians

1.9	102
2.16	26
18	23
3.5	17
4.1	134
13–18	163
5.11	30
20	31

2 Thessalonians

2.2	163
7	23
3.12	134, 141

1 Timothy

3.16	136
4.13	111

2 Timothy

4.12	51, 166

Philemon   10, 134

Hebrews

3.3–6	120
5.10	120
12—6.3	118
6.4	160
4–8	118
5	74
7.2	120
11	120
27–8	118
8.3	120
8–12	118
9.7	118
7ff	120
10.1–3	118

Hebrews—continued

10.18	108
25	108
12.18–24	120
13	142
13.15	108
15–16	108

James

2.5	23

1 Peter

1.2	23
3–12	107
3—4.11	61
12	22
20	168
2.5	74
9	107
3.18–22	136

3.19	46
21–2	139

Revelation

1.3	111
10	73, 163
4	109
4.1	109
2	163
8	109
11	109
5	109
5.9	109
12–14	109
7	109
7.10, 12	109
10.8–11	111
11	109
15	109
16	109
16.5–7	110
19	109

DATE DUE